Toxic Cultures at Work

Around the world and across industries, toxic workplaces are in the news. Taking a holistic approach, this book gives a succinct summary of how toxic cultures develop and shows how they can be remedied with practical takeaways for organisations.

Existing books on toxic culture either skim the surface of the latest scandal or take a theoretical approach of limited use to practitioners trying to improve their organisations. Now, organisational development expert James Cannon presents an all-in-one resource based on organisational and individual psychology research that offers actionable suggestions for required change. Cannon provides a framework to understand the complexities of a toxic culture, identifying eight drivers: power, leadership personalities, values, organisational design, formal and informal systems, relations with the external environment and individual systems of motivation and reward. The book also offers a comprehensive toolkit with questionnaires and checklists to manage and achieve cultural change.

Professionals and students in organisational psychology, business, and change management, as well as those with an interest in the political and social issues raised by toxic cultures, will appreciate this guide on how to tackle a problem that is much discussed but seldom solved.

James Cannon, PhD, specialises in organisational design and development, and has consulted with organisations around the world. He has run an extensive range of training courses for the Chartered Institute of Personnel and Development (CIPD) in the UK and has served as a visiting lecturer at Geneva University. He has been a fellow of the CIPD and the Chartered Management Institute (CMI) and a Manpower Society prize-winner, as well as being honoured by the UK government for his work in leadership development. He served at director level in human resources, information technology, and organisational development, and has been an independent consultant for over 30 years.

Toxic Cultures at Work

The Eight Drivers of a Toxic Culture and a Process for Change

James Cannon

Routledge
Taylor & Francis Group

NEW YORK AND LONDON

Cover image: ajr_Images – Getty Images

First published 2023
by Routledge
605 Third Avenue, New York, NY 10158

and by Routledge
4 Park Square, Milton Park, Abingdon, Oxon, OX14 4RN

Routledge is an imprint of the Taylor & Francis Group, an informa business

Library of Congress Cataloging-in-Publication Data
Names: Cannon, James, 1947– author.
Title: Toxic cultures at work : the eight drivers of a toxic culture
and a process for change / James Cannon.
Description: New York, NY : Routledge, 2022. | Includes bibliographical
references and index. |
Identifiers: LCCN 2022011458 | ISBN 9781032309361 (hardback) |
ISBN 9781032309354 (paperback) | ISBN 9781003307334 (ebook)
Subjects: LCSH: Corporate culture. | Organizational behavior. | Employee morale. |
Organizational change.
Classification: LCC HD58.7 .C3468 2022 | DDC 302.3/5—dc23/eng/20220309
LC record available at https://lccn.loc.gov/2022011458

ISBN: 978-1-032-30936-1 (hbk)
ISBN: 978-1-032-30935-4 (pbk)
ISBN: 978-1-003-30733-4 (ebk)

DOI: 10.4324/9781003307334

Typeset in Bembo MT Pro
by codeMantra

To Sue

Contents

About the author   ix

Acknowledgements   xi

     Introduction   1

Part A: Culture   13

1   **What is a toxic culture?**   15

2   **Organisational diagnosis**   29

Part B: Leadership – power, personality and values   43

3   **The toxic effect of power imbalance**   45

4   **Leadership: the dark triad – personality and the toxic individual**   58

5   **Values**   72

Part C: Organisation   89

6   **Organisational design: the toxic impact of structure and process**   91

7   **The informal organisation**   110

8   **Relations with the external environment**   126

Part D: The individual   **143**

  9   Motivation and communication   **145**

10   Reward   **160**

Part E: Solutions   **171**

11   Fixing toxic cultures: a strategy for change   **173**

Name Index   *187*
Subject Index   *190*

About the author

James Cannon specialises in organisation design and development, and has consulted with organisations in many countries. He was a visiting lecturer at Geneva University. He was a fellow of the Chartered Institute of Personnel and Development (CIPD) and the Chartered Management Institute (CMI), a British Psychological Society member and a Manpower Society prize-winner. He was also formerly special adviser to the CIPD. In 1989 he started his own consultancy as well as co-founding Cavendish Partners, a firm specialising in career counselling and coaching for senior executives. In 2016 he gained an award from the British Government for his work in leadership development.

He has written several books, including *Cost Effective Personnel Decisions*, the *Database Directory, Giving Feedback, Making the Business Case, Talent Management and Succession planning, Organization Development and Change* (both with Rita McGee), *Organization Design and Capability Building* (with Rita McGee and Naomi Stamford), and workbooks such as *Team Based Problem Solving, Career Review Workbook*, and the forthcoming *Aha! A user's guide to creativity* (with Robert Cannon).

He is a dual citizen and lives in the UK and Australia.

Acknowledgements

Many people have contributed, often unwittingly, to the development of the ideas in this book. Thanks are due to Rita McGee, Roger Niven and Farren Drury, with whom I have collaborated on many consulting assignments, for their many helpful comments. I am particularly indebted to students on courses and conferences around the world for their challenging questions, which have sharpened my own thinking. I have had the privilege of working with many clients and organisations over the years and I am grateful to them for the opportunity to learn from them as well as to contribute to them. Particular thanks are due to Peter Mutton for facilitating many opportunities. Many of the examples in this book come from these experiences. Finally, thanks are due to my wife Sue for her unfailing support in preparing this manuscript. However, what deficiencies there may be are all mine.

Introduction

In 2009, the British Parliament was rocked by an expenses scandal. Members of Parliament (MPs) had been claiming for such egregious items as pornographic films and cleaning a duck house. Unsurprisingly, the public were outraged. Some MPs went to prison for fraudulent claims, but the majority did not, as it was the norm to claim these expenses. It was part of the culture of entitlement. 'I work hard with long hours', one MP claimed and 'I don't have time to sort out my domestic expenses' (1). How had such a culture occurred that was so at variance with most citizens' view of what was reasonable?

In 2018, the Australian public were glued to their TVs each night as the daily proceedings of the Royal Commission into banking and the financial sector were shown. Royal Commissions are not usually compulsive viewing, but each night fresh scandals were revealed, including charging fees to dead people and legitimate insurance claims that were never paid, causing so much misery and even death to those with deteriorating medical conditions. A culture of 'greed is good' drove bankers to earn huge bonuses for unethical practices. How had this situation come about in some of the most respected institutions?

In 2019 in the USA, Harvey Weinstein, a movie mogul, was sent to prison for a series of sexual offences. The case gave birth to the 'Me Too' movement as it emerged that in the film industry (and indeed many others) a culture of sexually predatory behaviour was the norm. In a climate where women were faced with powerful manipulative men but earnestly desired to work in the film industry, such behaviours flourished.

In 2021, Canberra was rocked by charges of rape and sexual harassment amongst staff and even ministers in the Australian Parliament.

At Sony Music Australia, CEO Denis Handlin resigned, allegedly because of the toxic culture in the company. And so it goes on…

These are just some of the many examples of where normally law-abiding people were somehow caught up in systems of belief that condoned this behaviour. Why? How? And what should be done to fix it? In all these cases, leaders (and often new ones) had the task of changing these cultures and even years later, some doubt whether anything really has changed in these institutions. Certainly, in Australia, despite many recommendations made by the Royal Commission, few have been implemented and even fewer senior executives have been called to account, let alone sent to prison. This book aims to uncover the reasons why these toxic cultures occurred and how to develop the strategies to bring about change – in short, how to rediscover that moral compass.

There are a range of situations, including those marked by significant drama and infighting, where personal battles often harm productivity. In some examples, it is the reverse situation, where

DOI: 10.4324/9781003307334-1

seemingly effective organisations were miserable places to work, while in others, the organisations were quite harmonious, but their customers and taxpayers were cheated.

Toxic workplaces are frequently considered to be the result of toxic employers and/or toxic employees who are motivated by personal gain (power, money, fame or special status), and use unethical, mean-spirited and sometimes illegal practices to achieve their ends. However, there are many other drivers of toxic culture and manifestations of it. One wit summed up human behaviour as simply driven by three things – lust, greed and fear – and the examples above have ingredients of all three. 'People don't leave jobs; they leave toxic work cultures' – Dr Amina Aitsi-Selmi.

In this book I set out to explore eight drivers of toxic cultures, why they occur, how they are manifested and how they can be changed into a more productive way of working. These eight are as follows:

1. power and the toxic effect of imbalances
2. leadership personality and the dark triad
3. values
4. organisational design and the effect of structure and process
5. informal organisation
6. relations with the external environment
7. motivation and communication
8. reward.

Of course, there will be those who deliberately set out to commit crime for personal reward or cause harm through coercion. Intentional criminality is a psychological world of its own and I deliberately do not tackle this subject here.

So, what are the signs of a toxic culture?
There are two distinct categories:

•   Where unethical practices had caused harm to those *outside* the organisation – customers, shareholders, taxpayers or any other stakeholder. The cases of several Australian banks provided examples of this type of toxic culture, where the values of the organisation did not square with those outside. Their common characteristic was as follows:
    o   An arrogance towards their stakeholders – customers, voters, etc. – in the mistaken belief that as an institution, they were different and the normal rules did not apply to them. In recent times, the rise of Twitter and social media has provided an opportunity for push back, and in one study, some 18% of tweets were rude towards members of Congress in the USA (2).

Some have argued that this is a direct consequence of there being such strong demands for compliance to rules and norms that employees 'take it out' on external stakeholders.

•   Where beliefs and behaviours have caused pain and difficulty to those *inside* the organisation. This is harder to spot from the outside, but manifests in the performance of the organisation failing to achieve its potential – or even failing outright. Typically, these behaviours include yelling and verbal abuse, condescension, insults and put-downs, anger and disrespectful interactions. We can group these into six major categories:
    o   Incivility, where common courtesies are ignored.

o   Shaming, which involves humiliating others, sarcasm, excessive focus on the errors of others and critical comments about a person's characteristics (such as their height, weight or race) verging on the criminal, especially if it involves sexual or racial abuse.

o   Passive hostility, which involves the distrust of other opinions, passive-aggressive behaviour, turf wars and an unwillingness to accept any feedback.

o   Team sabotage, which involves attempts by an individual to monitor and control team members to their advantage and using authority and influence in the group to punish others for actions with which they do not agree.

o   Harassment, which involves behaviour, especially of a sexual nature, that has become silently condoned.

o   Ostracism. In strong traditional cultures, being 'sent to Siberia' was a way of dealing with those who did not accept group norms, particularly if it involved disclosing bad practice to management.

The health consequences of toxic behaviour are typically depression, anxiety, stress, fatigue and sickness.

These two distinct types of toxicity (affecting those inside and those outside the organisation) share some common characteristics. Both types of organisations have a dissonance between their underlying values and beliefs with the norms and conventions of society at large. Why does this come about in such diverse organisations? We will seek to explore this phenomenon in this book.

If we dig deeper into the stories of toxic cultures cited earlier, several features are apparent:

- In the case of the banks and other financial institutions in Australia, a strong bonus system of rewards was in place based on an assumption that in that industry, money motivates, which attracts people who are attracted by the possibility of big rewards. 'Greed is good' became the mantra. Those who achieved strong performance earned big rewards and became the role models for others, regardless of the way in which they had achieved that performance – the ends justified the means.

- Little or no oversight of accounting practices. Enron has become a well-known example of wilful corporate fraud and corruption. The scandal also raised questions about the accounting practices and activities of many corporations in the USA and was a factor in the enactment of the Sarbanes–Oxley Act of 2002. It contributed to the downfall of the Arthur Andersen company, which had audited them for years. There was a belief that projecting a stellar performance to the outside world was more important than the actual results, and so accounting practices were not followed in order to achieve that end.

- The MPs' expense scandal in the British Parliament was only exposed when a newspaper published expense claims. A belief that MPs were above scrutiny and that they were entitled to these expenses contributed to a lack of transparency and proper oversight. After this scandal, many government departments talked of the 'Daily Mail' test – in other words, if whatever was happening in the organisation resulted in headlines in the tabloid press, would everyone be comfortable with this? If not, then behaviour should change.

Let us examine some of the signs of a toxic internal culture that impact staff:

- In my work as a consultant, I often spend time in receptions waiting to meet someone. From doing this, you can immediately get a sense of the culture – particularly how friendly, how informal and how helpful their behaviour is towards outsiders. A sign that the culture is far from positive lies in characteristics that are the opposite of these. Conversations between receptionists about their private lives and destructive office politics whilst ignoring visitors in reception are often highly illuminating.

- Whilst different national cultures might determine the degree of formality in greetings (Germany and Japan tend to be more formal than the USA or Australia), it is what lies behind the formality which is indicative of a dysfunctional culture. When titles (both job-related and personal) are used to enforce hierarchy, status and power, this is indicative that there is a rigidity in the way that a company operates. These indicators are often reinforced by status symbols, such as where staff can park or which canteen they can use. The culture tends towards a 'command and control' type and is less flexible in times of change. This is also apparent when departmental boundaries have become walls and cliques form that inhibit others from interacting with them. Certainly, such a culture is less responsive to upward feedback.

- In the balance between initiatives to change some aspects of work and enforcement of the rules, the rules win out in less effective cultures. Given that few policies and rules are applicable to every situation, blind enforcement can lead to undesirable situations. The tragic case of factory fires in Bangladesh in 2016 and 2021, where the doors in a factory were locked for security reasons and no one had authority to open them, caused people to die inside when they were unable to get out. Rules that do not seem sensible when applied in practice can lead to underground avoidance, especially when there are punishments for breaking them. Avoidance is corrosive in a culture where in some instances the rules need to be enforced.

- Because culture is a difficult thing to clearly articulate, there may be a general unease or a realisation that things could be better, but an inability to identify what precisely is wrong, and so there is no easy prescription of how to improve the situation. This general malaise becomes manifest in moaning around the water cooler and unenthusiastic support for new initiatives which require effort. This malaise becomes particularly apparent when stories emerge that illuminate how people really feel. In one instance, a salacious poem that parodied the latest human resources (HR) initiative about flexible working appeared on a website which caused much mocking of HR (dubbed *Human Remains* in one organisation), even though the initiative would benefit many employees, especially those with families. The general level of trust in HR had broken down to such an extent that even the most positive initiative was met with cynicism.

- The sticks and carrots (punishment and reward) of motivation are a tricky balance to get right, but when the focus is only on infractions and punishment, lower morale is the likely result. An old naval joke decrees that 'the beatings will stop when morale improves'. This can be self-reinforcing, in the sense that once a lack of enthusiasm is discovered, sanctions and greater pressure are applied, resulting in a further loss of morale. This is often manifested in an unwillingness to take the initiative and a wariness of acting without referring upwards. Decision making slows down and frustration ensues. Stress is experienced by people at the frontline caught between customers and management, but with no authority to act. As one toxic manager put it, 'if they are doing a proper job, they won't hear from me, if they are not, they certainly will'.

- Another consequence of there being only a one-way flow of orders and no feedback is that plans and instructions that might make a lot of sense around the boardroom table are impractical on the shop floor or with customers. The result is only lukewarm acceptance or giving up at the slightest setback by those who have to carry out the instructions. The discussions between employees tend to be about how impossible or ridiculous these goals and plans are. A TV programme[1] featured chief executives going incognito to do basic jobs in their organisation, and the experience opened their eyes to how inappropriate some of the rules that were in place were.

- Achieving a level of communication that keeps everyone happy is difficult to accomplish, but when it is deficient, rumours flourish and the grapevine takes over as the major channel of information, causing confusion and panic. Complaints about communication is one of the earliest signs of cultural dysfunction. Language and perspective can hide or amplify cultural labels: 'One person's terrorist is another's freedom fighter.' A toxic and bullying culture might be described as 'a purposeful high-performance' culture.

- In these fast-changing times, creativity and innovation are important attributes for any organisation if it is to continue to re-invent itself in a sustained way. Encouraging an entrepreneurial and creative mindset requires a quite different culture and management style. No one has the monopoly on good ideas – they can come from anywhere, and creative cultures harvest those ideas from every part of the organisation and beyond. A certain arrogance that says 'we know best' by senior management or the new product division and rejects ideas from more junior staff or those in different roles or even from the customer is unlikely to survive for long.

- Fear is an overriding emotion in toxic cultures – fear of breaking the rules, of getting things wrong or of falling out of favour with the boss are all indicative signs of an unproductive culture. There might be shifting alliances and much politicking to gain power and influence; whispered conversations occur in the corridor that are at variance with what is said out loud. Indeed, 'double speak' is a characteristic of these toxic cultures. People fret and worry about who is up and who is down. High-level executives jockey for position and challenge one another for a favoured role or a plum assignment. No one is safe and everyone is on edge.

- One unintended consequence of positive psychology is 'toxic positivity', where in a desire to stay positive in times of difficulty and hardship, there is a fear of expressing real emotions and concerns, and inauthentic narratives and behaviour emerge. These narratives might include dismissing difficulties as merely negative choices ('choose to be positive') and urging positive thoughts ('look on the bright side' and 'all will be well tomorrow').

- The final sign of a toxic workplace is that there is no cohesion. The few people who laugh and joke with one another get suspicious sideways looks from people who are too afraid to drop their guard. Outspoken employees and non-traditional thinkers do not last long. They get frustrated and leave or they are invited to leave when their style clashes with the status quo.

We must be careful to avoid the adoption of a judgemental view of a toxic culture which is implied in the title of this book. Our only focus is on when such cultural characteristics as have been pointed out above have a poor and unintended impact on performance when seen from the viewpoint of the many stakeholders of any organisation. There is a tendency to form binary judgements – is this culture good or bad? However, we need to take a more nuanced view, as any culture will likely have good and bad consequences. Some of the cruellest leaders in history and some of the most toxic environments have nevertheless brought about substantial change to their societies and organisations. Culture is the product of everything that has gone before, and it is difficult to predict the likely outcome of a plethora of actions. Of course, many managers may not fully appreciate how their actions – the product of the needs of the moment – impact on the wider organisation. People do not set out to create a toxic culture. As such, toxic cultures should be seen as deviant behaviour rather than the intended outcomes of a particular strategy. The phenomena are then located in a complex web of factors which is amenable to analysis and is less the sole product of individuals.

Each chapter in this volume looks at a different driver of toxic cultures and explores ways of changing that specific driver. In Chapter 11, I discuss a more comprehensive strategy to change the culture of an organisation. Criminal behaviour is a subject on its own; however, some of the behaviour exhibited by some people in the various cases studied here has been criminal and in Chapter 1 I identify the legal consequences of toxic cultures for employees and organisations. My focus is on culture and how various factors conspire to create such unproductive ways.

PART A: CULTURE

Chapter 1 starts by considering what culture is and some of its dimensions, before identifying the characteristics of toxic cultures. What follows is a way of identifying when a culture has become toxic, both in terms of the behaviours that are seen and the effects on performance. In recent years, astronomers have managed to photograph a black hole, which of course consumes light. Before this, scientists only knew of the existence of black holes by the impact they had on the space around them. So it is with toxic cultures, which of course you cannot see; it is the effect on individual attitudes, behaviour and performance that gives the clue to its existence. It is the holy grail of organisations to perform to the maximum of their capability and it is a dramatic indication of the power of an effective culture when all the ingredients work together successfully.

Chapter 2 suggests ways of diagnosing toxic cultures and describes some simple tools and checklists to identify where toxicity may arise. These can be used as survey instruments as well as prompts for individual and group discussion. Precise measurement is difficult, and we need to be wary of spurious accuracy. Reactions of the major stakeholders are going to be the dominant guide. Indicators can be derived from labour turnover, absenteeism and grievances.

PART B: LEADERSHIP – POWER, PERSONALITY AND VALUES

Chapter 3 examines power and how different ways of exercising it influence organisational culture. The potential for power to corrupt is well recorded and the COVID-19 pandemic has provided a rich source of insight into how the locus of control has shifted towards different sources of power, in particular from employers to employees at home. Imbalances in the patterns of power are major factors in changing cultures to become toxic and in later case studies given in Chapter 8, the mapping of power imbalances is a crucial element in their explanation.

Chapter 4 identifies leadership at all levels as a major source of influence on culture and looks at individual personalities and how they distort cultures. The dark triad of the Machiavellian, the sociopath/psychopath and the narcissist, whilst rare in their extreme form, are all too common in their milder form, which results in manipulation. Leaders who get things done often use forms of manipulation as they must push against resistance arising from entrenched attitudes and fear of change. Yet macho management and the collateral damage that it leaves in its wake rarely create a sustainable long-term future. The difference between enthusiastic support and compliance arising from fear is sometimes difficult to spot and this chapter examines those critical 'moment-of-truth' behaviours that make the difference in this respect. When coupled with narcissism, where the focus is on the leader and how great they are, the purpose of the organisation becomes subordinate to their admiration and preservation.

Chapter 5 examines values and in particular how they form and what happens when they come into contention between competing values and goals. Making decisions is invariably based on our values and ethical positions, which arise from different philosophical assumptions. Our upbringing has much to do with forming our early ethical positions and in particular our sense of entitlement. An example of a training exercise is included, which is designed to show participants how to resolve differences in value choices. A key source of organisation tension is when the way in which performance is achieved conflicts with stated values. What wins – values or performance? Organisations have resolved this dilemma in various ways, and the case of Tylenol shows the beneficial impact of its adherence to its values.

PART C: ORGANISATION

Chapter 6 looks at organisational models that underpin our economies and explores organisational design where the poor design of structure and process results in role conflict, turf wars and errors caused by role confusion. So many errors in organisations are caused by interactions across organisational boundaries that are inefficient. Another sign that the organisational design is not fit for purpose is when it becomes unable to solve problems. Individual managers may appear impotent because no mechanisms exist for more coordinated action. When power rests in the hands of only a few (often extremely busy) managers at the top, an inability and unwillingness to solve the problem lower down develops.

Rules can become the source of toxic cultures arising from the best of intentions. Rarely do policies and rules cover every situation that people remote from the rule makers might experience, partly because of life experience and exposure. Few senior executives these days have worked their way up from the bottom and even if they had, the ways of operating today on the frontline with changing technology will be quite different from a senior executive's experience many years earlier. Another reason is that rules tend to be retrospective and based on the past, yet they need to be anticipating an increasingly uncertain future.

Watching, as I write, politicians and senior managers of all kinds wrestling with the COVID-19 pandemic illustrates how difficult it is to anticipate everything that might befall an organisation, let alone a country. When asked what he most feared, Harold Macmillan, a British Prime Minister in the 1960s, said 'events, dear boy, events'.

Chapter 7 explores systems of informal organisation for social groupings and the informal power relationships that provide one of the ways to bind groups together. The informal organisation is a powerful force and, once in opposition to the formal organisation, results in significant negative impacts on the organisation. Personal relationships form the backbone of the informal organisation and many examples of where quarantine and COVID-19 lockdown rules were broken occurred in situations where personal relationships were stronger than the formal rules. Convention, history and inertia also play their part in shaping the informal organisation, and, indeed, institutional memory is important in maintaining complex systems that have been built up over many years. Yet the dead hand of 'we have always done it that way' leads to a slowing down of initiative to improve or find better ways, and in due course a cynicism about the organisation. It was Maynard Keynes who famously remarked that not to change your views when the world changes was like a parrot that can only say 'it's going to be fine today'.

One byproduct of the informal organisation is the emergence of underground ways of working that ignore conventions and a growing tension between the old and the new. A desire by some to preserve the status quo leads to conflict and individual toxic behaviour, which can poison the organisational culture. Passive-aggressive behaviour and the growing array of toxic games and sexual liaisons such as those that occurred amongst staff at the Parliament in Canberra all serve to destroy working relations.

Chapter 8 looks at some of the examples of where external stakeholders are adversely impacted by a toxic culture and vice versa. Experience of these troublesome interfaces shows that checks, balances and clear value systems are imperative in sustainable relationships. A recent example is the aged care sector in Australia, when privatised home care turned from a social benefit into a financial business. The staffing model moved towards using many more casual employees from the gig economy, who in turn had to hold multiple jobs in many locations to make ends meet. When the COVID-19 pandemic came along, they became virus spreaders to the most vulnerable of communities, which suffered the highest number of deaths of any group in the population.

Another recent example is the US healthcare system, which, whilst it has been beneficial to the insured and the rich, has not served the poor and uninsured well, especially during the pandemic. We finish by looking at three case studies that illustrate the interaction of organisations with their environment and how they became dysfunctional: Crown Casinos, the US health industry and the Boeing aircraft company. Power imbalances between the different stakeholders provide an explanatory model of a significant cause of their toxic cultures.

PART D: THE INDIVIDUAL

Chapter 9 turns to the question of motivation and communication. There has been a long history of theories to explain motivation, from Maslow in 1943 to Herzberg in 1959, Alderfer in 1960s and 1970s, and the recent theory of Pink in 2011 identifying autonomy, mastery and purpose as the key drivers of motivation. Acculturation, often from an early stage in terms of identifying what is prized, lays the groundwork for aspiration. Incentives can take many forms depending on that aspiration – to be rich, famous, valued or significant. The list is long. In the examples given above, greed played a major role for bankers and their bonuses, and MPs and their expenses. Yet this is not true of many organisations or professions. Indeed, some of the hardest-working and most pressurised jobs – nurses, social workers, teachers and civil servants – are not well paid, and it is unlikely that people enter these careers for the money. Feelings of self-worth, security, helping others and the community at large play a bigger role in this respect. We explore how people become seduced by their motivators to engage in activities that are not beneficial to them. One aspect of motivation is the balance between the carrot and the stick - the balance between approach goals as opposed to avoidance goals.

In this chapter we also unpick why communication can lead to a lowering of morale. Too little, too late communication can lead to frustration and confusion; too much displaces other more useful uses of people's time, especially when it does not address employees' questions and concerns. Communication is one of the hardest aspects of a manager's job to get right and rarely do they manage to achieve it perfectly. In times of change when tactics need to evolve, ensuring everyone is on the same page with clear accountabilities and a direct line of sight in the transmission of information from top to bottom becomes a significant challenge.

Chapter 10 examines how reward can distort behaviour and lead to poor outcomes. Reward can be both extrinsic and intrinsic. A large amount of research indicates that money is a transitory motivator. Reward may not just take the form of money; power, promotion, influence, fame and patronage can all play their part in creating a toxic culture when a desire for these rewards become the dominant and overarching motivation for an individual.

PART E: SOLUTIONS

Chapter 11 lays out a strategic programme for cultural change and examines how to shift beliefs, attitudes and behaviours using a series of policies and practices. There is an old maxim in organisational development: 'you change the team, or you change the team'. In other words, there are two fundamental strategies to deploy: you change the dynamics of the organisation and how the system works with the players that you have, or you change the individuals in the hope that new people will work in a different way. Both strategies have their adherents and their strengths, but both have their limitations, and in this chapter, we explore how to navigate this minefield in order to achieve organisational, team and individual change. However, the first hurdle is to find a place to start and 'unfreeze' the situation, as invariably there is an unwillingness to change anything from many quarters. There is an old joke: 'how many psychologists does it take to change a light bulb? One, but the light bulb has got to want to change'. Too many people have a vested interest in the status quo, especially in terms of how people are rewarded. Change strategies have to be powerful and sustained in order to overcome these barriers and this is certainly one of the reasons why change programmes so often fail.

WHY THIS BOOK?

In a report by the SHRM in 2019 (3), it was found that toxic cultures had cost US businesses $223 billion in the previous five years and had driven 20% of US employees out of their jobs. A study of healthcare workers in the US (4) found that 25% of the sample believed that toxic behaviour was positively correlated with patient mortality and 49% stated that intimidation by another practitioner resulted in the misadministration of medication. Pearson and Porath (5) found that of those affected by toxic behaviour:

- 48% decreased their work effort.
- 68% said their performance declined.
- 78% said their commitment to the organisation declined.
- 12% claimed they quit as a direct result of toxic behaviour.

A recent analysis (6) points to the impact that incivility in political discourse is having in the USA. Hardly a year goes by without some fresh corporate scandal, and when the dust settles and the blame game is over, a more sober analysis invariably points at culture. Yes, there may be the odd rotten apple, but the assumption that most people in these enterprises are just trying to do the best they can has led to the following prevailing paradigm – treat people right and they will behave right. The right things as far as they can see are derived from what is expected and modelled by senior executives and what earns them rewards, which may only take the form of praise and respect, but are still powerful motivators. Different personalities will respond in different ways, and whilst we will see in Chapter 4 the role that toxic leaders can play, they do not account for most examples of deviant behaviour. There is an alternative view that organisations are an interstitial point of many competing interests, and it is the interplay of these that results in the culture that emerges. The bottom line (7) is that 49% of US workers were considering leaving their jobs, and in the UK, 64% of people in one survey described the negative impact that workplace culture had on their mental health (8).

My desire in this book is to explore these drivers of behaviour and help readers tackle toxic cultures for the benefit of all stakeholders.

A NOTE FOR READERS

This book is intended for two audiences. The first is those who wish to explore the subject of toxic cultures with reference to previous studies and cases. This might be someone studying culture or who has a specific professional interest in organisational development and change.

The other audience are practitioners in the field whose availability to study the subject might be limited, but who want to get the essence of what drives toxic cultures and how to change them. Each chapter ends with a summary of the key points, and Chapter 2 presents a number of basic tools to identify cultural characteristics that might not be beneficial to organisational effectiveness. Chapter 11 presents a practical process for culture change.

Notes and references are included at the end of each chapter.

NOTE

1 Under various titles: Undercover boss and Back to the floor.

REFERENCES

1 Report about former MP Sir Peter Viggers *The Independent* (7 September 2010). Retrieved 9 June 2022 from https://www.independent.co.uk/news/uk/politics/exmp-sir-peter-viggers-sells-duck-house-for-charity-2072007.html.

2 Theocharis, Y., Barbera, P., Fazekas, Z. and Popa, S.A. (2020) *The dynamics of political incivility on Twitter.* Sage Open.

3 SHRM (2019). *The high cost of a toxic workplace culture.* Retrieved 9 June 2022 from https://pmq.shrm.org/wp-content/uploads/2020/07/SHRM-Culture-Report_2019-1.pdf.

4 Holloway, E.L. and Kusy, M.E. (2009) Systems approach to addressing incivility and disruptive behaviours in health care organisations. *Advances in Health Care Management, 10*, 239-65.

5 Pearson, C. and Porath, C. (2005) On the nature, consequences, and remedies of workplace incivility: no time for nice? Think again. *Academy of Management Perspectives, 19*(1)*,* 7-18.

6 Boatright, R.G., Shaffer, T.J., Sobieraj, S. and Young, D.G. (2019) *A crisis of civility? Political discourse and its discontents.* Routledge.

7 Mirza, B. (2019, 25 September) Toxic workplace cultures hurt workers and company profits. Retrieved 5 April 2022 from https://www.shrm.org/ResourcesAndTools/hr-topics/employee-relations/Pages/Toxic-Workplace-Culture-Report.aspx.

8 Maher, C. (2021, October) Protecting your people: The importance of adopting a people-centric workplace culture. Retrieved 9 June 2022 from https://insight.culture-shift.co.uk/en/privatesector/protecting-your-people-the-importance-of-adopting-a-people-centric-workplace-culture.

Part A
Culture

What is a toxic culture?

INTRODUCTION

One day I went with someone to his bank in Sydney. He told his business to the receptionist and was asked to wait. After 15 minutes, he enquired when he might be seen, as nothing was happening and the staff were gossiping. After a few more minutes, a staff member put down their coffee and sauntered over to him and rather coldly dealt with his query, which required him to fill in a form and then go to the back of the queue. Eventually, he met the staff member again and, without any comment, she ticked it and slung it into an out-tray. 'OK' was all she said and signalled for him to leave. We left with a feeling of irritation.

Sometime later, I had cause to go to another branch of the bank to get my signature added to a business account. The service was perfunctory and the member of staff who dealt with me was critical of the way in which the minutes approving my addition to the account had been written. With a sigh, he said: 'I suppose I must approve it'. I felt like a naughty schoolboy and again left feeling irritated. These two experiences started me thinking about the culture of this bank that caused its staff to be so unfriendly to a customer. I have no reason to suspect that they were not otherwise sane, sensible citizens who were kind to their families and were just trying to do their jobs. However, the combination of rules, processes, pressures and behaviour of others had all left them with a reluctance to deal with customers in the way that they would probably expect for themselves. Culture has an extraordinary effect on behaviour.

There are many dimensions to this simple proposition and in this chapter, we explore culture and how it can become toxic both to those inside and outside the organisation.

WHAT IS CULTURE?

A popular definition of culture is: 'the way we do things round here'. As Fons Trompenaars in his pioneering work on different national cultures suggests: 'it is the way in which a group of people solves problems. It is not what is visible on the surface. It is the shared ways groups of people understand and interpret the world' (1). The same events can be given quite different meanings depending on the cultural lens through which they are viewed. Culture has a hidden aspect reflecting the values and beliefs (2) that we each bring to work, and this is manifest in our behavioural reactions and subsequence actions. Williams (3) defines organisational culture as 'the commonly held and relatively stable beliefs, attitudes and values that exist within the organization'. More simply, Farren Drury remarked that 'culture eats strategy any day', implying that culture has a greater

DOI: 10.4324/9781003307334-3

and more immediate impact on performance of an organisation compared to most strategic imperatives (4). The elements of culture are described as: 'the conscious and unconscious content and products of thought and reasoning. Culture pervades the decision making and problem-solving processes of the organization. It influences the goals, means and manner of action. It is a source of motivation and demotivation, of satisfaction and dissatisfaction. In short, culture underlies much of the human activity in an organization' (5).

The culture of organisations also affects society as a whole in the move towards corporate colonisation where 'the unobtrusive ways corporate meanings, instrumental logics, and managerial values dominate the ways we understand, think, and act in everyday life' (6).

SO WHAT IS THE IMPACT OF CULTURE ON ECONOMIC ACTIVITY?

In order to explain such a divergence between rich and poor countries, the early economists were obsessed with culture, a catch-all term encompassing a society's beliefs, preferences, and values. Adam Smith, the author of *The Wealth of Nations* (7), explored the ways in which culture helped or hindered capitalism. He argued that certain norms were required in order for market economies to thrive - most importantly, that people would be self-interested, but that they would satisfy their self-interest by adapting to the needs of others. Karl Marx, a few decades later, worried that a culture of 'oriental despotism' prevented the emergence of capitalism in Asia.

In his seminal work *The Protestant ethic and the spirit of capitalism* (8), Max Weber argued that a strong work ethic, the deferment of gratification (your reward is in Heaven) and the expectation of a sober God-fearing lifestyle facilitated capital formation. This was a vital ingredient in launching the industrial revolution. However, such simplistic explanations soon fall down when looking at industrialisation in Asia (9).

Theories abound as to how precisely culture influences economic activity. Is higher economic activity related to 'connections with strangers' (10)? Putnam (11) suggested that a culture where people 'read more newspapers, were more likely to participate in sports and social activities and voted' contributed to better government and more efficient economic transactions.

In order to grow, businesses must look beyond the founding family and learn how to involve and trust more than their relatives. There are variations in kinship practices and tightness of groups which affect the capacity of groups to organise large-scale ventures, as well as variations in their openness to external influences outside the kinship patterns. An old Chinese saying is that trust takes a lifetime to build and a moment to lose; it is described elsewhere as 'trust comes in on foot and leaves on horseback'. The development of social traditions about trust was critical to the formation of strong and enduring trading relationships. In the City of London, a founding principle was 'my word is my bond' and anybody breaking it would not survive long in the 'square mile'.

The application of science and data (emerging in the 17th century, often called 'The Age of Reason') to solve practical problems as opposed to a more philosophical enquiry by acquiring knowledge for its own sake contributed to economic development. James Suzman (12) traces the history of work in which he attempts to explain many of our cultural determinants of how we work and why they differ. For example, he argues that agriculture brought about a more regimented way of living because it was dictated by the seasons (planting and sowing) and the demands of different crops and animals (cows need milking). Female participation varies between societies and has deep cultural roots in farming traditions – ploughing takes strength and so men are more likely to do it, while herding is easier for women. Many other factors, including the emergence of legal systems about property and individual responsibilities, patterns of diseases often arising from colonialism and the legacy of the way in which they were governed, have all contributed to a society's culture.

The military have long sought to build a culture which encourages the will to fight – discipline, belief in serving your country, camaraderie and later honouring of veterans. At the battle for the French fort of Verdun in 1916, the Germans greatly underestimated the French motivation and grit to defend it. The casualties were huge (some say 300,000). Some research indicates that those who fought hardest had a low interest in material comfort and economic prospects. Team morale was high and team members bonded well together. The top priority of such fighters, says Richard Davis, shifted from the team (described as 'family') to another cause, 'a transcendental ideal that has become so sacralised that it would not be traded away for anything else' (13).

Overall, there is such a mass of factors that few definite conclusions can be certain about why cultures differ or their relationship to economies. All we can say is that history in all its complexity plays out today in the cultural norms and beliefs that a society holds, and these impact our every activity.

ORGANISATIONAL CULTURAL INGREDIENTS

With the culture of society as a backdrop, organisational culture is the product of the impact each and every stakeholder has on the organisation either internally or externally. It is a feedback loop in that every action an actor takes has some impact on others and they in turn react, influencing the initial actor and those who see and/or hear of it. Stories, particularly those involving some argument or emotional incident, will be talked about and spread because they are unexpected in the more formal setting of an organisation. This fund of war stories will in turn influence others going forward.

A critical judgement of any manager in times of change is whether to push on, face down their critics and resist any attempt to stop the process, or to pause and listen to them, back down and change course. There is a bias towards the former as it seems more heroic, but the latter requires more courage. However, the heroic manager might find it increasingly more difficult to lead a group of disgruntled employees who feel unable to voice their concerns or point out when small tweaks and modifications might make the whole process more effective. Far from being a collaborative effort, employees see it as 'the manager's personal change programme' and might at worst deliberately stand aside and watch it fail, believing that this will prove them right.

The following case illustrates the dilemma:

> *In a governmental organisation, a project was underway to introduce a new computer system that everyone would interact with. It had come about because the old system was inefficient and the vendor had refused to continue supporting it. However, the new system had many faults and user trials had not gone well. At a mass meeting, the project manager was faced with a barrage of criticisms and, clearly rattled and under pressure to get this system in place, finally snapped and told the audience it was going in as it was and they had better 'get over it'. Fortunately, the development was stopped and a radical new approach was taken that addressed many user concerns. However, the phrase 'get over it' entered the organisation's lexicon and it became a byword for insensitivity and lack of concern for the problems of others. The positive legacy on the culture was less arrogance on the part of IT project managers and a greater willingness across all projects to engage in a constructive dialogue in order to bring users with them.*

In most organisations, there is an expectation of 'rational' behaviour and so even the most extreme outburst must be justified in some way in order to make sense of it to both the instigator and those around them. However, the need to make sense of behaviour in organisations creates an incentive that is individually defined. Once defined, the culture is further nudged in that direction. The extent to which it is widespread depends upon both the influence of the instigator and the resonance of the incident with others. Indeed, humour from films like *The Death of Stalin* to comic strips like Dilbert illustrate how absurd some of the actions that go on in organisations seem to outsiders, and yet reasonable and rational to those inside. Once a plausible meaning is attributed to actions, it becomes internalised and what might have seemed odd to a new recruit on day one in a new organisation rapidly becomes normal. It should be noted that not everyone will share the same cultural beliefs and assumptions in an organisation and, indeed, given the tacit nature of many cultural norms, surveys across organisations do not agree on all aspects by any means.

Relationships, the engine that drives culture, are also socially constructed, and are affected for good or ill by the language used. A homeless charity initially described their residents as 'inmates', but that sounded like they were prisoners, so the charity reframed its 'clients' (which it thought was too impersonal) to become 'residents' and then 'guests' – euphemisms you might say, but it changed the attitude of staff over time towards being more respectful. Whilst this may appear manipulative, it is common practice. The change in language around racial prejudice and the description of skin colour has seen a transformation towards more socially acceptable words, which makes the use of old language seem even more provocative.

Culture becomes manifest in individual and collective behaviour, and whilst there is always some discrepancy between how individuals perceive their behaviour and the reality as experienced by others, there tends to be a bigger gap with more toxic individuals. Karl Weick (14) argues that we are all continually trying to make sense of the world around us and to interpret all the different cues we are given in order to ascertain how we should behave. When our perception of our behaviour collides with both our values and our feelings, we experience some discomfort. This in turn can lead to antagonistic feelings towards the organisation or to others around us, and our behaviour becomes similarly antagonistic and toxic. Toxic individuals have the capacity to justify their actions and to be able to tolerate critical feedback under the guise of 'this situation needs a strong leader', 'I'm being tough' or 'I'm being myself' – being 'authentic' or some other justification.

Schein (15) describes culture in three ways: artefacts, values and assumptions. Artefacts are the things you can see – like the furniture in the atrium, which says a lot about how an organisation wants to project itself. Values are shared beliefs we have and are often apparent when decisions are made. Assumptions are the unspoken beliefs. Other writers (16) have described culture as a web of stories, controls, symbols, rituals and routines, organisational designs and power structures.

Chapter 2 gives some tools to measure culture. All these instruments are worthy but imperfect attempts to capture a complex phenomenon.

FORMAL AND INFORMAL DRIVERS

Another way of looking at culture is by examining the formal and informal systems that operate in any organisation separately and seeing how each of these elements can result in beneficial or poor outcomes.

We can divide these elements into two sets of drivers. Figure 1.1 lays out the formal cultural elements.

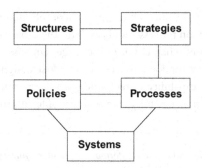

FIGURE 1.1 The formal cultural system

Structures involve roles and relationships between roles. Poor design is seen in role conflict and where there is confusion about responsibilities. A principle called subsidiarity (a principle enshrined in the European Union but imperfectly applied) dictates that discretion and decisions are pushed down to the lowest level that can be effective. Overcentralised control results in slower decision making (because it has to go up and down the chain), lower initiative ('it's the rules mate', 'higher than my pay grade') and inflexibility. A strict hierarchy gets in the way of coordination as it denies the possibilitiy of working across boundaries and asumes that each role covers the activities required without the need to liaise with others.

Strategy has been described as the road map for an organisation to reach its objectives and invariably involves a choice of route. Ineffective strategies result in wasted resources through pursuing routes that will not achieve those objectives in the most efficient way in terms of people, time, money and other resources. Conflict can often arise when individuals become so wedded to their strategy that there is a lack of appreciation and indeed flexibility in seeing others' viewpoints, and thus seeking some compromise to achieve better outcomes.[1]

Policies are the instructions about how to act in any situation. In establishing policies, which are invariably based on past experience, there is an assumption that the future will be much the same as the past. In times of crisis in particular, where little or no precedent can guide policy makers, the probability of policies turning out to be wrong is increased. In the recent pandemic, policy makers were having to deliberate between closing economies in a draconian way with the resulting collapse of the economy but the prospect of saving more lives, and favouring keeping everything open to faciitate the economy but at the expense of an overwhelmed health system and lives lost. Across the world we have seen a range of policy approaches, none of which has found the perfect balance between these two unpalatable scenarios. The legacy of those policies in terms of deaths and destruction of jobs will haunt politicians and their adminstrations for years to come. Whilst no one doubts politicians believed they were trying to do their best and were acting in the best interests of their countries, nevertheless the results were death and destruction.

Processes are the ways of producing outcomes and invaribaly involve hand-offs between individuals and departments. In a study conducted many years ago in American telephone companies, the researchers found that a very high proportion of mistakes occurred in the boundaries between departments because processes often cross organisation structures. Whilst a simple answer might be to change the structure (an all too common device), the reality is that there will always be organisational boundaries where hand-offs are required. Mistakes can incur costs, lost time from recovery and irate customers, all of which damage the organisation's reputation.

Our last formal element is systems which are inextricably tied up by processes. Technology can impose a degree of rigidity on processes and can limit the capacity and freedom for indiivduals to carry out different procedures when conditions change. Unexpected or infrequent actions that were not foreseen when the technology/processes were first designed can cause frustration and inadeqaute performance. The capability of technology to exert control remotely can give rise to damaging consequences, as it may not fully take account of local situations:

> *A car hire company wanted to gather more information for marketing purposes from their customers and established some questions embedded in the system dialogue that an assistant went through when a customer was renting a car. Car hire desks at airports are faced with a surge of customers as flights arrive. Invariably people want to get away as quickly as possible. The introduction of this additional dialogue slowed the process down and the queues became longer. The assistants became more stressed about this as they were faced with irate customers in front of them, whereas marketing was in head office a long way away. One day, an assistant found a way of bypassing the routine and life got easier as she processed customers more quickly and the queues got shorter. The customers were happy, but marketing didn't get their data.*

Where systems become too complex or too onerous for frontline staff, they take short cuts as the immediate pressures of the moment take precedence. In some situations where there is little oversight or a good understanding of the law (especially in complicated areas like finance), staff may even disregard the law.

Figure 1.2 lays out the informal cultural elements which are more diffuse and open to differing interpretations.

Soft systems include the style of leadership and the positive or negative impact on subordinates. The symbols of power are potent sources of motivation and control, but also of envy and rejection.

Values, as the label implies, are what we value, but are rarely comprehensively articulated. In recent years, organisations have focused quite frequently on specifying the corporate values, and we will look at these in more detail in Chapter 5. Suffice to say at this stage that there are two sources of difficulty. The first is when espoused values are different from what is observed in practice and is reinforced when performance outcomes that are achieved are rewarded, despite contradicting the espoused values. 'Walk the talk' is a common mantra for leaders and when

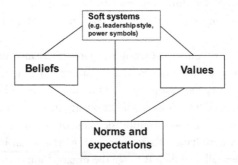

FIGURE 1.2 The informal cultural system

former American President George H.W. Bush said 'read my lips, no new taxes', people observed that taxes went up and as a result he lost all credibility and the election. The second source of difficulty is that individual values and corporate values are never likely to be totally congruent, even if lip service has been paid to them. Both these differences give rise to conflicts and disagreements. Values are difficult to spot, although in Chapter 5 I provide an exercise to try and harden up the visibility of values. It was the French philosopher Jean-Paul Sartre who is reputed to have said that we only really know our values when we make tough decisions, otherwise they are hidden by polite behaviour.

Our beliefs initially are based on our values that start to be formed from our earliest family experiences and are moulded and developed by subsequent life events. These in turn result in our beliefs about how the world works, how we should relate to it, how to behave in different situations and our expectations of others. Of course, beliefs should not be confused with 'objective truth', though if strongly held they may fuel our own 'psychological truth'. The rise of many conspiracy theories often occurs when beliefs (determined by many factors, including whom people trust) attain the status of truth in their eyes. We hold beliefs about many things that impact corporate culture, including: the environment in which the organisation operates (legal, ecological, political, financial and the marketplace), its performance, however this is measured (financial and personal as well as organisational, social responsibility and other outcomes), the appropriateness of the structure and processes of the organisation, its public perception and its treatment of employees. The extent to which employees accept these beliefs as correct is a measure of the strength of the culture, and once these become internalised and no longer questioned, they become harder to change. We carry our personal values and beliefs into the workplace, which can lead us to expect that any organisation we join will be congruent and accepting of them. Indeed, such beliefs are often unexamined and assumed to be universal. Therefore, it causes a shock when things turn out to be otherwise. When personal beliefs are not congruent with those espoused by the organisation, but due to the needs of a job, compliance is achieved, the result is to minimise wholehearted commitment, enthusiasm and discretionary effort, and subversive acts are increasingly likely.

The product of beliefs and values result in our norms of how to behave and expectations of what each social situation requires of us. A key question is who defines the norm and what is deviant behaviour? History is full of totalitarian regimes that sought to redefine what was acceptable behaviour and who was acceptable. Invariably, when others define norms with which we do not agree, rebellious behaviour arises, even if only in the mind. All social groups have shared norms that develop over time into rituals and mantras. When we unpack these, there are often shared values which provide the glue that causes these groups to stay together. When there is dissonance, toxic behaviour invariably ensues.

The nature of toxic cultures, why they occur and what drives them

The starting point of a toxic culture is when incivility takes hold. Everywhere in our world, the tenets of civilised behaviour appear to be breaking down – from extra-judicial killings of dictators and terrorists to toxicity in the workplace – 'snakes in suits', as one famous book put it (17). Indeed, in our postmodernist world incivility appears to be increasingly tolerated when it concerns any others who we don't like or respect. Rousseau, who famously remarked that he detested what another had said but would defend to the death his right to say it, would be unimpressed.

So why are we in this era of decline of so many of those hard-fought-for elements of civilised behaviour – the rule of law at its most basic and even more so of common courtesy in the workplace and the street? Why have we moved from a utilitarian (happiness before principle) and Kantian (principle before happiness) view of right behaviour to an egotistical view (if it is OK for me, it is OK)? Where do the roots of incivility lie? Is the cause the selfish gene that strives for survival and is emulated in organisational politics and societal oppression by one group against another? Or rather is it better explained at a sociological level as a pattern of forces, like the giant magnet in the Hadron Collider? There seems to be an increase in touchiness as we increasingly reach for our lawyers, or is this some symbiotic relationship that becomes self-fulfilling? The growing literature on trauma arising from a myriad of causes in our upbringing has been cited as the cause of psychological issues later in life (18).

Those who study the behaviour of animal colonies regularly report the collapse of delicately balanced structures into anarchy when overcrowding reaches a tipping point. A more intriguing and yet frightening theory might be that maybe incivility is the first sign of an overcrowded planet turning in on itself. Perhaps toxic behaviour is a product of a more stressful society and workplaces. It is most apparent in, for example, road rage or stress-related legal battles. The events in 2021 in North America, where riots occurred after the murder of a man of colour by a police officer, were the touchpaper for societal stress caused by years of discrimination and the brutal policing of minorities. Coupled with accelerating change of all kinds – technological, social, political and economic – and it is little wonder that many claim to experience extreme stress and be unable to function more frequently in everyday tasks (19). This finding points to a possible future increase in toxicity in cities and societies.

It is a curious paradox that you can live inches away from someone in an apartment block and not know them, yet in rural communities you can live miles away and know them well. Urbanisation destroys the lattice of social relationships that keep antisocial behaviour in check. In small communities the group memory ensures acts of incivility are not forgotten and can act as a further check against endangering relationships through the risk of ostracism.

Is toxic behaviour best explained neurologically? Neuroscientists suggest that under continuing stress, cortisol is raised and hypervigilance for threats means that people are closer to the edge more of the time. As the pressure of everyday life causes endless stress reactions (neurologically described as 'amygdale hijacks'), [2] we need to learn new coping methods, and invariably there will be times when we react inappropriately. The workplace has become increasingly insecure. Lifetime employment is a distant memory for most organisations and the stress caused by tighter deadlines, more demanding performance standards and minimum staffing levels results in the loss of the buffer that allows a more measured and polite way of behaving.

Regardless of the cause, organisational life and performance are being impaired by bad behaviour, especially that of leaders. It was Gary Chapman who remarked that when a workplace becomes toxic, its poison spreads beyond its walls and into the lives of everyone it touches. In tough times, there is a tendency for a nuanced and finessed management style to be abandoned in favour of more directive approaches. The exposure of employees to psychosocial hazards, 'little or no organisational support, poor interpersonal relationships, high workload, lack of autonomy, poor rewards and lack of job security' (20) all lead to both personal and organisational harm.

In June 2021, Denis Handlin, boss of Sony Music Australia for many years and a significant figure in the music industry, resigned. The press (21) reported 'allegations of bullying, harassment, racism and discrimination' throughout the organisation. The Guardian newspaper (22) reported a number of staff complaints that it was a 'boys club' and 'Sony was ruled by fear, like nowhere else I have worked'. Others described sexist remarks, 'arse groping' and only pretty young women attending a marketing event. These are typical indicators of a toxic culture and are not uncommon. What is surprising (and courageous) is that Sony removed such an icon in the industry, who was professionally successful, an officer of the Order of Australia, a board member of the Australian

Recording Industry Association and a major influence on many artists' careers. This showed that values and culture in the end were more important to a sustainable business than the performance and influence of one (very senior) man.

In the following chapters, we will describe many of the drivers of toxic cultures and will explain how they come about, but we should not seek to explain them away. The bottom line of toxic cultures is where individuals, regardless of their role or position in the hierarchy, find themselves working reluctantly out of fear or necessity and thus are unable to give of their best. This often arises when the behaviour and attitude of others causes them to be resentful and feeling unheard and unvalued. Externally, other stakeholders may feel similarly aggrieved because of the treatment they receive. A whistleblower in one of the Australian banks, pilloried for its immoral and illegal practices, remarked that the culture was toxic. He described the volatile, psychopathic behaviour of many managers where winning was everything, regardless of the consequences for their customers or staff.

Much of the evidence of toxicity comes from two major streams. The first stream is organisational sociology, which has catalogued a wide range of behaviours from the simple ways of 'manipulating my manager' to achieve personal goals, to more destructive behaviours such as sabotage, criminality and the pathology of destructive individuals. The second stream is the experience of HR managers who observe withdrawal from the workplace through formal grievances, absenteeism and ultimately staff turnover.

Cultures can become toxic over time through a series of actions that might seem mundane, but build to a tipping point. Amazon has become a titan of a company in the age of online shopping. In the USA, 50 cents of every retail dollar is spent through Amazon, making its founder Jeff Bezos the richest man on the planet. Over the years, various rumblings have emerged about its tough employee policies and low pay. In 2020 two tech engineers helped to organise a livestream event for warehouse employees to explain their COVID-19 fears. They were fired and a storm erupted at this vindictive behaviour, which prompted Tim Bray, a vice president, to resign and claim that Amazon exhibited a 'vein of toxicity' (23).

The business models of companies may also create the conditions that many would describe as toxic. An analyst at Goldman Sachs (24) in 2021 surveyed 13 peers and found that the average hours worked in a week was 98, with only 5 hours' sleep a night. A total of 77% of them had suffered abuse, and 75% had sought or considered seeking counselling because they experienced a decline in their mental and physical health. The possibility that they would not last long in those jobs was high. On the face of it, this may seem to be a straightforward example of an abusive organisation that exploited its junior employees. However, the reactions were less clear, making any definition of toxic culture much less universal. Reactions included 'what did they expect when they were paid so well?' and 'it's always been like that – never did anyone any harm'. Nevertheless, if an organisation has any sense of nurturing and retaining talent and building future capacity, then finding cultural norms which avoid negativity and harm, and are acceptable to the majority seems vitally important.

THE HISTORICAL CONTEXT

What is the root of a toxic culture? One culprit is postmodern ideas of relative values – what is OK for me is OK in general. The Judaeo-Christian philosophy created a set of rules of living that were so strongly enforced for generations that for many, it held in check more selfish and intolerant views of the world. Market economies work on a largely hidden assumption that competition is healthy, but needs to be regulated from time to time. The balance between freedom and control is in constant flux, being swayed by political philosophies and market conditions. However, competition when it becomes fuelled by personal conflict rather than just commercial interests begins to poison the companies and their practices, as well as the marketplace for all. The case study below of National Mutual (25) illustrates how a series of factors over many decades contributed to toxic relationships with its competitors and in the culture of the company to this day.

CASE STUDY: NATIONAL MUTUAL LIFE

National Mutual Life (NML) started in 1869 with a clear vision of solid values: 'our ambition is to be not necessarily the largest company but the best – and the best company is that which gives the best service to its policyholders and the community' (Andrew Newell, Chairman, in a 1923 speech at the annual meeting). It also set about making some pioneering changes to life assurance. Such worthy aspirations said nothing about how business was to be conducted, but in 1874 a handwritten note that was circulated to agents said scurrilous things about the company's competitors. This caused a series of claims and counter-claims and legal action for slander. It set in train a conflict with AMP, a 170-year-old wealth management firm that would have long-lasting consequences and established working practices that led to a toxic culture. John Templeton, a founding member of the NML senior management, was described as 'pugnacious'. He continued to have public arguments with AMP, other companies and with agents about the authorship of non-forfeiture conditions. The sensitive nature of several of the players meant that feuds and lawsuits became common, and the result was a far from calm-and-ordered approach to business. However, NML had become a pioneer which others followed. It is often the case that pioneers have a rough time to start with and maybe its combative style ensured its survival. In 1883, five insurance companies including AMP agreed to 'ban the twisting of business', a rebate to the life assured, comparison leaflets and appointing agents of another company without their permission. NML was not invited because AMP declared that only those who could be trusted were invited, further fuelling the animosity between them.

The issuing of vitriolic leaflets by both societies contributed to the friction. The consequence of this feud over many decades was to leave both institutions impaired in terms of their performance, and the present-day cultural problems of AMP may have some connection to this troubled past.

In recent times, this turbulence in the relationship between these companies has continued, with acquisitions and divestments between them and an ongoing civil action against AMP. Most recently, this toxic culture has become manifest in charges of sexual harassment and appalling leadership behaviour. We will discuss further aspects of the current situation in Chapter 4, but suffice to say that toxic cultures that have their roots in historical bad practices are prone to continuing these practices.

A counter-culture is always present to a degree when there is a divergence of interests. Traditionally organisational sociology has located the result of toxic cultures in employee misdemeanours and has often characterised them as the consequence of the struggles of labour versus management, being the representative of capital. Their misdemeanours are a source of rebellion against the system, a reaction to managerial dictats when management behaviour becomes onerous and seemingly unreasonable. Dramatic changes in the structure of industry, the shift to more knowledge work in offices and away from factories, from mass employment to greater contract and self-employment have challenged this view about the reasons for misdemeanours. Alternative reasons have been suggested arising from the structure and mode of competitive industries, reward systems and market economies. In recent times we have seen the divergence of interests between organisations such as banks and their customers, where the profit motive overrides consideration of customer needs, especially in times of hardship.

These changes have coincided or have driven changes in HR practice to create a more constructive culture, including the following:

- Shifts towards seeking to empower employees and focus on achieving effective managerial behaviour in a more democratic age.
- Positive motivation has become the focus rather than discipline and punishment.
- More processes and procedural discipline allied with legal prescriptions have become oriented towards mediation and negotiation involving everyone.
- Performance now assessed through metrics, feedback mechanisms and independent information systems, leaving less room for discretion or resistance.
- Greater opportunity for self-discipline and self-regulation.
- Strong cultures based on high consultation and participation, focused on engagement with the purpose of the organisation and the aligning of individual interests with it. The market is the source of discipline, especially when pension funds have become major shareholders of many corporations.
- A shift from bureaucratic control to control based on intrinsic interest in the tasks and supportive supervision – the supervisor as coach.

These changes have only partially ameliorated some of the industrial conflicts of old. The results have been a reduction in trade union membership and industrial disputes. However, toxic cultures of all kinds continue to flourish and despite efforts at greater transparency, resistance to (and in some cases crushing of) whistleblowers continues. The silencing of any opposition outside strict consultative lines has arisen as a new source of conflict.

Traditional sources of toxicity still persist, from the personal behaviour of influential leaders to unfair payment systems and the pressures many are under to perform, regardless of how this performance is achieved. When the ends become all-important, the means become subordinated, and individual and corporate values are sidelined.

LEGAL IMPLICATIONS

As we will show, toxic cultures become manifest in many ways, both overtly in the behaviour of leaders exhibiting characteristics of the dark triad (Machiavellianism, psychopathy and narcissism) (see Chapter 4) and more subtly in the passive-aggressive behaviour of the disaffected (see Chapter 7). Falsely accusing someone of misconduct is a type of passive-aggressive behaviour that is common in the workplace. Not only is such behaviour against most organisational policies, but it is also likely to be against the law. Making false statements of sexual harassment is a noted problem facing workplaces today. There is a growing desire to hold individuals accountable for the outcomes of toxic cultures, yet many of the characteristics of toxic cultures such as passive-aggressive behaviour are often difficult to prove in court, even when there is specific legal prescription against such behaviour.

In May 2021, seven former executives at France Télécom went on trial for 'moral harassment'. Prosecutors argued they should be held criminally liable for the suicides of 19 employees, the attempted suicide of 12 and the psychological harm experienced by eight others. Their conviction resulted in a year's jail term for former Orange chief executive Didier Lombard and a heavy fine for the company. The surprising thing is that a mechanism existed for holding them accountable. The prosecutors argued that the company's method of personnel management and the resulting culture put some employees at increased risk.

Legal prescriptions vary, especially in respect of employment, in different territories. In many jurisdictions, the following areas are where the law exercises some influence:

Legal threats to employers

- Unfair dismissal of employees, including constructive dismissal.
- Harassment, including bullying and sexual harassment.
- Discrimination. In the UK, there are nine protected characteristics under the Equality Act 2010: age, disability, marriage or civil partnership, pregnancy and maternity, religion or belief, race, gender, sexual orientation and gender reassignment.
- Stress. It is difficult for any manager to accurately assess whether an employee is subject to undue stress because of individual differences in interpreting stressors and resilience. However, once known, managers have a duty of care to mitigate stress. Case law in the UK has resulted in substantial damages being awarded to employees who have not been appropriately managed.
- Civil cases may also arise when fractious cultures result in slander (spoken) or libel (written).
- Where criminal behaviour by employees poses an existential threat to the enterprise. In Chapter 8, the case of Crown Casinos is used to illustrate the threat of condoning illegal behaviour.

Legal threats to employees

- There are legal threats to employees where a toxic culture results in retaliatory action, such as wilful damage or sabotage. Most jurisdictions have laws against intentional damage to another's property.
- Other actions might be embezzlement and misuse of assets, particularly for personal benefit as opposed to sabotage.
- Fraud against the company, employees and customers. Indeed, there may be a wide range of stakeholders who might argue that they have been defrauded. In December 2020, Flight Centre was accused of underpaying staff and may face legal consequences. A judgment is expected in 2022. This follows an earlier action where the company was found to have engaged in price fixing.

SUMMARY AND CONCLUSIONS

- Culture is the commonly held and relatively stable beliefs, attitudes and values that exist within the organisation.
- Many factors affect the relationship between the culture of society and the economy. This is mirrored at the level of the organisation.

- There are both formal and informal determinants of culture.
- There are numerous reasons why toxic cultures occur, but they tend to start with incivility and arrogance towards stakeholders. There are three elements that are pervasive in toxic cultures: overwork (workaholism) leading to exhaustion; presenteeism, where what is accomplished becomes less important than being present and visible (even if is only digitally); and, finally, authority that brooks no opposition, even when this may be in the best interests of the organisation. At the root of these issues is the lack of trust between managers and staff.
- Historically the rules that underpinned society were Judaeo-Christian, but this has given way to a postmodernist egocentric view of how to live.
- Toxic cultures within and between organisations can endure for years.
- We can locate the cataloguing of toxic behaviour in the work of organisational sociologists and HR specialists.
- There are many legal implications of toxic cultures for both employees and employers.
- To return to the Australian banks, the new CEO of the Commonwealth Bank of Australia (CBA) gave a *mea culpa* performance at the Royal Commission into finance and banking in 2018. This provided a chilling summary of how historically a respected institution can become a toxic culture marked by a long catalogue of abuses and corrupt practices. He said that it was 'a culture of too often putting profits before people, slow remediation, little or no consequences when scandals emerged, and CBA being too legalistic and defensive in its dealing with regulators'. He blamed governance failures on remuneration and incentive structures, which in some instances were not aligned to good customer outcomes (26).

NOTES

1 A good example is the Schlieffen Plan, which was created by General Count Alfred von Schlieffen in December 1905. The Schlieffen Plan was the operational plan for a designated attack on France once Russia, in response to international tension, had started to mobilise its forces near the German border. The plan could only be changed once Paris was reached. The rest, as they say, is history.

2 The amygdala is a collection of cells near the base of the brain. This is where emotions are given meaning, remembered, and attached to associations and responses to them (emotional memories). It is key to how you process strong emotions like fear and pleasure, with the resulting response of fight, flight or freeze.

REFERENCES

1 Trompenaars, F. (1996) *Riding the waves of culture*. Nicholas Brealey.
2 Schein, E. (1965) *Organizational psychology*. Prentice Hall.
3 Williams, A., Dobson, P. and Walters, M. (1993) *Changing culture*. CIPD.
4 Conversation with Farren Drury.
5 Williams, A., Dobson, P. and Walters, M. (1993) *Changing culture*. CIPD.
6 *Economist schools brief* – 9 September 2020.
7 Smith, A. (1776) *The Wealth of Nations*.
8 Weber, M. (2001) *The Protestant ethic and the spirit of capitalism*. Routledge (first published in 1930).
9 World Values Survey (2021). Retrieved 5 April 2022 from https://www.worldvaluessurvey.org/wvs.jsp.
10 Economists are turning to culture to explain wealth and poverty. *The Economist* (5 September 2020).

11 Putnam, R. (1993) *Making democracy work: Civic traditions in modern Italy.* Princeton University Press.

12 Suzman, J. (2020) *Work: A history of how we spend our time.* Bloomsbury.

13 Davis, R. (2020, 3 September) How to forecast armies will fight. *The Economist.*

14 Weick, K.(1995) *Sensemaking in organizations.* Sage.

15 Schein, E, (1985) *Organizational culture and leadership.* Jossey-Bass.

16 Johnson, G., Whittington, R. and Scholes, K. (2012) *Fundamentals of strategy.* Pearson Education.

17 Babiak, P. and Hare, R.D. (2006) *Snakes in suits.* HarperCollins.

18 Interview with Gabor Maté. Retrieved 5 April 2022 from https://1mb74417820q1ck2sr1ws5qz-wpen-gine.netdna-ssl.com/wp-content/uploads/2019/03/28-31-Interview-Gabor-Mate.pdf.

19 Hari, J. (2022) *Stolen focus.* Bloomsbury.

20 Aditya Jain - Nottingham University Business School. https://www.nottingham.ac.uk/.../focus-on-dr-aditya-jains-research.aspx.

21 Report in *Sydney Morning Herald* on Denis Handlin, 27 June 2021. Retrieved 9 June 2022 from https://www.smh.com.au/topic/denis-handlin-2rv.

22 Report in The *Guardian on 21 June 2021.* https://www.theguardian.com/culture/2021/jun/21/sony-music-australia.

23 The genius of Amazon. (2020, 20 June) *The Economist,* 18.

24 Goldman Sachs working conditions survey. Retrieved 5 April 2022 from https://drive.google.com/file/d/1jyeu-wvS3Z10xQ0BlMIDOkh_INoP_Nnb/view.

25 Street, E. (1980) *The history of the National Mutual Life Assurance Society, 1830–1980.* The Society.

26 Ferguson, A. (2019) *Banking bad.* HarperCollins.

CHAPTER 2

Organisational diagnosis

INTRODUCTION

It was Einstein who remarked that 'we will never be able to solve our problems at the same order of complexity we used to create our problems'. In this chapter several tools to measure aspects of culture are described in order to determine how dysfunctional it may be. These are largely survey instruments that rely upon honest assessments by key opinion formers. The first point to recognise is that organisations are systems of interconnected parts – people, technology, physical properties and the activities that flow through them. Change in one part impacts on another, and so before any prescription is possible, a thorough diagnosis is necessary.

MEASURING CULTURE AND CULTURAL TOXICITY

Toxicity may arise because of the unintended consequence of reasonable action, so what may appear to be obvious causes may not be the real reason. Oliver Sachs, a clinical neurologist, talks of being more aware of our 'peripheral vision'. It should be borne in mind that there are many drivers of culture, including the following:

- The work itself and the way it is organised.
- The technology used and the degree of freedom given.
- Routines and processes for getting work done and the degree of bureaucracy involved in checking and controlling.
- The composition of the workforce and the skills and attitudes they bring to the work.
- The leadership style.
- The type and variety of customers and the organisation's approach towards serving them.
- The way in which staff are rewarded.

We will explore these in subsequent chapters.

Peter Senge (1) identified several problems that can occur because of not considering organisations as systems:

- Today's problems come from yesterday's solutions.
- The harder you push, the harder the system pushes back.
- Behaviour grows better/worse before it grows worse/better (the lag effect).

DOI: 10.4324/9781003307334-4

- Faster is slower (because more mistakes occur).
- Systems have integrity (dividing an elephant in half does not produce two elephants).
- The consciousness that created the problem is part of the problem (Einstein).

The following case study is illustrative in this respect:

> *The purchasing department of an airline managed to negotiate a saving on plastic bags, which the airline used in large quantities, in return for using a thinner material. The bonus scheme for purchasing managers was based on their savings made against targets. The sacks were used for rubbish collection on the aircraft and elsewhere. However, the costs of cleaning the aircraft went up overall because the thinner material kept breaking, spilling contents on the carpets in the aircraft, but this cost was borne by a different department from the purchasing department, whose members received their bonus.*

NATIONAL CHARACTERISTICS

Over many years, researchers have sought to link measures of culture with success (however measured) of a society. Power distance between groups of people has been described by Gert Hofstede (2). He suggests that there are six dimensions of national culture: power distance, uncertainty avoidance, individualism/collectivism, masculinity/femininity, indulgence and long-term orientation. This is of particular interest when examining differences between countries. Korea, for example, has a high-power distance index (PDI) where there is high deference to hierarchy. In low PDI countries such as the Netherlands and Sweden, there is less deference and greater equality. In organisations, it is suggested that high PDI cultures are less likely to accept feedback, let alone criticism, from more junior staff. This is sometimes associated with poorer outcomes, greater miscalculations and lower morale, especially where bosses are not competent. Power imbalances in organisations can also be a source of friction and are a major factor in cases of bullying and harassment.

In his book *The culture map*, Meyer (3) describes other dimensions: communicating, evaluating, leading, deciding, trusting, disagreeing and scheduling. Netflix uses this tool to compare cultures in the regions in which it operates to help them understand each other's culture, and where tensions and frictions might arise.

Fons Trompenaars (4) identifies other orientations or dimensions which differentiate country cultures. These include how universal decisions and rules across all relationships can be, whether individual effort is recognised, how emotional leaders in public life can be, whether relationships are specific to a role, and whether status is achieved by accomplishment or birth. They give the clue as to where conflicts are more likely to arise in and between those societies.

At a business reception, an American was sounding off about how Asian businesses were so corrupt because they gave contracts to their friends and family. 'You can't trust them', he said. A Thai businessman who was listening said: 'But if you don't trust your friends and family, why should you trust a stranger more?'

These cultural differences give an idea as to why some organisational cultures do not translate well internationally. For example, American culture, which stresses individual freedom and enterprise, does not sit so well with Asian cultures, which are suspicious of individuals standing out, preferring to be part of the team (a Japanese saying states: 'The nail that sticks out gets hammered down'). In Eastern cultures relationships are important to establish before doing business in order to determine whether there is trust between the parties. In Anglo-Saxon cultures, where there is a strong tradition of the rule of law, legally binding contracts are more likely to be required before any relationship building. However, we should bear in mind that these cultural assumptions are not universally true.

ORGANISATIONAL CHARACTERISTICS

Turning to some of the indicators of toxic cultures in organisations, one quick way of determining the health of a culture is the degree to which difficult subjects can be aired. The 'corridor conversations' that occur before or after a meeting and that are not reflected in the discussions in the meeting are a test of the openness of the culture and the extent to which sacred cows cannot be challenged – in essence, what can we not talk about. As we will see later, one consequence of highly narcissistic leaders is the compliant and sycophantic behaviour of subordinates that seeks to hide the truth in order to gain favour (and keep their jobs).

Another way to identify a toxic culture is the extent to which it is interfering with the achievement of the organisation's goals by the degree of friction caused by the culture. Organisations to some degree experience friction by virtue of the formal rules and processes, and the informal differences in norms that might exist. Excessive caution or bureaucracy can slow the organisation's processes such that they become an inhibitor of performance. A recent example has been the slow rollout of vaccines during the COVID-19 pandemic in the EU due to the coordination deemed necessary across all Member States. This was in contrast to the nimbler, now post-Brexit UK, which felt no such inhibitions and frictions.

Roger Harrison (5) in an early paper identified four dimensions of organisational cultural differences:

- Power orientation, as we have just seen, where control of people and the environment is paramount. The geometry of power can flex depending on whether it is exercised through authority derived from position, personal charisma, the balance of competing interest groups, perceptions, values and norms or through dialogue and persuasion (6).
- Role orientation, which is typical in bureaucracies where there is a focus on structure and formal relations between functions. Hierarchy and status are important.
- Task orientation, where the focus is on getting the job done and involves flexibility in tasks and structures.
- People orientation, where the emphasis is on consensus achievement, a culture of helping each other and respect for individuals.

INDICATORS OF A TOXIC CULTURE

There are several indicators of a toxic culture to examine, but before doing so, it is important to consider whether we are using the right indicator.

The following story provides an illustration of this:

> *One day a man came out of a bar after dark and dropped his ring in the gutter. He walked to the nearest lamppost to look for it. An observer asked him why he was looking there rather in the dark gutter. 'Ah', he said, 'it's lighter here.'*

It's tempting to look at indicators and metrics that are easy to examine and measure, but are they the right ones? It is easy to be beguiled by leaders who look good, but are not necessarily doing things that produce a productive culture.

Labour turnover

Leaving an organisation occurs for many reasons, but trends across an organisation can be indicative of its climate and health. A recent study (7) showed that 'affective commitment' and 'normative commitment'[1] are negatively correlated with leaving intentions. The reasons people give for why they leave are notoriously skewed towards those reasons that allow for the possibility of return at a later date. Nevertheless, changing patterns can give an indication of the climate - for example, 'personal reasons' are indicative of a reluctance to say the real reason and often point to problems with an individual's boss or the organisation as a whole. Leaving for more money especially when that is not supported by the facts, is indicative of feeling undervalued.

Absenteeism

National statistics point towards differences between organisations and sectors. Public service tends to be higher than finance, and construction, other than amongst sub-contractors, higher still (8). Organisations and countries that have little or no sick pay schemes typically also have lower rates of absence. At the start of the pandemic, the virus spread quickly in the USA, which was partly explained by people struggling to come in to work because there was little or no sick pay.

Absenteeism for health issues does arise. However, colds and back sprain are sometimes seen as euphemisms for a day off. Absence patterns only have a loose connection with actual illness and may be for both domestic reasons (children, elderly parents, medical appointments, etc.) and indicative of a frustration at office politics and the office climate. Absence is an indicator of a lack of engagement. Indeed, some employers have offered 'duvet days' to encourage honesty about these low motivation days. This is based on the belief that a day spent in bed might refresh the person to come back more productively in the future.

Time off can be a reward and in some factory situations, payment and absence are linked. Historically, pay day has been associated with a low rate of absence, and absence can depend on the day of the week (it is highest on Mondays and Fridays). Much has been written about the relationship between absence and income[2] according to job type (9). Absence may cause specific bottlenecks if the right staff are not in place at critical times. Telephonists were often found to have some of the lowest rates of absence. If a telephonist goes sick, they know that the workload will not decrease and their colleagues, with whom they work closely and usually in close proximity, will have to work harder. This may be an incentive to struggle in when there is a positive culture (although the pandemic has stopped this), but it can easily be a source of manipulation and control in more negative environments.

Absence is also lower where fear of dismissal is greater, especially during probation periods. Absence has traditionally been seen as a litmus test of engagement, but we must be wary here, as recording systems might not catch the manager going to the dentist or taking a half-day after visiting a client. A shift has occurred away from 'presenteeism' - i.e., you are only seen to be working if you are sitting at your desk - towards a focus on deliverable results. This plays well for a more mobile workforce, but relies on trust and metrics of expected outcomes. For those with time-bound expectations (e.g., picking up children from school at a specific time), the idea of time at work being less important than output results in 24/7 working. This can be exhausting and stressful, made all the more so by modern technology, which doesn't acknowledge down time and compounded by trans-global organisations wrestling with time zones. Managerial action to control absence has been likened to squeezing a balloon: put pressure in one part and absence bursts out in another way. A drive to reduce lateness in an engineering factory resulted in high levels of absence! Employees realising they would be late (and penalised) decided it was better to turn round and go home, claiming to be sick.

Grievances

Organisations usually have formal grievance procedures, and how these change over time can be indicative. The more informal airing of grievances is a more sensitive test of climate. Toxic cultures may become apparent to some of those involved, but this rarely becomes crystallised until some significant failure occurs. That failure may be commercial, but is often associated with a scandal where values and beliefs are questioned.

The following case study is illustrative in this respect:

> *The Australian Federal government was in the spotlight when an investigative TV programme (10) exposed the sexual antics of two Cabinet ministers and brought to light the toxic culture in which young female staffers suffered at the hands of powerful and predatory men. Earlier, a senior politician got his staffer pregnant and as a result the Prime Minister at the time (Malcolm Turnbull) issued a decree that sexual relations with staff should be forbidden. It was labelled the 'bonk ban', but seemed to do little to curb the excesses. In the subsequent analysis, several ingredients caused this toxic culture to develop. A combination of men in powerful positions (usually well versed in influencing and persuasion through getting elected) lonely from being on their own away from family, pressure and late nights, close working relationships and invariably alcohol, and young staffers at early stages in their careers and wanting to avoid offence or getting a reputation for being difficult, led to the latter being tempted/coerced to be supine for the good of their career.*

The power imbalance adds pressure and creates an air of entitlement. The case above give rise to some added criticism for the hypocrisy of promoting 'traditional family values'. whilst at the same time cheating on partners at home. It is often propounded that government ministers need to be above reproach in order to set a good example, not least because of the need to avoid being compromised and blackmailed.

A significant driver of a toxic culture is when there is a blatant wrong such as illegality or inappropriate (especially sexual) behaviour, and a blind eye is turned to this. This gives a licence to the perpetrator to continue and generates increasing frustration amongst victims, especially if an appeal is made to senior management, who may demonstrate wilful blindness or an inability to act. Wilful blindness can occur when whistleblowing is seen as too dangerous to the person or the organisation and there is a need to be able to claim 'I didn't know what was going on'. A recent case in the Australian Defence Force highlighted the culture of condonement to poor behaviour of those in positions of power which led to illegal killings of civilians in Afghanistan.

As we have discussed earlier, there are many factors that influence culture and certain behaviours that result in poor performance however measured. The following checklist in Table 2.1 is a simple way of identifying how toxic a culture might be.

A simple diagnosis framework is given in Table 2.2 which sets out some of the major parameters in the process that all organisations will go through to achieve some output. Table 2.3 identifies areas to investigate.

TABLE 2.1 Checklist of factors that contribute to toxicity

Factor	Indicator
The values of the organisation are unclear	People at all levels behave expediently regardless of the impact on others
The values are stated but rarely articulated	Values do not enter everyday discourse
People don't walk the talk	People's behaviour is incongruent with their values
The organisation does not meet the needs of its various stakeholders	Conflicts arise between stakeholders
People are not treated with respect	Abuse and bullying are commonplace and tolerated
There is little or no feedback from stakeholders and little effort to improve in light of it	Feedback is confused with criticism and is avoided
Managers turn a blind eye to behaviours which are known to be bad but are seen as expedient and productive	Decisions and actions are short term and only address selective interests
There is favouritism and intrinsic and extrinsic rewards are made irrespective of merit	There is a popular understanding of who is in or out of favour, and no attempt at any objective assessment process.
People are unclear on their roles or objectives and pursue their own agendas	There is a lack of coordinated action and errors often occur
People play politics	There is withholding of information from others to exert power
Organisational design focuses on departmental performance at the expense of a more holistic view	There is rivalry and conflict between departments, resulting in competition, not cooperation
Teamwork is poor and there is no support for each other when problems arise	Slow reactions and errors occur; there is blaming of others over errors
Commitment to 'stay and finish the job' is low	People leave work at the finishing time regardless of the state of their work

TABLE 2.2 A framework for diagnosis

Input	Transformation	Output
Money	Resources to product	Product
People	Individuals to a team	Impact on stakeholders
Technology	Harnessing technology to	Unintended consequences
Property	specific outputs	
Information		
Constraints (legal, environmental)		
Energy		

TABLE 2.3 Areas to investigate

INPUT	Indicators of a positive culture	Indicators of a negative culture	Area to address?
Money	People see remuneration as fair	High turnover to seek higher pay	
	Organisation is properly funded Costs are not an undue burden on the financial model	Funding crises Costs create an undue burden on the costs structure of the organisation, causing other areas to be squeezed unreasonably	
People	Positive satisfaction scores Discretionary effort is exhibited	High turnover, absenteeism and grievances	
Technology	Enables work to be done easily and effectively	Rigidity and inefficiencies, causing aggravation and negative impact on performance	
Property	Surroundings provide a workspace that enables effective performance	Poor conditions adversely impact recruitment and retention	
Information	Timely information facilitating decision making	Lack of or incorrect information Slow production of data	
Constraints	Frictionless activities	Illegal behaviour arises to overcome legal constraints in order to achieve goals Justification of why things cannot be done	
Environmental	Genuine effort to be socially responsible and sustainable in terms of environmental impact	Scores badly on environmental metrics – pollution, energy use and social concerns	
Energy	Meets best practice in energy use and conservation	No attempt to use energy wisely	
TRANSFORMATION			
Resources to product	End-to-end efficient design with minimum effort and delay	Inefficient processes created piecemeal	
Individuals to a team	High in group solidarity and smooth teamworking	No team synergy	
Harnessing technology to specific outputs	Technology designed to be fit for purpose	Off-the-shelf solutions that are inappropriate	
OUTPUT			
Product	Meets all required standards and approval of all stakeholders	Significant shortfalls in all output metrics	
Impact on stakeholders	Expectations are managed and met	Widespread discontent	
Unintended consequences	Minimised	Surprise at management's inability to anticipate the consequences of their actions	

Below are two questionnaires to provide a more specific diagnosis. The first is a Cultural Audit Questionnaire (11), which aims to survey opinions on a series of questions in order to produce a profile for subsequent analysis and deeper discussion.

CULTURAL AUDIT QUESTIONNAIRE

The following statements seek to differentiate cultures and are based on empirical evidence that there are nine principal dimensions of organisational culture. The aim of the tool is to audit a culture along these nine major dimensions in order to identify where change may be required. It can be used in several ways:

- As a survey tool to identify the perceptions of a group of respondents.
- As a prompt for a discussion about what the culture of the organisation *should* be.
- As a diagnostic instrument to identify where there may be cultural difficulties.

To use the Questionnaire, place a cross against each statement depending upon your degree of agreement/disagreement according to the scale below:

SA – Strongly Agree, A – Agree, N – Neutral, D – Disagree, SD – Strongly Disagree.

Then, using the scoring sheet below, calculate a score for each of the nine factors.

Finally, plot the average score for all respondents on the sheet that then follows (with a large group, you may wish to mark the maximum and minimum as well).

Now consider the following:

- Where are the areas that are not assisting the organisation in reaching its goals?
- How does it compare against the ideal?
- What actions might change these beliefs towards the ideal?

Organisation unit to which the questionnaire applies.

Date of completion: _____   Job of respondent:_____

Organisational level:_____   Function:_____

		SD	D	N	A	SA
1	People agree with the stated vision and values of the organisation					
2	People generally behave in a way consistent with the values					
3	The values represent the best way of acting to deliver results					
4	People are generally treated fairly					
5	This is a demanding organisation and sometimes demands more than is reasonable					
6	There is a reasonable balance in the organisation between what is expected of people and their ability to deliver					
7	There is no prejudice in the organisation					
8	People are treated with respect					
9	Not everyone is treated the same way					
10	Most people get along well in the organisation					
11	There is much conflict between factions in the organisation					
12	People have their differences but are always dealt with amicably in the organisation					

13	People are committed to achieving their objectives					
14	People do not associate their work with the company goals					
15	People see achieving their goals as critical to company success					
16	People trust management reports and statistics to be accurate					
17	Management reports are written to give a good impression					
18	A serious view is taken of reporting information incorrectly					
19	People are encouraged to develop their skills to the maximum					
20	The organisation tries to learn from its mistakes					
21	Staff rely solely on people's past experience					
22	There is real synergy amongst our teams					
23	Teams are always in conflict					
24	Teams do better than every member working individually					
25	I trust the organisation to do the right thing					
26	I think the organisation often has a hidden agenda that it does not share with staff					
27	I feel comfortable with the organisation because it does things in the way that I would expect and is right					

Scoring sheet

Now circle the letter from the questionnaire above in the table below and identify the number below it. Record the total for each factor on the right. For example, if I strongly agree with Question 1, circle, SA and count 5. Add this score to those from the other two questions and enter the total.

A   Q1   Q2   Q3   Total

SD	D	N	A	SA		SD	D	N	A	SA		SD	D	N	A	SA
1	2	3	4	4		1	2	3	4	4		1	2	3	4	4

B   Q4   Q5   Q6

SD	D	N	A	SA		SD	D	N	A	SA		SD	D	N	A	SA
1	2	3	4	4		1	2	3	4	4		1	2	3	4	4

C   Q7   Q8   Q9

SD	D	N	A	SA		SD	D	N	A	SA		SD	D	N	A	SA
1	2	3	4	4		1	2	3	4	4		1	2	3	4	4

D   Q10   Q11   Q12

SD	D	N	A	SA		SD	D	N	A	SA		SD	D	N	A	SA
1	2	3	4	4		1	2	3	4	4		1	2	3	4	4

E   Q13   Q14   Q15

SD	D	N	A	SA		SD	D	N	A	SA		SD	D	N	A	SA
1	2	3	4	4		1	2	3	4	4		1	2	3	4	4

F

Q16						Q17						Q18				
SD	D	N	A	SA		SD	D	N	A	SA		SD	D	N	A	SA
1	2	3	4	4		1	2	3	4	4		1	2	3	4	4

G

Q19						Q20						Q21				
SD	D	N	A	SA		SD	D	N	A	SA		SD	D	N	A	SA
1	2	3	4	4		1	2	3	4	4		1	2	3	4	4

H

Q22						Q23						Q24				
SD	D	N	A	SA		SD	D	N	A	SA		SD	D	N	A	SA
1	2	3	4	4		1	2	3	4	4		1	2	3	4	4

I

Q25						Q26						Q27				
SD	D	N	A	SA		SD	D	N	A	SA		SD	D	N	A	SA
1	2	3	4	4		1	2	3	4	4		1	2	3	4	4

Cultural profile

Now plot the average score for all participants.

Factor	Description	Negative	1	2	3	4	5	Positive
A	Identification with vision and values	Alienation						Loyalty
B	Equity – balance between expectations and actions	Injustice						Fairness
C	Treating others equally	Prejudice						Respect
D	Consensus amongst staff	Discord						Understanding
E	Commitment to achieving goals	Unconnected						Confidence
F	Integrity of Information	Deception						Honesty
G	Process of mutual development	Regression						Growth
H	Group dynamic	Conflict						Synergy
I	Alignment with organisational beliefs	Suspicion						Trust

What to be aware of

This is one approach to measuring a selection of cultural dimensions. It is not exhaustive and may well benefit from being combined with other tools. For example, the next tool looks at a specific team and is based on the work of Patrick Lencioni (12). It can be used as part of a team development exercise and as a diagnostic. The team can complete it and aggregate the results before embarking on a discussion on how to improve the way they work. Alternatively, it can be used as a survey tool by an independent assessor as the basis for determining a more generalised process of team improvement.

The questionnaire highlights the areas that all teams need to work on:

- Build trust through establishing clarity of mission and purpose together and behaving consistently with mutually agreed ground rules.

- Overcoming fear of conflict by learning to debate constructively and not confuse differences of views with personal attacks.
- Building commitment to team goals by encouraging the primacy of team goals over individual goals.
- Establishing clarity of personal accountability and holding people to it. An indicator is how people react when things go wrong; some people will look at themselves and what they have done to find the cause, whilst others will look for who to blame. The reverse is true when things go well, with some looking to see who to thank and praise, and others attributing success to themselves.
- A relentless focus on getting successful results based on a clear understanding of what success looks like.

TEAM ASSESSMENT

Use the scale below to indicate how each statement applies to your team. Try to rate the statements as honestly as you can:

1. usually
2. sometimes
3. rarely
    1. --- Team members are passionate and unguarded in their discussion of issues.
    2. --- Team members challenge one another's deficiencies or unproductive behaviours.
    3. --- Team members know what their peers are working on and how they contribute to the collective good of the team.
    4. --- Team members quickly and genuinely apologise to one another when they say or do something inappropriate or possibly damaging to the team.
    5. --- Team members willingly make sacrifices (such as budget, turf and headcount) in their departments or areas of expertise for the good of the team.
    6. --- Team members openly admit their weaknesses and mistakes
    7. --- Team meetings are compelling and not boring.
    8. --- Team members leave meetings confident that their peers are completely committed to the decisions that were agreed on, even if there was initial disagreement.
    9. --- Morale is significantly affected by the failure to achieve team (as opposed to individual) goals.
    10. --- During team meetings, the most important - and difficult - issues are put on the table to be resolved.
    11. --- Team members are deeply concerned about the prospect of letting down their peers.
    12. --- Team members know about each other's personal lives and are comfortable discussing them
    13. --- Team members end discussions with clear and specific resolutions and calls to action.
    14. --- Team members challenge one another about their plans and approaches.
    15. --- Team members are slow to seek credit for their own contributions, but quick to point out those of others.

Absence of trust	Fear of conflict	Lack of commitment	Avoidance of accountability	Inattention to team results
Q4	Q1	Q3	Q2	Q5
Q6	Q7	Q8	Q11	Q9
Q12	Q10	Q13	Q14	Q15
Total	Total	Total	Total	Total

Interpreting the scores:

  8–9: not a problem.
  6–7: could be a problem.
  3–5: indicative of a problem to be addressed for effective team functioning.

Finally, summarise your findings in the table below.

TABLE 2.4 Culture mapping[3]

Significant cultural characteristics	Areas of possible toxicity	Areas of development	Measures of success

SUMMARY AND CONCLUSIONS

- In this chapter we have explored how to determine whether a culture is toxic and whilst there are no perfect measures, these tools may give some indication of areas to explore. Ultimately, the measure of whether an organisation is a safe, productive and engaging place to work is whether people are less stressed, more effective and breathe a little easier, and the needs of all the stakeholders are met.
- There are national characteristics that differentiate societies, and various dimensions have been shown as a way of understanding them.
- Organisations are systems of interconnected parts and in order to understand how toxicity occurs, we have to make the connections between these parts.
- Organisations have different dimensions which differentiate toxic cultures.
- The measures of a toxic organisational culture are shown in labour turnover, absenteeism and grievances, as well as more qualitative indicators.

NOTES

1 Affective commitment is defined by Meyer and Allen (1991) as an emotional relationship, and normative commitment as a sense of obligation and moral duty towards the organisation (see reference 7).

2 There is an old oft-quoted joke: why do you only work four days a week? Because I can't earn enough working only three.

3 Note: these cultural audit tools were developed with Rita McGee, who has given permission for their inclusion.

REFERENCES

1 Senge, P. (1990) *The fifth discipline.* Random House.

2 The 6-D model of national culture. Retrieved 9 June 2022 from https://geerthofstede.com/culture-geert-hofstede-gert-jan-hofstede/6d-model-of-national-culture.

3 Meyer, E. (2014) *The culture map: Breaking through the invisible boundaries of global business.* Public Affairs.

4 Trompenaars, F. (1996) *Riding the waves of culture.* Nicholas Brealey.

5 Harrison, R. (1972) Understanding your organisation's character. *HBR, May–June, 119–268.*

6 Boonstra, J.J. and Gravenhorst, K.M.B. (1998) Power dynamics and organisational change: A comparison of perspectives. *European Journal of Work and Organisational Psychology,* 7(2), 97-120.

7 Moreira, A. and Cesario, F. (2021) Organisational commitment as a reducer of turnover intentions: Which component (affective, calculative, and normative) is the best predictor? *Academia Letters, Article 3636.* https://doi.org/10.20935/. AL3636. See also Meyer, J.P. and Allen, N.J. (1991) A three-component conceptualization of organizational commitment. *Human Resource Management Review,* 1(1), 61–69. https://doi.org/10.1016/1053-4822(91)90011-Z.

8 ONS. *Sickness absence in the UK labour market – 2020.* Retrieved 5 April 2022 from https://www.ons.gov.uk/employmentandlabourmarket/peopleinwork/labourproductivity/articles/sicknessabsenceinthelabourmarket/2020.

9 Pfeiffer, C. (2010) Impact of wages and job levels on worker absenteeism. *International Journal of Manpower,* 31(1), 59-72. See also Hopkins, T. (1990) *The relationship between absenteeism and the amount of overtime worked in various job classifications in a metal fabrication plant.* Western Michigan University.

10 ABC, *4 corners programme,* 9 November 2020.

11 Cannon, J. and McGee, R. (2016) *Organisational development and change.* CIPD. See also Cannon, J., McGee, R. and Stanford, N. (2010) *Organisation design and capability building.* CIPD. Further insights were gained from Hemsley Fraser: http://www.hemsleyfraser.co.uk/Learning Solutions.

12 Lencioni, P. (2002) *The five dysfunctions of a team.* Jossey Bass.

Part B

Leadership – power, personality and values

Part 6

Leadership – power,
personality and values

CHAPTER 3

The toxic effect of power imbalance

INTRODUCTION

The exercise of power, whether through violence or subtle influence, has intended and unintended consequences on the culture of the environment in which people participate. It was Lord Acton who suggested that power corrupts. One of the key drivers of toxic leadership is the pressure created by the '4th Industrial Revolution' (mechanisation, mass production, automation and now digitisation) (1). Competitive pressures have led to toxic decisions and illicit behaviour - for example, Volkswagen and the diesel test fraud (2).

The global pandemic has added further pressure to quickly respond to changed imbalances in market conditions, where there have been few precedents to guide policy. The result has been disruptions in staffing expectations of the employment contract, both legal and psychological. Digitisation and home working have blurred any strong view of the working day, with work for some meaning being on duty 24/7. The results have been tiredness to the extent of burnout and mental health issues. A UK study (3) showed a deterioration in the mental health of the population; in particular, women with degree-level education and young adults (those aged 25-34 and 35-44) were impacted most. These groups went through the highest levels of psychological distress during the pandemic.

COVID-19 has changed the balance of power in many contexts, not least in employment, where home working and new definitions of 'essential workers' have arisen. The popular press has described working from home (WFH) as the 'pyjama revolution' (4) as there is no longer the need for more formal attire.

In this chapter we explore the nature of power and how it is exercised in different contexts, and focus in particular on the impact that different power relationships have on the toxicity or otherwise of culture. This chapter lays the foundations on this subject, as we will touch on power and its implications throughout this book.

POWER AND RELATIONSHIPS

Farrell et al. (5) examined power in personal relations and suggest that there are four facets:

1. Power differs across relationship domains. Different parties in the relationship have more or less influence depending on the subject.

DOI: 10.4324/9781003307334-6

2. Power includes the decision process, and influences who makes and how decisions are made in the relationship.
3. Power reflects interdependence. The greater the interdependence, the more likely it is that compromise will occur. Where reciprocity becomes unbalanced, the opportunity for coercion and toxic behaviour increases (6).
4. Resisting influence is a type of power. This may be exercised in many ways, some of which are subversive and destructive, as we shall examine later on when looking at the informal organisation.

Whilst this study was in the context of personal relationships, these facets translate to all relationships, including those that operate in the world of work and organisations.

POWER MAPPING

The balance of power is one of the oldest and most fundamental concepts in international relations theory (7). This balance of power theory suggests a model of equilibrium as the condition most likely to result in peace. In the organisational literature, there has been discussion of the 'proper' and 'improper' use of power (8) and the concept of optimum power to achieve effective and sustained performance. Tang (9) has suggested a tool for mapping power along two axes – influence (from most to least) and support (from support to oppose), as shown in Figure 3.1.

In Chapter 8, we examine three recent case studies of organisations that have come under scrutiny for their toxic cultures. We will use the map (figure 3.1) as a tool to summarise the balance of forces on these organisations which has led to their suboptimal performance.

POWER AND AUTHORITY

Power is wielded in organisations to establish priorities, issue instructions and push for performance. Inherent in this process are sanctions if actions are not fulfilled. Power is vested in rules and policies because it provides credence to the enforcers (often HR). Leadership in modern organisations emphasises the use of soft power (i.e., persuasion and encouragement), but there is the always the hidden threat of sanctions and, ultimately, dismissal.

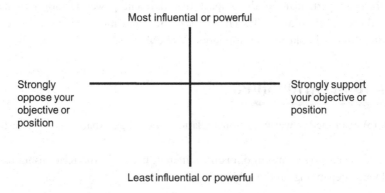

FIGURE 3.1 Power mapping and analysis

Authority also accrues to those who control resources, technical skills, knowledge, legal power and access to those who command these resources (10).

At the contracting stage of the employment relationship, there are both legal and psychological aspects of the agreement (11). Social exchange theory and equity theory (12) suggest that there is an individually defined need contribution balance that, once unbalanced, has negative consequences in terms of motivation and potentially subversive behaviour. The increase in industrial action in Kellogg's (13), points to a growing sense of inequity in the effort-reward relationship, especially during the pandemic, where flexibility was required but the 'rewards' often entailed furlough, short-term working and redundancy. Even for those in work, incomes have risen only slowly, if at all, in many territories and industries.

Power and position are important drivers of culture. Hofstede's concept of power distance (14) is an indicator of social inequality. Where power is exercised in a particular way that is not expected or agreed, it can be perceived as leading to a sense of entitlement to personal rewards, but also to command others in an arrogant and unfeeling way. Recently, pressures on business leaders (15) have caused a decline in the traditional civility between employer and employee, and unrelenting pressure for performance and the erosion of personal privacy:

> This person does not share and wants to control all situations. She is one of the most difficult people that I have ever worked with; she shames, blames, and micromanages all aspects of the treatment. Only she can be right! She needs to be involved in everything. She belittles the team, undermines their delivery of care, points out all errors, and prevents others from learning and being accountable for their performance (16).

Common characteristics of overcontrolling behaviour is a certain arrogance that the person knows best and an unwillingness to listen to advice, especially when it goes against their preconceived ideas. The belief that they are better than others come from a lack of self-awareness reinforced by a fear of being shown to be lacking and a self-belief that only they have the wisdom to deal with any situation or make all decisions. Alternatively, it may stem from a sense of inadequacy and hence a need to control the situation to avoid any challenge. This has the effect of limiting initiative or experimentation with new ideas. This behaviour has negative consequences for organisations working to accelerate the pace of innovation, where a more open style that encourages challenging the status quo will yield the best results (17).

CASE STUDY IN A GOVERNMENT DEPARTMENT

In 2020, a government department went through a process of reorganisation and finance departments were merged. In the battle for positions in the new slimmed-down structure, the 'winning' boss immediately began to put his people in key positions, and several staff from the other department lost their jobs. The rest of the staff carried on with their projects as they believed nothing much would change.

One manager decided to use his discretion and make a decision for himself, the like of which he had done many times before with the blessing of his previous boss. However, the new boss carpeted him for exceeding his authority and though he grudgingly accepted it was the right decision, he believed that he should have made the decision. This same scenario played itself out with several other employees. The new boss believed that there had been a lack of control and he had to centralise decision making. The result was poor and slower decisions because he did not have all the information about the projects in the merged department. Staff were left somewhat bruised and reluctant to take any decisions. They began to apply for other jobs and soon some left. Because of budget constraints, no replacements were recruited and project deadlines slipped, causing conflict with other departments and a further lowering of morale amongst those who had to interact with them.

The working climate further deteriorated when due to enormous pressure to meet previous deadlines, some mistakes were made and disciplinary action was taken. Staff felt this was unfair and a petition was raised to have this action rescinded, which was refused. The new boss declared that standards and disciplines had to be maintained, but failed to realise that it was his own actions that were contributing to the problem. Eventually he was dismissed and the slow road to recovery began. It had taken less than a year to reach this stage, but it took at least two years to recover from it.

There are several ways in which power is exercised in organisations and the strength of each of these depends on 'four contingencies of power' (18): substitutability (is there an alternative?), centrality (how central to success is the issue at stake?), (degree of) discretion, and visibility (outside of the parties). Each of these ways can be corrupted and each can also change the locus of control. The legitimacy of different ways in which power is exercised comes from the discourse surrounding both the outcomes required and the route to achieving them (19).

Influence can be described as exerting power without authority or responsibility for the consequences. Covey (20) describes concentric circles from a core of what you can control, through influence, to an outer circle of concern but with little or no influence. The individual who spreads false rumours, undermines official instructions or reduces support for the mission can be highly destructive. When the intention is to use such behaviour for personal gain as opposed to delivering the organisation's mission, it becomes harmful to the intended organisational outcomes and sets norms and expectations about the future conduct of other employees. However, those with authority may deliberately downplay that power source and seek to influence events more subtly, in the belief that it may be an effective strategy to get their way rather than using direct instruction.

A characteristic of influential people in toxic organisations is their destructive interpersonal skills. This often arises from the desire to manipulate in order to exert power or to at least limit any damage to their self-image or credibility with others. Two types of behaviour are particularly damaging:

- Personability. A recent study (21) suggested that it may be that manipulative bosses are not really trying to *be nice* with employees after an abusive tirade, but, rather, are attempting to *fake nice* in order to manipulate their social image without actually changing their behaviour. In other words, some bosses are skilled at looking good after an episode, leading employees and senior executives to forgive and forget — until the next tirade occurs and the cycle continues. If this is true, employees and organisations may be unknowingly enabling toxic boss behaviour by being too forgiving of it.

- Impression management. Offending bosses in the study above reported taking multiple steps to maintain their social image. Specifically, they reported that they engaged in impression management behaviours, such as doing small favours for employees with the express purpose of getting employees to view them more favourably, while also engaging in self-promoting behaviours like highlighting how hard they work or showcasing past successes. However, these bosses did *not* admit to engaging in behaviours aimed at genuinely repairing the damage done by this abuse, such as offering a sincere apology. Unfortunately, it appears that toxic bosses don't change as much as we would like them to - instead, the bad behaviour tends to continue or often gets worse. Even when abusive bosses may appear genuinely repentant after a tirade, they usually have ulterior, self-interested motives.

However, we should be aware that manipulation and 'impression management' are intrinsic requirements of a number of roles, such as advertising, selling and spying! When recruiting for jobs like this, it is important that individuals know when to use these skills and when not to.

Other ways in which power is exerted include the following:

- *Personal respect and charisma*
  Charming persuasion from a boss who you respect is how the best leaders operate. This shift in power relationships can be characterisied as a move towards a conceptualisation of power in socialised terms (i.e., power is for benefiting the organisation and helping others) and away from power in personalised terms (i.e., power is for advancing one's personal agenda, status and prestige) (22).

- *You have something that others want*
  This can lead to blackmail, and several recent sexual harassment cases stem from this misuse of power. The 'Me Too' movement exposed how powerful movie moguls and others abused their position with victims whose future careers they believed depended on acquiescing to their wishes. Control of resources (budget, staff and information) can also be subverted towards benefiting the controller rather than the organisation.

- *Authority that derives from holding a position*
  Positions usually come with the power to sanction or reward. The formalising of hierarchy, reporting relationships and authority can lead to abuse, with subordinates forced to do personal work for the boss or be their foot soldiers in political games. Confusion arises when there is insufficient clarity about roles and boundaries, resulting in turf wars and a lack of authority to resolve disputes.

- *Collective power*
  Social groups that have shared interests exert power through their strength in numbers. The trade union movement was founded on such a principle. Its legitimacy may come from the strength of their convictions, or from the processes (often seen as democratic) that underpin their decisions and subsequent actions.

- *Representative or referential*
  In situations where someone is issuing instructions on behalf of another, it is assumed that this representative is accurately reflecting the wishes of the person with authority. Where the messenger distorts the message due to their own agenda, authority is undermined when the bias is revealed. The chain of command is brought into question and can lead to a slowdown in decision making as there is a lack of trust in the transmission system of messengers. The representative may be referring to others in order to avoid any blame falling on themself. We explore the role of communications in toxic cultures more fully in Chapter 9. A variation occurs where someone is influenced by or has a protective umbrella of someone with power (not necessarily by virtue of the authority vested in their position). This referential power may come from a toxic individual who is effective at manipulating others. It may also come from an expert.

- *Information and expertise*

  Where organisations are reliant on experts with specialist knowledge, especially when there is no source of challenge, wrong decisions might be made. Withholding information that can help others is a way of exercising power and is typical of political infighting. This is most likely when no one is in full command of the facts and the context. Making technical decisions without the context can be dangerous. The following case illustrates this:

> *A naval commander was testing a new torpedo, but had not been told that the torpedo had a self-destruct device if the torpedo failed to hit its target and turned round. In the test the torpedo failed to launch, and the commander ordered the ship to turn round to go back to port, with disastrous consequences (23).*

One problem with authority based on expertise is that the expert may not necessarily be a good role model. Historically, it took a long time for the medical profession to adopt good hygiene practices. The first advocate of cleanliness was Aulus Cornelius Celcus of ancient Rome. It was not until the 19th century that the importance of hand hygiene in hospital settings was recognised for the first time when influential leaders promoted it (24). In a recent case in a workshop, the designated person for safety was a poor example and when challenged for cutting corners, his reply was that he was an expert and knew how to cut corners safely. There is a maxim that you have to learn the rules before you can break them, but it is difficult to shift cultures if there are not sufficiently good role models doing the right thing on a consistent basis.

- *Coercive power which can best be described as bullying*

  It is a question of interpretation when tough management becomes coercive bullying. Coercive behaviour can also arise from personality factors which we will explore further when examining the so-called dark triad of Machiavellianism, psychopathy and narcissism.

THE BULLY

Harassment and bullying have always been a feature of organisational life, often stemming from inadequate managerial capability, tough targets, stress and other conditions. It can take many forms (25) and can include impossible targets, physical threats or attacks, sarcasm, offensive jokes, bad language, slander and libel, pestering, stalking and coercion.

The psychology of toxicity starts with individual reactions to threats. The consequences at work and at home can be numerous (26): fear, stress, anxiety, illness, absenteeism, lack of commitment, energy and enthusiasm, poor performance and low productivity, resignation and high labour turnover, conflict, poor morale, accidents and poor quality of work produced.

Abusive behaviour has many negative consequences for subordinates. It reduces collective efficacy, supportive behaviour to other team members (as everyone is looking out for themselves) and affects life beyond the workplace: 'Employees report feeling emotionally drained, experience lower well-being, and even increased conflict at home' (27).

Bullying can start by picking on a person and abusing them. Tactics include shaming another through humiliation, sarcasm or pointing out errors. Bullies' manipulative and controlling behaviour can be quite subtle and insidious. Onlookers in the organisation might turn a blind eye, being glad it's not them who is in the firing line and afraid to interfere because of possible reprisals. It results in a complicit silence with no one prepared to call it out. The recipient might come to see it as normal and similarly afraid to challenge because of the repercussions. When humiliation is used, the victim might come to believe that they are in some way to blame through their lack of competence or be seen as overreacting. Whistleblowers in these situations have to display even more courage as they are likely to invoke yet more bullying.

Bullying can be described as 'strong management' and much depends on who commands the narrative. However, bullying is aggressive demands that are unreasonable and treats the victim with little or no respect. It is concerned with the bully's sense of frustration and entitlement to do what they please. Harassment is a form of bullying and is unwanted conduct that affects the dignity of the person affected. Strong management is legitimate and is based on reasonable demands and constructive and fair feedback to employees, and is designed to achieve outcomes that everyone wants. It is sometimes difficult to distinguish between the two, and the aggressive manager may believe that their brand of strong management is required to improve morale.

The bully often comes from a place of insecurity or inadequacy. The realisation that they have control over others through bullying, that they may go unchallenged and that they can enjoy the feeling of controlling others can be a powerful drug to them. Organisations that have a culture of bullying might be able to get compliance in the short term, but there is a wellspring of resentment that builds over time. The bullied seek to get out, to subvert, to survive – all strategies designed for self-preservation and not geared towards becoming the best they or their organisation can be.

The following case illustrates how one person changed the dynamics of a situation where she had been bullied:

> *A manager bullied his secretary, who was a mild-mannered woman, by unfair criticism, putting her down in front of others and making her look stupid. She was good at her work, but needed the job, otherwise she would have left. After telling her friend about him, the friend remarked that he sounded like a baby in his playpen throwing his toys around. The following day he was ranting at her about a trivial matter. In the moment she saw him as a little baby and said: 'now don't get yourself upset, just calm down and you'll get over it' and walked out. He was stunned that she had answered back, and she was stunned that she had the courage to stand up to him. After that, the dynamic between them began to change and he was no longer so belligerent, and she was more forceful in answering back.*

The story poses a question as to what signals people give that encourages or discourages bullying behaviour. If you reduce the signs of vulnerability, you change the perception of the potential bully. In helping people to deal with relational problems, we run the risk of disempowering them. As a doctor said, 'the more we help people, especially when they might be able to help themselves, we disempower them, ultimately making them more dependent in the future and less able to fend for themselves'. What are we to do?

In Japanese there is a word 'Pawahara', which means 'power harassment' and is used to describe the abuse supervisors heap on their subordinates. In a hierarchical society like Japan where respect for seniority and age is a key feature, subordinates put up with behaviour that other more equal societies would not tolerate. Honda Soichiro, the founder of Honda, was renowned for throwing things at subordinates when he was angry (28). The occasion of such abuse in many organisations seems to be growing and a third of workers in Japan had experienced power harassment. Japan's Ministry of Health, Labour and Welfare defines five types of harassment: physical attacks, mental attacks, social isolation, excessive demands and privacy infringements. In 2020 the Ministry suggested that: 'What bosses see as tough love can come across as hurtful to junior employees, especially as behavioural norms change between generations.'[1] Despite new laws to crack down on this behaviour, there is little real sanction and so little likelihood of a dramatic improvement. South Korea has a similar problem called 'gapjil', the authoritarian attitude of senior managers who abuse their power and shout at employees, insisting on them working unpaid all night and at weekends, and on running personal errands for them.

Who are the bullies? They come in all shapes, sizes and genders. It should be noted that gender stereotypes tend to downplay the evidence of female bullying, believing that it is more prevalent in males. Gender differences in impulsivity, dominance and aggressiveness appear in all cultures and from a very early age – but also for cultural reasons. Amongst women, manipulation (sometimes downplayed as 'feminine wiles') is a more dominant characteristic. 'Women tend to be more devious, deceptive, charming and manipulative, whereas men are more likely to be described as aggressive and harassing' (29).

POWER AND COVID-19

One dramatic change that the COVID-19 pandemic has brought about is a shift towards remote working. Public health stay-at-home orders have legitimised a desire that many have wanted and have limited the power of employers (30). A total of 40-60% in advanced economies are allegedly working remotely (31). This is apparent in the rising property costs in remote and beautiful parts of the country, as people realise that they can work remotely and enjoy the view without the cost, time or stress of commuting, Individuals freed from commuting have reported spending longer at work and being more productive by being able to control communications more and avoiding unproductive office gossip. In one study, only 15% reported being less efficient working from home (32).

However, working from home has many aspects that have not been so beneficial both to employers and employees. It might at first seem like a benefit, but isolation at home, sometimes with children present, tends to increase stress rather than reduce it. Incidents of domestic violence have risen, even amongst priests (33). For employers who are used to seeing their employees working at their desks, remote working requires greater trust and clearer identification of how to identify good from bad performance as opposed to observing whether employees are looking as if they are working. Opportunities for mentoring and informal induction have become more limited and tools for tracking progress on projects have had to be more accurate as there is no longer the opportunity to 'manage by walking about' (MBWA). For the low-trust micro-manager, remote working is stressful: 'he became obsessive micromanaging every single aspect of our working hours and finding smallest things to critique … our stress levels were high knowing that at any moment our boss could check on us and we were all collectively going crazy' (34). It appears easier to say rude or threatening thing over Zoom than in person.

Working hours have also become more flexible during the pandemic. For some, this has been a blessing, with greater opportunities to integrate childcare and other domestic duties with work. However, flexible hours can be a double-edged sword with telephone calls late at night and little opportunity to be off duty. As a result, there have been calls for greater clarity on boundaries and acceptable behaviour relating to work. The Victorian police in Australia have agreed to allow officers to switch off their phones when they are off duty. The ILO (35) guidelines on working practices have also been dusted down and quoted in more cases in Europe.

The negative aspects of home working have been described as a lack of more casual interactions that might have benefited problem solving and consensus formation (36). This is particularly apparent when inducting new recruits into informal routines and ways of working. New employees have found it hard to get into the cultural norms and meet people face to face. Nevertheless, home working has shifted from a privilege to a right borne out of necessity, as evidenced by the resistance some employers are facing in attempting to restore full-time office attendance. One legal firm proved the fears that people would not work when they were at home to be groundless. They found that expenses were down and revenue was up, and they distributed the excess profits to all staff. The findings also showed that 61% of employers are planning to make moderate to extensive changes in order to allow more hybrid working, reflecting the views of 90% of employees, who said they want flexibility in terms of when and where they work (37).

Some employers have viewed home working as an incentive for staff retention and strategically positions them ready for restrictions and lockdowns that might occur in a future pandemic. Others have taken a more robust approach to encouraging employees to return to the office. Facebook and VM Software amongst others have promoted the idea of adjusting salaries to the cost of living in the place of work, i.e., at home (38). A study of Microsoft employees in 2019-20 found that remote working makes people's collaboration practices more 'static and siloed' (39), which has implications for long-term remote working, where innovation based on collaboration is key to future success.

The increase in turnover, called by some 'The Great Resignation',[2] can be described as employees reassessing their priorities and reasserting their right to choose how they work. Nilanjana Roy describes them as 'Time Millionaires', as they choose lifestyles that give them more personal fulfilment. In several industries and countries, restrictions on labour mobility have shifted power to those with crticial skills (40). For example, fruit pickers in Australia have won improved pay and conditions as a result of the limited availability of foreign workers. In the USA, 4.3 million (2.9% of the national labour force) Americans left their jobs in August 2021, the highest number on record. In the UK, vacancies have surpassed 1 million for the first time (41). The reasons given include overwork and underappreciation, fear of contracting COVID-19 and the weakenng of ties to their organisation: 'we're experiencing a severe global labour shortage that has tipped the balance of power towards workers' (42). Deferrment of career moves as a result of the pandemic has also contributed to this surge, with some saying that home working has caused them to reassess their career goals and working life. In one survey in the UK, 24% said they planned to move jobs within three to six months (43). Microsoft claim in this survey that the figure is higher, with 40% across the world considering future moves. It is hardly surprising that Gartner have identified that staff retention is the number one strategic imperative for organisations.

This shift in power to employees has societal implications as well; workers, such as delivery personnel who have traditionally been seen as low-skilled and subject to constant cost-cutting through increased pressure, performance measures and periodic change of employer through outsourcing, have been found to be essential in the pandemic with so many at home. They have also run an increased risk of contracting the virus. There is now a new appreciation of medical, security, construction and retail staff. Increased reactions against lockdowns and vaccine mandates have fuelled a growing resentment that some can enjoy increased freedom whilst others cannot. This rise in inequaliity has implications for societal cohesion (44):

The pandemic has rewritten the psychological contract or employment deal that was forged during the eras of neoliberalism and austerity. Today's workers want to be seen as people – complex, messy, colourful, diverse, flawed, fabulous humans. That means that they

(Management) need to rethink how work is done in the post Covid world and rethink how they attract, retain and manage their people (45).

A decline in commuting has implications for city property, services, cafes, retail and transport, and health and safety, whilst working remotely and massive government support in many countries has led to increased public debt and a legacy for future generations to repay, further fuelling resentment towards the actions (however important at the time) of past governments.

The resolution of these employer–employee tensions are likely to trigger conflict over questions of fairness, equality and employee power, as well as labour mobility, disruption in wage rates and the emergence of a wider range of hybrid employment arrangements. Economists believe (46) that post-pandemic office workers will continue to work 1.3 days away and the hybrid model of working will become the norm (47). Questions remain over how to foster team cohesion and creativity, remote leadership and knowledge sharing in that changed working environment.

TABLE 3.1 Effects of working from home (WFH) during the COVID-19 pandemic.

Effect	To employees	To employers	To society
Positive	- More control over their working day - Better able to integrate family and other responsibilities into work patterns - Time and travel cost savings as a result of less commuting - Some report greater personal efficiency	- Savings in office and business travel costs from proven remote working protocols - Greater chance of retention? - Useful test of technologies to support new ways of working	- WFH allowed society to function whilst pursuing public health stay at home orders were in place - Greater flexibility in the labour market?
Negative	- Blurring of start and finish times ('the 24/7 job') - Loss of social contact - Fewer opportunities to see good performance in action - Greater onus on managing your own career - Mental health issues - Increased domestic violence - Conflict between home schooling and home working	- Less control over employees time spent on activities - Less opportunity for informal mentoring and coaching, particularly with new employees - Greater difficulty in transmitting institutional memory - Reluctance of employees to return to their office due to health concerns, lack of child care close to work, etc. - Lower team cohesion? - The 'Great Resignation' (4.3 million employees left their jobs in the USA out of a working population of 160 million) - Increase in unionisation - 'Higher communication and coordination costs' - 'Static and siloed' collaboration practices	- Increased social tension between those 'essential workers' whose work cannot be done remotely and those able to work from home - Disruptions in supply chains - Disruptions to businesses that rely on office workers commuting to inner cities (cafes, bars, dry cleaners, etc.) - Impact on public transport

SUMMARY AND CONCLUSIONS

- Imbalances in power relationships are a major cause of toxicity.
- Power mapping gives an indication of where power imbalances might lie between stakeholders.
- The COVID-19 pandemic has shifted the power relationship between employers and employees.
- There are multiple ways power is exerted, including:
  - influence through personability and impression management;
  - personal respect and charisma;
  - having something that others want;
  - authority from position;
  - collectively;
  - representative or referential;
  - information and expertise;
  - coercive.
- Bullying is a significant cause of a toxic climate that arises from a power imbalance.

NOTES

1 Quoted by *The Economist* about Inao Izumi, of Cuore C Cube, the consultancy that defined Pawahara.
2 Coined by Anthony Klotz at Texas AM University in May 2021.

REFERENCES

1 World Economic Forum. *Fourth Industrial Revolution*. Retrieved 11 April 2022 from https://www.weforum.org/focus/fourth-industrial-revolution.
2 Hotten, R. (2015, 10 December) *Volkswagen: The scandal explained. BBC News*). Retrieved 11 April 2022 from https://www.bbc.co.uk/news/business-34324772.
3 Patel, K. et al. (2021) Psychological distress before and during the COVID-19 pandemic: Sociodemographic inequalities in 11 UK longitudinal studies. Retrieved 11 April 2022 from https://www.medrxiv.org/content/10.1101/2021.10.22.21265368v1.full.
4 Free exchange: The pyjama revolution. *The Economist* (30 October 2021).
5 Farrell, A.K., Simpson, J.A. and Rothman, A.J. (2015) The relationship power inventory: Development and validation. *Personal Relationships, 22*(3), 387-413.
6 Emerson, R.M. (1962) Power dependence relations. *American Sociological Review, 27*(1), 31-41.
7 Levy, J.S. and Thompson, W.R. (2005) Hegemonic threat and great power balancing in Europe, 1495–2000. *Security Studies, 14*(1), 1–30.
8 Singh, A. (2009). Organisational power in perspective. *Leadership and Management in Engineering, 9(4), https://ascelibrary.org/doi/full/10.1061/(ASCE)LM.1943-5630.0000018.*
9 Tang, A. Power mapping and analysis. Retrieved 11 April 2022 from https://commonslibrary.org/guide-power-mapping-and-analysis.
10 Salancik, G. and Pfeffer, J. (1977) Who gets power - and how they hold on to it. *Organisational Dynamics. Winter.*
11 Restubog, S.L.D. and Kiewitz, C. (2015) Psychological contracts. In *International Encyclopedia of the Social & Behavioural Sciences (Second Edition).*Elsevier, pp. 366-371.
12 Bizshifts-trends. The equity theory: Principle of balance, fairness, justice... in the workplace: Workers' perceptions about fairness does matter (August 2014). Retrieved 11 April 2022 from https://bizshifts-trends.com/equity-theory-fairness-justice-business-workers-perceptions-fairness-workplace-matter.

13 Kellogg's workers have gone on strike in October 2021 claiming that they are 'tired of corporate greed'. Retrieved from https://www.reuters.com/.../kellogg-warns-earnings-hit-workers-strike-2021-11-04.

14 Hofstede, Geert H. (1997). *Cultures and organisations: Software of the mind* (second ed.). McGraw-Hill.

15 Coldwell, D.A.L (2021) Toxic behaviour in organisations and organisational entropy: A 4th Industrial Revolution phenomena. *SN Business Economics, 1*(5., https://doi.org/10.1007/s43546-021-00079-0

16 Kusy, M.E. and Holloway, E.L. (2010) Disruptive and toxic behaviours in healthcare: Zero tolerance, the bottom line. And what to do about it Retrieved 22 June 2022 from https://www.academia.edu/38388895/May_Jun_2010_335_340_pdf.

17 Cannon R. and Cannon J. (2022*) Aha! A user's guide to creativity*. Austin Macauley (in press).

18 McShane, S.L. and Von Glinow, L.M. (2013) *Organisational behaviour: Emerging knowledge, global reality*. McGraw Hill.

19 Armstrong, P. (2015) The discourse of Michel Foucault: A sociological perspective, *Critical Perspectives on Accounting, 27*: 29–42.

20 Covey, S.R. (2013) *The 7 habits of highly effective people*. Simon & Schuster.

21 McClean, S.H., Courtright, T., Smith, A. and Yim, J. (2021, 19 January) Stop making excuses for toxic bosses. *Harvard Business Review*.

22 Torelli, C.J. and Shavitt, S. (2010) Culture and concepts of power. *Journal of Personality and Social Psychology, 99*(4), 703–723.

23 Arkin, W.M. and Handler, J. (1989) *Naval accidents 1945–1988*. Neptune Papers.

24 History of cleaning in healthcare. *European Cleaning Journal* (2012) Retrieved 9 June 2022 from http://www.europeancleaningjournal.com/magazine/articles/special-features/history-of-cleanliness-in-healthcare.

25 Stephens, T. (1999) *Bullying and sexual harassment*. CIPD.

26 Priesemuth, M. (2020, 19 June) Time's up for toxic workplaces, *Harvard Business Review*.

27 https://anti-bullyingalliance.org.uk/

28 Lessons from 100 columns, *Economist – 13 June 2020*.

29 https://anti-bullyingalliance.org.uk/

30 Remote-first work is taking over the rich world. The *Economist* (30 October 2021).

31 Dunlop, T. (2021) Has the pandemic changed the way we work for good? Retrieved 12 April 2022 from https://www.eurekastreet.com.au/article/has-the-pandemic-changed-the-way-we-work-for-good.

32 Barrero, J.M., Bloom, N. and Davis, S.J. (2021*) Why working from home will stick*. National Bureau of Economic Research.

33 National Anglican Family Violence Project (NAFVP) (2021) National Anglican Family Violence research report. Retrieved 12 April 2022 from https://anglican.org.au/wp-content/uploads/2021/08/1.-NAFVP-Research-Report.pdf.

34 'Nikolina', quoted by Hickok, J. (2021, 5 April) Why toxic workplace cultures follow you home. *BBC*.

35 Labour standards on working conditions. Retrieved 12 April 202 from https://www.ilo.org/global/topics/dw4sd/themes/working-conditions/WCMS_560706/lang--en/index.htm

36 EY (2021) Work reimagined: Global employer survey. Retrieved 12 April 2022 from https://www.icmif.org/wp-content/uploads/2021/06/ICMIF-EY-Work-Reimagined-Presentation-June-2021.pdf.

37 Randstad survey of job mobility (2021). Retrieved 9 June 2022 from. https://www.randstad.co.uk/employers/workforce-insights/rebr-report.

38 Kolakowski, N. (2020, 15 September). These tech companies want pay cuts for remote workers. Retrieved 12 April 2022 from https://insights.dice.com/2020/09/15/these-tech-companies-want-pay-cuts-for-remote-workers.

39 Microsoft (2021) The next great disruption is hybrid work – are we ready? Retrieved 12 April 2022 from https://www.microsoft.com/en-us/worklab/work-trend-index/hybrid-work.

40 McEwan, A. (2021, 29 October) With the Great Resignation, Australians are ditching pre-COVID burnout and pursuing better work-life balance. Retrieved 12 April 2022 from https://www.abc.net.au/news/2021-10-30/great-resignation-australians-quitting-jobs-work-balance-covid/100566922.

41 Dunlop, T. (2021) Has the pandemic changed the way we work for good? Retrieved 12 April 2022 from https://www.eurekastreet.com.au/article/has-the-pandemic-changed-the-way-we-work-for-good.

42 Wiles, J. (2021) Great Resignation or not, money won't fix all your talent problems. Retrieved 9 June 2022 from https://www.gartner.com/en/articles/great-resignation-or-not-money-won-t-fix-all-your-talent-problems?sf253544625=1.

43 Gibbs, M., Mengel, F. and Siemroth, C. (2021) *Work from home and productivity: Evidence from personnel and analytics data on IT Professionals*. Becker Friedman Institute.

44 Yang, L., Holtz, D., Jaffe, S. et al. (2022) The effects of remote work on collaboration among information workers. *Nat Hum Behav 6*, 43–54, https://doi.org/10.1038/s41562-021-01196-4.

45 Wiles, J. (2021) Great Resignation or not, money won't fix all your talent problems. Retrieved 9 June 2022 from https://www.gartner.com/en/articles/great-resignation-or-not-money-won-t-fix-all-your-talent-problems?sf253544625=1.

46 Lund, S., Madgawkar, An., Manyika, J., Smit, S., Ellingrud, K. and Robinson, O. (2021) *The future of work*. McKinsey & Company.

47 Barrero, J.M., Bloom, N. and Davis, J. (2021) *Survey of working arrangements. November updates*. WFH Research. See also Barrero, J.M., Bloom, N. and Davis, S.J. (2021) *Why working from home will stick*. National Bureau of Economic Research Working Paper 28731.

CHAPTER 4

Leadership

The dark triad – personality and the toxic individual

INTRODUCTION

An ancient saying is 'the fish rots from the head down' and there have been many leaders in history (such as Hitler, Mao and Stalin) who could claim to have had devastating effects on their countries. What is it about such individuals that they can wreak such havoc and why have they been able to get away with it, at least for the most part and for a time? In this chapter we explore something of that pathology and how it can become so destructive. Our focus is on organisations rather than nations, but many of the same characteristics of national leaders are apparent at the level of smaller social groupings. For the most part, we are not dealing with 'destructive leadership' (1), but rather toxic leadership, where the intention may be positive, but the effect is negative. Employees might reinforce this toxicity by acquiescing with leader's fixations (2), and indeed there may be little or no distinction for the recipient between destructive and toxic behaviour.

Leadership has been described as creating the conditions for people to do their best work, and the extent to which people feel negative emotions can inhibit performance. The most significant influence on culture is the behaviour of those in leadership. So, what are the characteristics of leaders that lead to toxic cultures? 'The standard you walk by is the standard you accept' was said by General Morrison of the Australian Army. He was referring to the treatment of women, but his comment has relevance to the behaviour of leaders at all levels in all organisations and to all people. How you spend your time and attention is a key choice for senior leaders, given that there is never enough time to do everything. These choices are determined by their vison of the future, their philosophy of management and their formula for success, personal preferences often honed through personal values and conventions, interests and capability. At issue is how these choices are made and whether there is 'wilful blindness' in the exercise of them. Gladys Berejiklian, former New South Wales (NSW) premier, was caught on the phone saying to her disgraced former partner that she 'didn't want to know that' when he started to tell her of some shady deal (3). Moral legitimacy is questioned when those setting the rules are not whiter than white. Boris Johnson, the UK Prime Minister, has similarly lost authority through disregarding COVID-19 rules that were set by his government.

A tension that is never resolved in all profit-driven organisations is what behaviour is appropriate to make that profit. How far should you push to the boundaries of legality? What means justify the ends? Recently, in the USA, several CEOs made an open statement (4) that their businesses were not *only* about profit for its shareholders, but recognised that they had social obligations to a wide range of stakeholders, not least to employees and how they were treated. This signalled a

DOI: 10.4324/9781003307334-7

shift from the simple message that business was about profit and challenged the view that it was *the* only duty of managers to maximise profits by increasing sales and squeezing costs, including employee remuneration and benefits.

COVID-19 has shown up a range of leadership styles from national leaders to deal with the pandemic, from denial (Donald Trump in the USA) to early firm action (Jacinda Ardern in New Zealand). Sweden has shown a middle path of avoiding mass lockdowns by urging individual responsibility. Faced with rising cases and deaths, it shifted strategy to rapid tracing and testing in order to isolate clusters early on (as NSW did, in contrast to Victoria, in Australia). The Swedish approach was to urge everyone to use every means possible to avoid contagion (face masks, social distancing, hand washing, etc.), but at the same time giving people freedom as to how they would respond. It sought to balance and weigh up in a pragmatic way the trade-offs in any policy. Even though this approach has not been totally successful, the Swedish government have managed to take the population with them in a way that policies in America have not done. The lesson for all cultures – both national and organisational – is to always seek trade-offs between freedom which encourages responsibility and initiative (most of the time for most of the people) and central control that results in uniformity and clear guidance, but runs the risk of losing support, especially when rules appear unreasonable to some groups and those who are irked by any outside control.

There was a hope that working from home, as so many have done during the pandemic, might give some relief from the worst elements of office politics and toxic leaders. The picture that is emerging is not so simple. Those leaders who tended to micro-manage became worse, checking up on their staff far more than before because of their inability to see them working at their desk. Performance management based on 'presentism' became impossible and sorely tested whether they could trust their staff. Hannah Hickok (5) reported cases where the use of software such as TeamViewer and Hubstaff encouraged some managers to become obsessive about checking up on their staff. 'Physical presentism' can stimulate several unhelpful behaviours. One men's outfitter in New York used to sell a second jacket with a suit. This meant you could leave one on the back of your chair so that no one knew if you had gone home.

THE EFFECTIVE LEADER

Many writers agree that the most important traits for being an effective leader are trustworthiness, vision and expertise (6). We seek leaders who genuinely display a degree of humility and whose values of integrity and transparency are more likely to lead to positive team behaviour. Highly influential leaders are described as charismatic and authentic, and deploy certain behavioural characteristics in the way in which they influence people, including high levels of eye contact, active listening, careful questioning and deploying interest in the answers gained, with often humour and courtesy. They display emotional, organisational and strategic intelligence (7).

Highly influential leaders build diverse teams. Discrimination in all its forms – age, race, sexual orientation and educational background - can lead to stereotyping of those who are different with a negative impact on performance. There is considerable evidence that a diverse workforce is better for creativity and problem solving, and, where one is customer-facing, better matched to the world outside (8). Of course, leadership has to be learnt and in many professions, technical competence – e.g. in law, accounting or technology - does not automatically give people the necessary skills. People will forgive mistakes if they are accompanied by an openness and a willingness to correct them.

THE CHARACTERISTICS OF TOXIC LEADERS

In contrast to effective leaders who create high levels of trust, engagement, discretionary effort and productivity, incompetent leaders leave their followers anxious, alienated and with unproductive work habits. People rarely leave bad companies; they leave bad managers.

One way of identifying poor employee engagement is the degree of scepticism employees show to new initiatives, often exemplified in the sarcastic humour shown. Moore (9) described what poor leaders do:

They kill enthusiasm.
They kill emotion and passion.
They kill explanation of why we do what we do.
They kill engagement with our goals.
They kill reward by rewarding the wrong things.
They kill culture.
They kill trust.

The behavioural characteristics of poor leaders are numerous, with each having an individual twist. Whilst imposter syndrome[1] is common, the poor leader has long since suppressed such doubts. A simplistic way of describing the drivers of bad human behaviour is the seven deadly sins: lust, greed, sloth, wrath, envy, pride and gluttony. We will come across most of these sins as we examine how individuals can create toxic conditions in their organisations.

It is likely that at some point senior managers will experience criticism that may seem unfair. It requires a degree of maturity to accept it and implement change. The poor leader is likely to react by rejection and even a desire to retaliate. Ken Henry, former chairman of National Australia Bank, was heavily criticised in the Royal Commission into Misconduct in the Banking, Superannuation and Financial Services Industry and described as 'hubris wrapped in arrogance surrounded by conceit' (10).

In a recent article Tomas Chamorro-Premuzic (11) argues that those who recruit and appoint leaders should focus more attention on distinguishing confidence from competence. It was Hazlitt, the 18th-century philosopher, who said 'as is our confidence so is our competence'. Confidence is required to have a go at something new, to resist giving up when things go wrong, and through practice to become competent. But it becomes a problem when overconfidence coupled with a lack of awareness results in arrogance.

Warren Buffet is reputed to have remarked that when he saw companies building a new corporate headquarters, he sold the shares. He had learnt that success can breed a certain arrogance and a belief that they no longer needed to be aware of their competitors. In essence, they shifted more towards enjoying rewards rather than being hungry and competitive. Leona Helmsley, dubbed the 'Queen of Mean' and the doyen of a famous hotel in New York, was rich and famous, but her arrogance also led her to ignore the rules and remark that paying taxes was only for 'little people'. She ended up going to jail for tax fraud.

In an earlier study, I found that amongst several reasons why people became self-employed was the desire to get away from toxic culture environments that were plagued with politics and inappropriate behaviour (12).

A recent case in Australia illustrates the huge consequences of poor leadership. The recent scandal involved Bo Pahari, a senior manager at AMP, a financial service company, who was demoted and fined as a result of sexual harassment against a subordinate. A short time later, he was promoted to a new senior role because he was a high performer and that clearly weighed more in his superiors' decisions. His promotion demolished any perception that the culture had changed and resulted in widespread outrage from shareholders and clients over the revelations. Finally, he was forced to resign. The former sex discrimination commissioner Elizabeth Broderick commented that 'it also signals that any substantiated claim of sexual harassment against a senior leader charged with setting and driving employee engagement and organisation culture may severely impact their ability and credibility to hold a leadership position' (13).

There are other aspects of the AMP culture that worked against a long-term sustainable culture intended to encourage people to stay and give of their best. Pahari described his approach as 'Orca one' because he encouraged his people to hunt like a pack of orca whales. In the wake of the banking and financial scandals, highlighted in the Royal Commission, this behaviour was in direct opposition to the more ethical approach that AMP was trying to deliver to rebuild its tattered reputation. Its new chairman, Debra Hazelton, has the task of creating a more inclusive and diverse but less bureaucratic culture. This aim is not unique to AMP and these are elements of the cultural mix that all organisations strive to address.

One consequence of individual managers whose behaviour is deviant or unproductive is that they give licence to others to follow their example. If the boss swears and yells, it is hardly surprising to see other more junior managers doing the same. Some have described the resulting shift required of leadership as a move towards needing a 'social licence' to oper-ate[2] (14). Apart from diversity and inclusion, the licence should include standards of ethical behaviour at all levels and in all transactions. The emergence of ESG[3] as a standard to deter-mine appropriate business for investment is a manifestation of this.

Other common causes of unproductive behaviour are as follows:

- Inadequate skills of influencing and persuasion.
- Projection of their inadequacies on to others.
- Stress and overload.

THE SKILLS OF PERSUADING AND INFLUENCING

Effective leaders combine having high expectations of people and what they can do (often beyond what they think they can do themselves) along with strong personal bonding that generates a sense of trust, security and belonging – 'I have a legitimate place in this team'. Gregg Popovich, the head coach and president of the San Antonio Spurs, was rated as one of the most successful basketball teams and was described by an assistant coach Chip Engelland as follows: 'he delivers two things over and over: he'll tell you the truth, with no bullshit, and then he'll love you to death' (15). In retirement, Al Decker, one of the founders of Black & Decker, would make an annual visit to each plant round the world and as he walked down the production lines, he would stop and chat to a worker, asking about their family, often based on remembering something he had been told the last time he had visited. People saw this and believed that he cared. Bullies, narcissists and psychopaths show no indication that they care for their people.

The underlying skill is summed up in an ancient saying: 'If you wish to be understood, seek first to understand'.[4] Deep listening and a generative dialogue are at the heart of effective influencing. One dimension that has a strong relationship to performance is conscientiousness. Those with high levels of influence want to do a good job and the converse is also true. When things go wrong is a decisive moment for leaders and the culture that is created. It is a moment of truth when a leader understands how their behaviour impacts the culture for good or ill.

PROJECTING THEIR INADEQUACIES ONTO OTHERS

The manifestation of personal problems of leaders and their inability to deal with them may appear in many ways; some of the more dangerous include alcoholism, mental illness and physical aggression. These may also be manifest in the workplace and the consequence of this behaviour may lead to ostracism, breakdown in communication and poor performance of others.

STRESS AND OVERLOAD

When people are under stress, their behaviour can become irritable and uncivil. The response to incivility can be 'people can't sleep, they get sick, their relationships suffer, and they lose the enjoyment of going to work' (16). It can easily spread – backstabbing, gossip angry outbursts, condescension and verbal sabotage. These are difficult to address legally or through discipline as they are not as overt as bullying or harassment, yet can be equally insidious and devastating to those affected.

Fear is a major driver of behaviour and has been explored as early as Charles Darwin in his last book *The expression of the emotions in man and animals* (17). Henry James, a pioneer in psychology (18), showed that emotions were often beyond conscious control. We might check our facial expression when hearing the sentence of a court, but we are unlikely to be passive when chased by a bear. The autonomic nervous system controls many of the body's functions without conscious thought, such as breathing. The sympathetic system acts to stimulate processes, such as increasing blood pressure when the body is facing a threat (19), whereas the parasympathetic system will act to reduce it and restore the body to a normal balanced state. This pioneering work, subsequently amplified by the emerging neuroscience into the brain processes that underpin fear, gives us a clue that the irrational behaviour that we find in those who are stressed and or fearful may well be only partially controlled by the individual. Even though they may be conscious of what they are doing, they may still be unaware of why it is occurring and be unwilling or perhaps incapable of easily stopping it [5](20). We will explore fear more in Chapter 9 on motivation.

The perpetuation of toxic cultures arising from poor leadership can be as a result of leaders recruiting people in their own image and, because of their narcissistic tendencies, recruiting less competent people to ensure these people don't show them up. Over time, there is a degradation in the quality of the leadership team to the detriment of the organisation as a whole. The problem is taken as reinforcement for the narcissist's belief that they are better than anyone else and therefore indispensable. One consequence is the emergence of rotten apples.

The rotten apple theory, whereby it only requires one disruptive individual to spread dissatisfaction amongst many, is a consequence of bad leadership. A study by Felps et al. (21) describes the effect of the rotten apple on a group. Their experiments catalogue how certain behaviours encourage others to follow their lead, with the resulting loss of team effectiveness. He describes three archetypes that reduce team effectiveness: the aggressive and defiant, the slacker, and the depressive. However, his research also found the kind of leadership behaviour that neutralises this behaviour, which in essence is creating a sense of safety and security in a team where people feel they belong. When people feel connected (like family, as some would describe it), they become much more effective, especially when this is compounded with a belief in their purpose. Such groups become powerful and able to perform anything – for good or ill. The influence of Bill Papas on the Forum Finance group, which is now embroiled in a massive case of fraud, is indicative of how one man can corrupt a whole company (22).

PERSONALITY AND THE DARK TRIAD

There are many characteristics that separate people and can be the cause of irritation and conflict. An example of one characteristic that separates people is the extent to which they do things early as opposed to at the last minute, and is the cause of much friction in organisations. Micromanagement can seem stifling to the recipient, yet to the manager who is highly detail-conscious and is fearful of mistakes, it seems necessary. Getting the balance right between giving freedom and keeping control is a skill many managers fail to learn. So, the underlying personality differences might facilitate the emergence of more toxic behaviour. Other demotivating characteristics include being continually negative and giving little respect to others, often compounded by differences in race and gender.

More sinister factors can have a damaging effect on culture. Moshagen (23) proposed personality factor D to encompass individual traits that in essence increase personal utility at the expense of others, accompanied by beliefs that serve as justifications. They suggest that personality factor D is correlated with egoism, Machiavellianism, narcissism, moral disengagement, spitefulness, self-interest, psychological entitlement, psychopathy and sadism. The dark triad (and some argue it is a tetrad) focuses on Machiavellianism, psychopathy and narcissism (with sadism as a fourth).

Machiavellianism

Machiavellianism is a personality trait centred on manipulativeness, callousness and indifference to morality. Richard Christie and Florence Geis used edited and truncated statements inspired by Machiavelli's works to study variations in human behaviour (24). Their *Mach IV* test, a 20-question, Likert-scale personality survey, became the standard self-assessment tool and scale of the Machiavellianism construct. Those who score high on the scale are more likely to have an elevated level of deceitfulness and an unempathetic temperament (25).

Sociopaths and psychopaths

Board and Fritzon (26) surveyed British senior managers and concluded that 'the prevalence of histrionic, narcissistic and compulsive personality disorders was relatively high'. Whether these characteristics are a result of nature, nurture or both is an open question, but psychopaths do show different brain responses to emotional triggers compared to non-psychopaths. Brain imaging has shown that the limbic system in psychopaths does not activate to the same degree as the norm, though cognitively it does. The implication is that the impact that psychopaths and sociopaths have on organisations can be highly effective in their pursuit of their agendas and achieving their goals, but destructive in the longer term to those around them and their organisations (27).

There are different types of psychopaths (28):

- The manipulative, with a particular competence in interpersonal persuasiveness.
- Talkers rather than doers, but who are skilled in playing politics.
- The braggarts, showmen and bullies, who display macho behaviour and react aggressively to any threat to their self-image.

Signs of psychopathy are superficial charm, insincerity, egocentricity, manipulativeness, exploitativeness, independence, rigidity, stubbornness and dictatorial tendencies (29). The manipulative psychopath lives without conscience, guilt or loyalty to anyone but themselves and is superficial, grandiose, deceitful, impulsive, irresponsible and lacking in empathy. They behave badly in the workplace for the fun and the chaos it creates. Whilst one individual might be manageable, their attitudes and norms can spread like a virus. It begins to divide people into those who follow and those who do not. It can become a rebellious movement and encourage others who are disaffected with the organisation to exhibit these behaviours because they see others doing it. This is common when organisations become criminal subcultures, where staff ignore the law and everyone goes along with it. Similar descriptions of this behaviour might be described as *antisocial personality disorder* (30).

Earlier, we identified that psychopathy and sociopathy – antisocial behaviour disorders - are a common characteristic amongst those leaders who are highly effective in overcoming difficulties and opposition because they have little or no concern for the collateral damage inflicted on innocent people. Their lack of empathy may be disguised by their language of describing emotions, but they don't feel them. An example is Dr Spock in *Star Trek*, who responds to emotionally charged situations as 'interesting' or 'fascinating'. Sociopaths, whilst capable of empathy, are affected by the norms of their environment and allow some commitment to a sense of right and wrong.

Estimates of the percentage of psychopaths and sociopaths in society range from 1% to 4%. In one survey (31) it was reported that 15% of the prison population are psychopaths and are more likely to reoffend, as they have little remorse for their crimes. The proportion of those with psychopathic traits is greater in certain professions, including banking, law and the media. This is not surprising as psychopaths are attracted to environments where they can maximise their influence and rewards, without being emotionally affected. Many people imagine psychopaths to be serial killers as shown in films. Some killers diagnosed as psychopaths have been described as soulless. While it is true that some killers are psychopathic, it is also true that many more people in 'respectable' jobs have psychopathic tendencies.

The earliest authoritative work on psychopaths was by Hervey Cleckley (32) with his book *The mask of sanity* published in 1941. He found that whilst intelligent, they didn't learn from their experience, being too bound up with their own worldview. They tended to disregard others' views or described adverse circumstances as the fault of others and therefore as requiring no change from them. Psychopaths are also liars or skilled at gilding the truth to show themselves in a good light. Their lack of empathy and understanding of others' emotional reactions make them able to push through tough decisions, but with great collateral damage to any people affected.

The Psychopathy Checklist-Revised (PCL-R) is used to identify psychopathy and must be administered by a trained practitioner in a face-to-face interview. Factors emerging from the 20-item test are correlated with narcissism and borderline personality disorder. A version called the PCL:SV lists traits under four domains (33), which are as follows:

- Interpersonal, where the person is assessed as superficial, grandiose and deceitful.
- Affective, where the person lacks remorse, empathy and doesn't accept responsibility.
- Lifestyle, where the person is impulsive, lacks goals and is irresponsible.
- Finally, antisocial, where the person has a history of poor behavioural controls.

WHY ARE PSYCHOPATHS TOLERATED?

- They can be very charming as they have found this to be effective in manipulating people to their agendas.
- They display characteristics that in some contexts are seen as desirable – taking charge, making decisions and getting others to do things. In reality, this often emerges as bullying. A moderate dose of psychopathy might be very useful in some jobs requiring forcefulness in terms of getting things done. In a time of crisis, people curiously want leaders who appear to have a special insight into what needs to be done, regardless of the tenuous link to reality and the lies that underpin their views.
- They step up when tough change has to be implemented as they are usually unmoved by the fallout caused in people's lives.
- They respond well to minimal rules and so can more easily exploit their ideas, unfettered by corporate bureaucracy and controls.
- There are toxic protectors who are apologists for them, because they may be recipients of past favours or future opportunities.
- There are toxic buffers who believe that for all their faults, this individual, because of their performance or potential, must be retained and so act as a form of go-between.

As we will discuss in Chapter 5, the dilemma for a manager of a psychopath lies in whether to reward their high performance or tackle their behaviour at the possible expense of performance. Psychopaths operate by taking advantage of weaknesses in assessment at hiring and, later, by a culture that frowns on whistleblowers and that rewards achievement above all other things. Environments that are heavily controlled create fewer opportunities to be manipulated, but in the natural rhythm of organisational life, controls increase until they become burdensome and are then followed by greater tolerance for a freer approach. It is then that the psychopath can begin to work as they are invariably rule breakers.

The psychopaths tend to have a talent for 'reading' people and working out how they can get others to subscribe to their way of thinking. They work on their ability to present themselves to others and sometimes watch themselves in action, partly to confirm to themselves how clever they are, but also to use all their charms to manipulate others. In so doing, they present themselves to others in a way that is most likely to gain their following and acquiescence.

Goffman's book on the presentation of self (34) describes how we all construct an image of others based on small pieces of data – clothes, titles, qualifications and manners – and we usually assume the best of them until reality proves otherwise. The con artist may be an expert at presenting a mask of sincerity and integrity, playing on people's gullibility and vulnerabilities. This is done solely with the aim of gaining some advantage, but with a callous disregard for the feelings of others. The narcissist will receive attention and flattery, the anxious will be reassured, and others might find them fun. 'Few will suspect that they are dealing with a psychopath who is playing up to their particular personality and vulnerabilities' (35).

Anthony Levandowski, the technologist who led Google's self-driving car project, was sentenced in August 2020 to 18 months in prison for stealing company secrets on his way to another job. Levandowski's lawyers said that he made a life-changing mistake, but it didn't come out of the blue. Levandowski openly flouted Google's rules for years and exercised bad judgement. In 2011 an incident reported in the *New York Times* (36) described when Levandowski took a Google driverless car on a freeway before it was ready and swerved to avoid a collision in a way that seriously injured his colleague. Instead of reflecting on whether his forbidden test drive was irresponsible, Levandowski seemed to regard it as a useful data-collection exercise, which is a common feature of those who care little for others.

This type of behaviour was lavishly rewarded, until Levandowski left Google and the company turned against him. And he is not the only rule-breaking genius who Google loved. Determined, confident and rule-bending people have created successful companies and world-changing inventions. Apple once made a TV advertisement entitled 'here's to the crazy ones', praising those who broke the conventions and rules of the day to make breakthrough innovations. That makes it easier, perhaps, to shrug off the occasional company implosion or federal prison sentence.

One of the consequences of the psychopath arising from their aggressive view of organisational life is that they assume that everyone thinks as they do. They view business as a corporate jungle where it is a dog-eat-dog world and politics of all shades is fair game. So, it is OK to get what you want, regardless of the damage done to others. You are either a winner or a loser. Given their low boredom threshold, they gain a thrill from gaming the system and taking high-risk actions. They seek situations where they can take advantage of others, make a killing and hide their actions. They typically want money, power, fame and sex. The combination of manipulative charm and narcissism results in a gathering of loyal followers seen in many cults. They believe that they are entitled to unquestioning support. In these scenarios, victims are treated as expendable and with little remorse if things go wrong.

SO HOW DOES THE PSYCHOPATH REACH POSITIONS OF POWER AND INFLUENCE?

1. The so-called 'Peter Principle', whereby people get promoted beyond their level of competence, is amplified by psychopaths through their ability to lie convincingly about their achievements. The result is that they are easily hired and promoted. Interviews are the perfect game for the manipulative psychopath to use all their charm to get the job. That's the aim rather than actually doing it. Once in place, they take parasitic advantage of the situation for

their own ends. In examining CVs, be aware that psychopaths cross the line between marketing their skills and experience, and outright lying and exaggerating about experience. The ability to brazenly lie comes from having no conscience about their actions.

2. Personality is complex and many people are only dimly aware of how they come across because they rarely think of it. To the psychopath, this is a constant awareness. Their view of themselves as skilled, intelligent, attractive, etc. is presented in a way that supports this view, even to the extent of lies and deceits being employed to achieve it. The aim is for others to interpret their personality in the way they want. Once this is shattered by others seeing through the falsehoods and challenging the person, several outcomes can occur. It is a moment of truth, and the challenger can be rejected in aggressive ways - perhaps labelled as a liar, loser, faker, enemy, etc. To others, these reactions may seem extreme, but to the skilled psychopath who has built up a loyal following, they begin to believe that the challenger is wrong or at best disloyal. Another reaction might be to mobilise supporters who, by showing their strength in numbers and conviction, demonstrate to the world that the challenger is wrong. Another alternative is to deny reality. The events of 6 January 2021, when the Capitol Building in Washington DC was stormed because people believed falsely that the election of Joe Biden as President had only been achieved as a result of a manipulated vote reflected the loyal following that Donald Trump had aroused, regardless of the truth.

3. The author once was misled by an individual who had little or no regard for the truth:

> *Recruiting once for a position and following an interview, the author believed he had found the ideal candidate. Proudly, he showed the CV to his boss, who went to his filing cabinet and produced a different CV but with the same address. It transpired that the candidate made a living out of claiming travel expenses to interviews and made up a different CV each time depending on the job.*

We make judgements about people very quickly – some studies would indicate in the first few minutes. We then filter out any information that disagrees with our earlier view and retain any that supports our view.

There have been many studies in the biases that occur when interviewing staff. The following is one example:

> *In a historical study of interviews, a marginal candidate for a job was interviewed and presented to a number of interviewers. At the end, the interviewers who would have selected the candidate remembered twice as many positive things as negative things, and the reverse was true of those who would have rejected the candidate.*

The psychopath recognises this and ensures that first impressions are very favourable. Charming interactions convince the doubters, especially in jobs that require strong interpersonal skills. Their followers – 'Pawns' and 'Patrons' - invariably invoke cognitive dissonance by filtering out the positive and negatives, and only remembering the positives. Detractors, by way of contrast, readily identify devious, deceitful, manipulative and underhand behaviour. To the psychopath, everyone is seen for their potential to give them what they want. So, their first step is assessment. Is the person open to flattery about their skills, behaviour, attractiveness, position, etc. and how can they be turned into a fan, or through soft blackmail, to not reveal the psychopath's weaknesses? They use impression management by pressing others' 'hot buttons' and for many who lack attention from others of any kind, such attention can be beguiling. This is further reinforced when connections are made – similar interests, values, beliefs or histories – even when these are fictitious. This gives rise to a belief that this new 'friend' will be a source of support. When the psychopath no longer needs this 'pawn,' they might manipulate the narrative to demonstrate that they are the victim of some event and are merely trying to defend themself. They might also transfer blame to others.

It becomes a source of bewilderment and frustration when a 'pawn' is dumped because of a failure to meet the psychopath's needs and their usefulness has passed. Abandonment by the psychopath is common as they feel little emotional connection to those they have manipulated. There is the curious phenomena of self-blame by the victim when the psychopath turns against (or ignores) their followers. The victim wonders what they did wrong and then forgets the episode, partly out of embarrassment at being conned. They in turn collude with others through silence, and the toxic psychopathic behaviour is perpetuated and reinforced.

NARCISSISTS

Higgs (37) concluded from many studies of bad leaders that narcissism is the primary cause of bad leadership. Fame increases narcissism and the male sense of sexual entitlement, as we can see by the numbers of high-profile powerful men like Harvey Weinstein who have been called out and brought to justice by the 'Me Too' movement. Donald Trump infamously said 'I'm automatically attracted to beautiful women – I just start kissing them. It's like a magnet. Just kiss. I don't even wait. When you're a star, they let you do it. You can do anything. Grab 'em by the pussy. You can do anything!' (38).

The narcissistic personality has some common characteristics with the psychopath and the sociopath. They exhibit behaviours described as cold, callous, cynical and lacking in remorse. 'They appear indifferent to social repercussions and social welfare' (39).

The narcissist finds criticism of any kind difficult to handle and responds invariably by lashing out and, if possible, firing/removing the critic. The result is a sycophantic court where there is no challenge. In medieval times, the court jester was the only person able to speak truth to power and not get his head cut off. The narcissist needs such a person, but it is almost impossible for that relationship to survive.

The narcissist feels self-important and is preoccupied with fantasies of their brilliance, how successful they are and their power to change things. They will exploit others for their ends, which are always for personal accolades and recognition. To highlight their own superiority, they will denigrate anyone who disagrees or gets in their way. However, they are brittle and once their flawed personality is exposed will either lash out or collapse. Denial is a common way narcissists deal with any situation that undermines their view. They have an unreasonable sense of their entitlement to compliance with their wishes and constant praise for their efforts.

SO, HOW DO WE DEAL WITH NARCISSISTS AND PSYCHOPATHS?

There are clear lessons from the research on narcissism. Anything which leads to giving a sense of superiority and entitlement is bad news. At the interpersonal level, especially if it is at the extreme, it is difficult for change to occur. Any challenge will be rejected. So, the first steps to take are as follows:

- Accept them for who they are, but not be seduced by their superficial manipulative charm.
- Be clear on your own boundaries and what you are not prepared to do.
- Be aware that they may try to manipulate by making you feel guilty or arousing sympathy.
- If you have the power and the backing of colleagues, recognise that the narcissist will make idle promises, so hold them to account. This may take courage if the narcissist is your boss.

At a societal level, hierarchies based on wealth, race, sexuality or gender need to be challenged. Economic inequality leads to more narcissistic behaviour than exists in more equal societies. In parenting and education, we should beware the narcissistic pitfalls of privilege. A sense of superiority and entitlement leads to exploitative and even cruel behaviour. If lack of empathy is a core component of narcissism with devastating results, then we need to engage in programmes that are proven to raise empathy in schools. There is a clear need for anti-entitlement programmes asserting an ethic of care for others as an ideal to live by, instead of 'me first'.

SUMMARY AND CONCLUSIONS

- Leadership is about creating the conditions for people to do their best work. The impact that poor leadership has on the culture of the organisation is significant.
- Toxic leaders behave differently from effective leaders.
- Poor behaviour arising from inadequate interpersonal skills is exacerbated when leaders are under stress.
- 'Rotten apples' can infect the whole organisation.
- Simple personality differences might be the cause of friction, but the tendencies of some leaders to exhibit the dark triad of Machiavellianism, psychopathic/sociopathic, and narcissistic characteristics can do great damage both to the mental health of individuals who become subject to their behaviour and to the health and performance of their organisations.
- Poor leaders' skills of manipulation and deceit result in their survival in organisations longer than might be considered logical once their motives and behaviour become apparent.

NOTES

1 Impostor syndrome refers to an internal experience of believing that you are not as competent as others perceive you to be.
2 Simon Mawhinney, MD of Allan Gray, described as 'contrarian investors', suggested that 'Companies must have a social licence to operate above all else or ultimately it will be your company's downfall.' It wasn't the move the strategists wanted, but AMP realised the game was up.
3 ESG is the acronym for Environmental, Social and (Corporate) Governance, the three broad categories, or areas, of interest for what is termed 'socially responsible investors'. They are investors who consider it

important to incorporate their values and concerns (such as environmental concerns) into their selection of investments.

4 Often attributed to Stephen Covey, but an earlier reference is to St Francis of Assisi.

5 Fight or flight in Walter Bradford's memorable phrase in 1915.

REFERENCES

1 Einarsen, S.L., Aasland, M.S. and Skogstad, A. (2007). Destructive leadership behavior: A definition and conceptual model. *Leadership Quarterly, 18*, 207-216. http://dx.doi.org/10.1016/j.leaqua.2007.03.002.

2 Coldwell, D.A.L. (2021) Toxic behaviour in organisations and organisational entropy: A 4th Industrial Revolution phenomenon? *SN Business Economics, 1*(5): 70.

3 'You are my family': Gladys Berejiklian faces ICAC for inquiry into her conduct as NSW Premier. Retrieved 9 June 2022 from https://www.news.com.au/national/nsw-act/politics/gladys-berejiklian-to-face-icac-in-inquiry-into-her-conduct-as-nsw-premier/news-story/f17b4b94c8f9d2c862fafe637c1f62b6.

4 Business Roundtable (2019, 19 August). Business Roundtable redefines the purpose of a corporation to promote 'an economy that serves all Americans'. Retrieved 12 April 2022 from https://www.businessroundtable.org/business-roundtable-redefines-the-purpose-of-a-corporation-to-promote-an-economy-that-serves-all-americans.

5 'Nikolina', quoted by Hickok, J. (2021, 5 April) Why toxic workplace cultures follow you home. *BBC*.

6 Mayer, C. (2013) *Firm commitment: Why the corporation is failing us and how to restore trust in it*. Oxford University Press.

7 Goleman, D. (2013, December) The focussed leader: How effective executives direct their own and their organisations' attention. *Harvard Business Review*.

8 McKinsey (2020) *Diversity wins: How inclusion matters*. https://www.mckinsey.com/featured-insights/diversity-and-inclusion/diversity-wins-how-inclusion-matters

9 Moore, J. and Sonsino, S. (2007) *The seven failings of really useless leaders*. MSL Publishing.

10 Ferguson, A. (2019) *Banking bad*. HarperCollins.

11 Chamorro-Premuzic, T. (2020) How to spot an incompetent leader. *Harvard Business Review*. Retrieved 12 April 2022 from https://hbr.org/2020/03/how-to-spot-an-incompetent-leader.

12 Cannon, J. (2003) *Moving into self-employment*. Unpublished PhD thesis, Birkbeck College, London University.

13 AMP Capital's Boe Pahari steps down as CEO following harassment furore. Retrieved 9 June 2022 from https://www.infrastructureinvestor.com/amp-capitals-boe-pahari-steps-down-as-ceo-following-sexual-harassment-furore/ (infrastructureinvestor.com) For further commentary on the case, see also Pahari 'made a lot of money' for AMP Capital. Retrieved 9 June 2022 from. https://www.afr.com/companies/financial-services/pahari-made-a-lot-of-money-for-amp-capital-20200706-p559i5.

14 Gluyas A. (2021) Contrarian Simon Mawhinney spares no one in his comeback fight. Retrieved 9 June 2022 from https://www.afr.com/markets/equity-markets/contrarian-simon-mawhinney-spares-no-one-in-his-comeback-fight-20210930-p58w88.

15 Black, W. (2015) *Psychopathic cultures and toxic empires*, Frontline Noir

16 Coyle, D. (2108) *The culture code*. Bantam Books.

17 Darwin, C. (1859) *The expression of the emotions in man and animals*.

18 James, H. (1890) *The principles of psychology*.

19 Kusy, M. (2011) Toxic workplaces. *HR Edge,* Fall.

20 Fratzl, A. et al. (2021) 'Flexible inhibitory control of visually-evoked defensive behaviour by the ventral lateral geniculate nucleus'. Retrieved 9 June 2022 from https://www.cell.com/neuron/fulltext/S0896-6273(21)00657-7?_returnURL=https%3A%2F%2Flinkinghub.elsevier.com%2Fretrieve%2Fpii%2FS0896627321006577%3Fshowall%3Dtrue#%20.

21 Felps, W., Mitchell, T. and Byington, E. (2006) How, when, and why bad apples spoil the barrel: Negative group members and dysfunctional groups. *Research in Organisational Behaviour*, 27, 175-222.

22 *Greek City Times* (2021, 27 July) Forum Finance Group: The entity at the centre of staggering $400m fraud allegations Is 'open for business'. Retrieved 12 April 2022 from https://greekcitytimes.com/2021/07/27/forum-group-the-entity-at-the-centre-of-staggering-400m-fraud-allegations-is-open-for-business.

23 Moshagen, M., Hilbig, B.E. and Zettler, I. (2018). The dark core of personality. *Psychological Review, 125*, 656-688.

24 Christie, R. and Geis, F. (2010) Some consequences with taking Machiavelli seriously. In Borgatta, E.F. and Lambert W.W. (eds.). *Handbook of personality theory and research* (pp. 959-973). Rand McNally

25 Spielberger, C.D. and Butcher, J.N. (2013) Advances in personality assessment. Routledge.

26 Board, B.J. and Fritzon, K. (2005) Disordered personalities at work. *Psychology, Crime & Law, 11*(1), 17-32.

27 Boddy, C.R. and Taplin, R. (2016) The influence of corporate psychopaths on job satisfaction and its determinants, *International Journal of Manpower, 37*(6), 965-988. https:// doi.org/10.1108/IJM-12–2015–0199.

28 Board, B.J. and Fritzon, K. (2005) Disordered personalities at work. *Psychology, Crime & Law, 11*(1), 17-32

29 Babiak, P. and Hare, R.D. (2006) *Snakes in suits*. HarperCollins.

30 See also https://ajp.psychiatryonline.org/doi/10.1176/ajp.152.8.1228

31 Black, W. (2015) *Psychopathic cultures and toxic empires*, Frontline Noir.

32 Cleckley, H. (1941) *The mask of sanity*. William A. Dolan.

33 Hart, S.D., Cox, D.N. and Hare, R.D. (1995) *Manual for the psychopathy checklist: Screening version (PCL:SV)*. Toronto PCL.

34 Goffman, E. (1956) *The presentation of self in everyday life*. Doubleday.

35 Babiak, P. and Hare, R.D. (2006) *Snakes in suits*. HarperCollins.

36 Shira Ovide (2020, 6 August) On tech. *New York Times*.

37 Higgs, M. (2009) The good, the bad, and the ugly: Leadership and narcissism. *Journal of Change Management, 9*(2), 165-178. See also Friedman, H. and Fireworker, R. (2021) The biggest threat to an organisation during the information age: narcissistic leaders. *Academia*. Retrieved 12 April 2022 from https://www.academia.edu/65134154/The_Biggest_Threat_to_an_Organization_During_the_Information_Age_Narcissistic_Leaders.

38 *ABC News* (2020, 18 September) Donald Trump made vulgar comments about women during taping of *Access Hollywood* episode in 2005. Retrieved 12 April 2022 from https://www.abc.net.au/news/2020-09-18/donald-trump-access-hollywood-vulgar-comments-women/11402244?nw=0&r=Interactive.

39 Babiak, P. and Hare, R.D. (2006) *Snakes in suits*. HarperCollins.

Values

INTRODUCTION

In the USA, following the collapse of Enron, an energy company, some years ago, a Senate inquiry found a culture of arrogance and greed that cared little for the law or consequences for the company's customers. Despite the calls for new and tougher forms of regulation, the conclusion of a Senate inquiry was that no regulation could ever substitute for leaders of all kinds of organisations having a 'moral compass'.

In tough, competitive, commercial businesses, it is easy to be cynical about anything other than making money. So, what is a moral compass, why is it necessary and how is it formed? The simple answer is that it comes from our early upbringing and the way we learnt about right and wrong. Early influences such as parents, friends, teachers, pastors and experiences are all important in this process. The application of this moral compass depends on how we weigh up alternative options in everyday life, and the balance between our concerns about others and ourselves. However, there is more to it than this and in this chapter we will explore how values are formed, how they become subverted and the benefits of pursuing an ethical approach in organisations.

WHAT ARE VALUES?

Values are typically defined in two ways. The first way is in connection with the weight we give something and indicates our preferences. We might value one car more than another for many reasons. The second way implies something that is correct, often in a moral sense. We value honesty and integrity.

But how do we know what our values are? It was Oscar Wilde who remarked that: 'A cynic is a person who knows the price of everything and the value of nothing.' It is not a subject that people think frequently about. It's easy to hold the value of, say, 'excellence in everything' and 'integrity', but those behaviours require courage, energy and consistent application in order to truly exhibit them in practice. Clearly what we value can only be seen in the light of the decisions we take and the behaviour that results.

Here is a story about morality and you are asked to decide who is the worst villain in the story. It is based on the story of Abigail and the river:

DOI: 10.4324/9781003307334-8

> *One day Anne wanted to cross town to be with her lover Frank. However, her car had broken down, so she approached John, a taxi driver, to take her there. As she had no money, he suggested that he would be pleased to take her if she had sex with him. Disgusted, she rejected his offer and turned to her friend Ron for help. He was busy and did not want to know. So, reluctantly, she accepted John's terms and fell into the arms of her lover Frank. However, when Frank learnt what she had done in order to meet him, he rejected her. Unhappy but resentful, she turned to a renowned hard man Bob to go and beat up Frank. As the sun sets on this unhappy scene, we hear Anne laughing at Frank's misfortune.*

So, who is the villain and what emotions do they arouse in us?

- John – because of his manipulation of a vulnerable woman? Our disgust at his immorality?
- Ron – because he did not have the courage to stand up to John? Our desire to have acted, but a fear that we might not and be like Ron?
- Anne - because of her morality and desire for revenge? Her lack of regard for her honour?
- Frank – because he could not forgive Anne for an act that arose out of her love for him? Our contempt for his callousness?
- Bob - for gratuitous violence? Our fear of violence?

The likelihood of resolving the question is low, as each person will have a different view depending on the weight they give to different values. Below is a summary of five different approaches which underpin our judgements about what is right, and the possible positions that each of the actors in this story might take to justify their actions:

- Utilitarian: action is judged by its consequences – the numbers affected and the effect on their well-being. Happiness before principle (Anne? Ron?).
- Kantian: action is judged by whether you would wish everyone to act as you do. Principle and duty before happiness (Frank?).
- Aristotelian: action is judged by whether the greatest good for the greatest number leads to human flourishing (John? Anne?).
- Social contract: action is judged by whether it acknowledges the unwritten contracts that bind society together - both rights and obligations (Bob?).
- Egoism: action is judged by self-interest (John? Ron?).

The utilitarian position places a value on expediency – just get the job done to achieve the right result, regardless of the rules. This approach is sometimes taken in organisations when staff are under pressure or time is short. The problem arises when a similar situation occurs in the future and following the rules would take more time or procedures. There is then a greater tendency to continue bypassing rules and procedures, resulting in a lack of commitment to due process.

In contrast, in the Kantian approach (named after the German philosopher Emmanuel Kant), principles need to be followed regardless of the effect. This usually occurs in legal cases where the law is clear. The 'ends' of justice having been seen to have been done justifies the 'means' of a trial. For example, when the 'means' of promoting a product are by lying about its quality, the ends of greater sales can never be justified, and society establishes laws to protect consumers in this case.

The Aristotelian ethical position (named after the Greek philosopher Aristotle) of the greatest good for the greatest number underpins the creation of laws. If you drive the wrong way down a one-way road because it is quicker to your house, it is against the law as the one-way system is framed for the greater good rather than individual convenience. There are occasions where a strictly legal position offends our sense of fairness and natural justice in some way. In practice, the law is often tempered with mercy, as this might be seen to be the greater good.

This position is also reflected in the difficulty of establishing good HR policy. For example, equal pay for equal work is based on a principle of fairness – the greater good for the greatest number, which is translated into job evaluation schemes and pay policy. However, from an individual perspective, this may not seem fair as any policy cannot consider every nuance of differences between jobs. Each of us will have a different perception of what is fair to us in any particular set of circumstances. Where there are significant numbers of people that see policy as unfair because it does not fit their circumstances, it increases the danger that they will find ways round the policy.

The social contract position is much less clear because it relies on customs and norms, which may not necessarily be agreed by everyone. When there is the cry 'but we have always done it this way', it is indicative that this social contract has been challenged. A recent example was where Barnardos, a children's charity, scrapped Mother's Day on the basis that in a more complex society, children are not brought up only by mothers. However, this offended many as mothers hold such a traditional position in society. The issue is how to retain a balance between what is achieved and how it is achieved.

An egotistical ethical position as a guide to action is determined by what is in my best interests. The demands for personal freedom and the resistance to anything that curbs this drives the political agendas of the far right in America. The gun lobby take this position, but there are invariably poor consequences of this for others. In the USA in 2019, the number of deaths by firearms (including suicides) reached 40,000.

It is this last ethical position that underpins aggressive performance management, and the result, as we saw with the banks, is poor results for customers. In more reasonable situations, there is a realisation that poor outcomes for customers in due course backfire and a 'do as you would be done by' policy is a better long-term position to adopt. Where personal or sectional interests outweigh any ethical position, a toxic culture emerges – at least as seen by some of the differing stakeholders.

The manner in which the COVID-19 pandemic was dealt with says much about the ethical position of leaders when weighing up the health and survival of the population against the demands of the economy.

PERFORMANCE AND CULTURAL VALUES

One of the hardest decisions any manager can take is to remove a high performer who presides over a culture that does not adhere to the cultural norms that are espoused. Denis Handlin of Sony Music Australia (see Chapter 1) paid that price because of the allegations made against him. These 'mavericks' are often tolerated for a long time. It is interesting to contrast what was meted out to Handlin with the promotion given to Bo Pahari at AMP, who was accused of sexual harassment. This resulted in a furore and a wave of protest. Culture matters and symbolic acts – removal on the one hand and promotion on the other - are the true indicators of the culture organisations want to create. Figure 5.1 illustrates the possible outcomes of this (1).

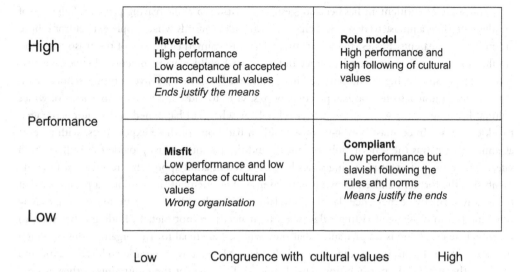

FIGURE 5.1 Performance versus congruence with cultural values

Note: This model was developed with Rita McGee who has given permission for its inclusion.

THE ROOTS OF VALUES AND ETHICAL STANDARDS

Upbringing

Children learn what they live is a short set of homilies by Dorothy Law Nolte (2) in which she lays out the consequences of how a child is treated with the resulting behaviour as an adult. Values are established early in life, being copied from parents and sources of significant influence such as teachers. These influences often set unrealistic expectations of entitlement, however worthy they may be. Through our upbringing, we also acquire prejudices and unconscious biases.

Entitlement

In India poverty was defined as the inability to feed oneself. In England poverty was defined as being without a TV and a holiday.[1] Whilst no one would challenge the improvement in living conditions for millions across the world, it is salutary how our definitions of need as opposed to want change over time. These beliefs stem in part from a comparison with others: if they have it, why don't I have it? This is fuelled by a more fashion-conscious age where young people want the latest trainers or mobile phone to ensure their street cred. Norms of what is cool morph into norms about what is essential. The earliest credit card in the UK was labelled with the tag line 'take the waiting out of wanting'. Conspicuous and instant consumption has become the norm, which in turn has fuelled an envy for what others have. More depressingly, one study showed that half the population will readily cheat to get what they want if they think they won't get caught (3).

A culture of entitlement has been a noted feature of young people in several countries. It encourages less tolerance for conditions that require extra effort to achieve them. What our forebears fought and died for becomes assumed, commonplace and subject to complaint if unavailable, rather than being viewed with gratitude.

This sense of entitlement has been suggested as relating to child-rearing patterns. 'The age of entitlement' (4) is a phrase to describe a change in attitudes towards what people expect from those around them – parents, bosses, the government – and is claimed to be one of the reasons behind conflict in society. Lareau found distinct differences in child-rearing practices between socio-economic groups. In higher-income families, children had intensive lives outside school, with extra tuition, music lessons, football practice, books, visits to museums and a whole array of wider cultural learning. They were quizzed after school for what had happened and were encouraged to ask questions. In contrast, lower-income children had none of these experiences, with parents assuming that it was the school's job to educate and the parents' job to provide food, shelter and safety. These two different parenting styles lead to different adult approaches to life. Lareau comments that the former children grow up with a sense of entitlement. Perhaps it is a possibility that these early formative experiences lay the foundation for adults who expect more from their environment and so challenge existing rules when their needs are not met. In finding other ways to meet their needs, there is no guarantee that they will be beneficial for the organisations of which they are part, or the customers and other stakeholders. Maybe lower-income children assume and accept authority and do not question what happens? They accept the constraints as they assume that others know best.

Piff (5) conducted a series of real-life experiments which showed, for example, that people driving more expensive cars and newer models were four times more likely at a crossing to cut up drivers of lower-status vehicles. They were three times less likely to yield at a pedestrian crossing. Drivers of the least expensive cars *all* gave way to pedestrians. Intrigued by this, Piff conducted laboratory experiments and found 'the richer the meaner' effect. The richest students were meaner and more likely to consider stealing or benefiting from things for which they were not entitled than those from lower-income backgrounds. Piff said that 'upper-class individuals feel more entitled, are less concerned with the needs of others, and at times were prepared to behave selfishly, even unethically, to get ahead'. It's not just rich and famous men who can behave like this. The scandal over a so-called 'Triwizard Tournament', organised by privileged boys at Shore, the elite Sydney private boy's school, reeked of entitlement. Their plans for 'Muck Up' day were racist, misogynist and cruel: 'spit on a homeless man', 'have sex with a woman over 80 kilograms' or a woman who 'scored' a lowly 3 out of 10 for looks, have sex with 'an Asian chick', and 'shit on a train' (6). Such behaviour is deeply concerning in times of mounting inequality.

Wealthier people were more likely to agree with statements such as 'I honestly just feel more deserving than other people'. They were also vainer, being more likely to rush to a mirror and check themselves out if a photograph was being taken. They drew larger circles to represent themselves than they drew to represent other people. Piff''s laboratory experiments revealed that even when poorer people were simply primed to think of themselves as wealthy, this increased feelings of superiority and entitlement, and they began to behave selfishly. When people look down on others, they tend to acquire the belief that they are better than others, more important and more deserving. This led to bad behaviour – for example, helping themselves to more sweets meant for children in a laboratory next door – than if they were primed to feel disadvantaged. Piff noted: 'That suggests it is more the psychological effects of wealth than the money itself.' Strikingly, Piff found that in unequal societies, higher-income people were less likely to give money to charity than poorer people when compared to more equal societies.

It is not only wealth which can increase narcissistic behaviour. Patriarchal society asserts the superiority of men over women and gives them a greater sense of entitlement. It is hardly surprising then that research shows that narcissism is higher in men than women. Research also shows that male entitlement and a sense of superiority can have appalling consequences for increased sexual aggression and predation, and is a key factor in domestic violence. Those who have a sense of entitlement also tend to be assertive in getting it, making them appear selfish to some or in other situations single-minded in order to achieve their goal:

> *A famous tech company was fighting a lawsuit about its monopoly position and a meeting was arranged with the government lawyers. At the appointed time, the tech company team did not appear. When questioned, they replied that they assumed that the government would come to them.*

That's an arrogant sense of entitlement!

Sadly, entitlement to the good things of life places constraints on one's ability to enjoy simple pleasures. A 2016 Case Western University study found that entitlement – 'a personality trait driven by exaggerated feelings of deservingness and superiority' – can lead to an unending cycle of negativity. Lead author Joshua Grubbs (7) said: 'At extreme levels, entitlement is a toxic narcissistic trait, repeatedly exposing people to the risk of feeling frustrated, unhappy and disappointed with life.' Narcissists will promote themselves as highly optimistic, ready to conquer and control, yet when they cannot, they crash. It's a fragile optimism.

Where does entitlement come from?

- Several forces came into play which affected child-rearing practices in advanced economies. Birth control resulted in smaller families and children became more subject to the care of parents. In a large family, parents would provide the basics, but socialisation was often the product of multiple children interacting with each other. Survival was about needs, not wants. In the 20th century, Benjamin Spock and other child specialists began to encourage a more child-centric approach to upbringing, including feeding on demand rather at set times, giving children choices (e.g., about what they would wear) and being more attentive to their wishes. A time of rising prosperity after the Second World War meant that children enjoyed more toys, clothes, food, etc. The cumulative result of all these small changes is to confirm to the child that they have some agency in their lives and as these benefits accrued, so they became accepted as the norm. Once anything becomes accepted, it moves from being a benefit to a right.

- A very obvious example of the impact of small families on children's sense of entitlement lies in China, where the one-child policy has resulted in 'the little emperor syndrome', where excessive attention from parents and grandparents and provision of material benefits (that the parents didn't have) have resulted in 'spoiled brats', as one commentator has called them.[2]

- Modern democracies, particularly in Europe, have established a range of health and welfare benefits. The National Health Service in the UK, 'free at the point of delivery', is the sacred mantra which whilst widely admired is often the subject of abuse. In one example an ambulance was called because someone's condom had broken. What is free is more difficult to evaluate and value, encouraging a greater pressure to deliver. Where resources are insufficient to meet every need, triaging results in non-life-threatening cases being subject to waiting lists. Criticism arises when individuals feel that their needs have a higher priority and the system of triaging is unfair.

- Christopher Caldwell's book *The age of entitlement* (8) was described by Jonathan Rausch in the *New York Times* (9) as 'provocative and pessimistic', and he puts forward a critique of Caldwell's views that 'radical individualism, free-market fundamentalism, and unfettered globalisation' have resulted in the decay of social norms and civil society institutions over the last several decades. Nevertheless, progressive policies towards conferring more rights upon citizens have the unintended consequence of encouraging the belief that such provisions should be universally available, which are not always realistic, given limited resources and the capacity of systems to deliver to every citizen. When rights become emphasised and responsibilities less so, entitlement becomes more pronounced.

- There has been considerable focus in recent years on challenging racial discrimination in many societies, most noticeably with riots in America. Despite progressive legislation, racial prejudice runs deep. A fear of those who are different places an onus on justification of your position and your right to hold it. Whilst any independent view is a privilege to maintain, especially in the face of evidence that it is misplaced, the right to hold it is seen as an entitlement in a liberal democracy.

- Politically, control of culture and ensuring that political philosophy is in line with cultural norms is much more likely to win an electorate's mandate than narrow ideological agendas.[3]

Individual differences

It is easy to assume that others will share our values – integrity, honesty, pride in a good job done, respect of others, etc. – but studies (10) point to each of us having a unique contour map of attitudes and behaviours that we value. These are only really apparent when choices must be made and there are those who can make choices that to them seem reasonable, but seem bad to the rest of us – for example, the high-pressure salesman who sees meeting his target as more important than selling the product that the customer really needs, or even the scamsters and other fraudulent actors on the internet who justify their actions by 'caveat emptor'.[4] Money is seen as more important than the victim, who is out of sight and mind. Those who have had bad experiences and commit such acts may see them as legitimate payback for past injustices. For some, there is a twisted awful logic, such as the paedophile who convinces himself that he is 'educating' his victim. There will also be those who see it all as a game and gain a thrill from conning others.

Cultural differences

In a famous historical book *In search of excellence* (11), the authors identified several features of successful companies. One area varies considerably between companies because there is no perfect answer and much depends on their values. It is sometimes called 'tight loose' and signifies the balance between policies that are tightly controlled by a few senior people and those areas of discretion that can be determined further down the organisation depending on local circumstances. The clash of values between tight control and delegated authority is a particular point of friction. So many factors determine the balance – the work, personality and management style, history and norms from elsewhere. The clash between two approaches becomes apparent in mergers. Acquisitions and mergers have a poor record of success and have more to do with ego and the drive for size in the belief that somehow size will deliver synergies and efficiencies. The overhead cost from bureaucratisation that comes with size often significantly reduces any savings that might have been forecast.

Tax evasion is a problem for all tax authorities, partly because there is no universal acceptance of the system of taxation. This is due to perceptions of unfairness, unwillingness to fund some of the activities governments engage in and resistance to deductions of some of their 'hard-earned' cash. Several strategies emerge to counter evasion: heavy penalties, persuasion by using nudge-type psychology and greater participation in setting spending priorities, especially at the local level. In some countries (e.g., Greece), tax evasion (as opposed to legal avoidance) became so universal by the many schemes in operation that norms had shifted to a point where it was considered foolish not to evade tax.

Germany has been a successful manufacturing country and the backbone of the economy are the Mittelstand, usually family firms embedded in the local community that have a reputation for quality products, investing in the skills of the workforce and with prudent investment to ensure minimum debt. These values have built loyal and flexible workforces, with sufficient reserves to weather many economic storms. Local taxes in Bavaria are related to the viability of the economic base, thus ensuring a close and supportive relationship of employment and an alignment of the interests of the financial institutions and their customers.

Contrast this with a report by the Australian Securities and Investments Commission (ASIC) which found that '75% of the customer arrangements from the big four banks and AMP were not in the interest of clients' (12). The Australian Royal Commission into banking and financial institutions set out six principles that all companies should adopt as a minimum (13):

- Obey the law.
- Not mislead or deceive.
- Act fairly.
- Provide services that are fit for purpose.
- Deliver services with reasonable care and skill.
- When acting for another, to do so in the best interests of that other.

Espoused values are rarely totally congruent with values in practice, as demonstrated by behaviour exhibited and the choices made, but it is a measure of the toxicity of a culture when the espoused values diverge greatly from those actually practised. Corruption flourishes when there are few checks on human failings aggravated by a lack of transparency. Corruption appears in many forms, but there are principally four, according to Yuen Yuen Ang of the University of Michigan (14):

- Theft of money, materials or position, though it may be seen as a rightful compensation for some act of service - for example, the local official who takes a payment for a licence and then keeps it for himself.
- Grand theft', where the leader of an organisation treats its revenues as his own personal account. Dictatorships around the world enjoy this benefit.
- Money paid for a service to be speedily provided. Passing through Lagos Airport, a minder once 'kindly' steered the author speedily through customs and immigration for $50, compared to the normal queue of several hours.
- Payments made for access to favoured contracts and other privileges. A recent example was a payment made of $10,000 to sit next to the prime minister of a country at a dinner where contracts were discussed.

Many of these forms are disguised as payment for a service and the legitimate has a fuzzy edge with the shady.

All these forms of corruption stem from a lack of accountability to legitimate oversight bodies such as a regulator or parliament. A good test is if the transactions were made public ('the Daily Mail test'), would they be seen as legitimate? Different values will respond to this question in different ways. In Nigeria many of these 'service' payments have become so commonplace that few would comment if these were made public. Nevertheless, they all distort efficient economic processes and the allocation of resources, as well as generating resentment amongst those excluded from such opportunities.

One area where there is a considerable culture clash relates to the assistance given to relatives. In some countries, it is seen as a family duty to help relatives into jobs. This becomes particularly onerous when the individual is appointed to a position of great influence. It is by no means restricted to some countries, as cases emerge from all around the world of giving a job to a wife or buying a place at university.[5] One consequence of the recent clampdown on corruption in China is greater aversion to risk amongst officials of all kinds. Corruption, after all, does oil the wheels of commerce and society at large.

ETHICS AND BUSINESS

Do business and ethics mix? N.R. Narayana Murthy, one of the original founders of Infosys, one of the most successful Indian IT companies, and its leader for over 20 years, set out with the intention of 'creating wealth legally and ethically'.

Consider these quotations:

Business is a sphere where ethical demands do not apply because the sole responsibility of business is to maximise profits for shareholders. (Milton Friedman, economist)

Sustainable development like building a successful business requires the integration of social, environmental and economic considerations for the long term. (Vicky Kemp, World Wildlife Fund)

Stakeholder analysis suggests that to ignore any one stakeholder leads to a long-term decline. (French and Bell, experts in organisation development).

Stakeholder capitalism poisons democracy, partisan politics poisons capitalism, and in the end we are left with neither capitalism nor democracy. (Vivek Ramaswamy – entrepreneur)[6]

Despite Ramaswamy's and Friedman's positions, recent events have turned against that view, with several CEOs now recognising the value of taking a more balanced view of the many stakeholders in a business. The debate about ethics was given a further impetus by a report (15) which showed the economic benefit of more ethical behaviour, prompted by research that found that only 54% of Australians generally trust people they interact with. The outcome of their research is an initiative called 'The ethical advantage', a report that uses three new types of economic modelling employing extensive datasets and research sources to put forward the case for pursuing higher levels of ethical behaviour across society.

For the first time, the report quantifies the benefits of ethics for individuals and for the nation, and the findings are compelling. They include the following:

- A stronger economy: if Australia were to improve ethical behaviour, leading to an increase in trust – average annual incomes would increase by approximately $1,800. This in turn would equate to a net increase in total incomes of approximately $45 billion.

- More money in Australians' pockets: improved ethics lead to higher wages, consistent with an improvement in labour and business productivity. A 10% increase in ethical behaviour is associated with an increase of up to 6.6% in individual wages.
- Better returns for Australian businesses: unethical behaviour leads to poorer financial outcomes for business. Increasing a firm's performance based on ethical perceptions can increase the return on assets by approximately 7%.
- Increased human flourishing: people would benefit from improved mental and physical health. There is evidence that a 10% improvement in awareness of others' ethical behaviour is associated with a greater understanding of one's own mental health. Transparency helps to keep people honest and it reinforces a self-image of an upright citizen, which is a trait to which most people would probably aspire.

The report also identifies five interlinked areas for improvement for Australia and its approach to ethics, supported by 30 individual initiatives:

- Developing an Ethical Infrastructure Index.
- Elevating public discussions about ethics.
- Strengthening ethics in education.
- Embedding ethics within institutions.
- Supporting ethics in government and the regulatory framework.

These are hardly revolutionary proposals and are not confined to Australia, but these give encouragement to those who champion higher standards in business and public life. The world's most ethical companies have historically outperformed others financially, demonstrating the connection between good ethical practices and performance that is valued in the marketplace (16). Ethical considerations include: governance, leadership and reputation, environmental and societal impact, and ethics and compliance.

ENFORCING ETHICAL STANDARDS

As part of their professional standards, financial advisers in Australia must comply with a Code of Ethics (17). The Code is a set of standards and core values designed to encourage higher standards of behaviour and professionalism for financial advisers. There are 12 high-level ethical standards for financial advisers to meet, including the following:

- Acting in the best interests of clients.
- Avoiding conflicts of interest.
- Ensuring clients give informed consent and understand the advice they receive.
- Ensuring clients clearly agree to the fees they will pay.
- Maintaining a high level of knowledge and skills.

As well as complying with the Code of Ethics, all existing and new financial advisers must take the Financial Advisers Standards and Ethics Authority (FASEA) Code of Ethics bridging course. This course can be done separately or as part of an approved degree.

Different organisation types will espouse quite different cultural values, and those who knowingly join these organisations will to some extent accept their culture and values. The armed services require discipline and, in times of conflict, the ultimate sacrifice. Such expectations would be considered unreasonable if you join the post office!

In organisations, the guardian of corporate values is often laid at the door of HR, and their role encompasses both clarifying and articulating the values for new recruits, monitoring how well the organisation and particularly leadership is demonstrating the application of these values in everyday behaviour and decisions, and finally administering sanctions to those who transgress.

HOW ETHICAL BEHAVIOUR BECOMES SUBVERTED

There are very few people who would admit to themselves that they are wholly bad. We may fall short of the standards to which we aspire; we may make mistakes and bad judgements, but usually we still harbour a belief that deep down there is a good person trying to do the right thing. We judge ourselves by our good intentions, but unfortunately others judge us by our actions and words. We are often judged in hindsight, which is easy for others to do, but seems so unfair when we had to make the decision without the benefit of hindsight.

Values pose dilemmas in terms of when we must make choices, and the pressures come from many sides to decide what necessarily may not be the best option. There may be the need to satisfy others – perhaps expediency, or our own needs for money, or we may succumb to our weaknesses (the seven deadly sins). Once we have fallen from the standard we espouse, especially if we have been open about it, others may take the lead from us.

In Edward Snowden's account of his time at the CIA, the espoused values of government (18) were at variance with reality. He describes the thrill of the technical possibilities of being able to spy on every citizen as the driver of their actions rather than any ethical constraints. It was an example of the means justifying the ends. When abuse of power and betrayal of trust become the norm in large corporations, patterns of behaviour are established that make it easier for others to do the same. Where there are no clear ethical standards and whistleblowers are fearful of raising issues, abuse flourishes.

The ethical dilemma that employees might face in a toxic culture is whether to speak up with the aim of bringing about change to a more beneficial culture, where all might prosper, but with the risk that those in power might feel threatened and terminate their employment. The union leader who organises a strike against poor wages might lose, with the result that supporters might lose money and their jobs, or might win but cause the firm to fail in the process. Navigating a path forward requires an ethical understanding of what is right, but also the wisdom to determine the most practical course (19). So how do we deal with these cultural values that allow or even encourage toxic cultures?

CHANGING THE ETHICAL LANDSCAPE

Many organisations in recent years have focused on seeking to articulate a set of corporate values. Regrettably, many of these statements, good in themselves and the product of much honest endeavour, are rarely publicised to the extent that people know them and it is even rarer that they are translated into specific behaviour.

CASE STUDY 1: EXERCISE IN LEADERSHIP IN ACTION: MANAGING THE DILEMMAS WE FACE

An organisation decided to crystallise its cultural aspirations by articulating a set of value statements. These included words like 'professionalism', 'integrity', 'teamwork', 'community' and 'take action'.

These were high-minded aspirations, and few would challenge them, but they were hardly in a form that would shift behaviour. They set about several activities.

On the leadership programme that all aspiring managers went through, they carried out two exercises, the first of which involved examining common dilemmas people faced when translating the values into everyday decisions, and the second identifying behaviours that they had experienced that showed the values in action, and the reverse, where behaviour had flouted the value.

EXERCISE: LEADERSHIP IN ACTION – MANAGING THE VALUE DILEMMAS WE FACE

The values we espouse are undoubtedly a worthwhile aim. However, we only really know our values when we have to make choices, and that often poses dilemmas. Followers are entitled to expect from their leadership a degree of clarity about how these dilemmas should be resolved. The clearer the expected behaviour is understood, the easier it is for followers to do the right thing and therefore the less leaders will need to closely supervise.

The values of the organisation are stated as follows:

- Professionalism.
- Integrity.
- Teamwork.
- Community.
- Take action.

EXAMPLES OF POSSIBLE DILEMMAS

The values help us make decisions, but what happens when values are in contention? Identify what course of action would be wise in the following dilemmas.

The exercise is designed to identify how we can manage better the ambiguity of competing values.

Professionalism, but at what cost?

Professionalism encourages staff development and the acquisition of skills to deliver good-quality work. This takes time and resources, and can deflect people from the practical requirement of delivering products on time and to a competitive price. How do we get the balance right?

A situation arose where a new product was being launched about which there had been some doubts about the quality of its manufacture. There were considerable cost implications in remanufacturing and in the time delay to launch, not least in losing market position, yet it was known that there might be consequences in reputation in launching a poor product. How would you have dealt with this dilemma?

Integrity, but will the truth always lead to better results?

Integrity encourages us to question when we see things are wrong and to be honest with others and ourselves.

Giving an assurance of confidentiality to a counselling client is critical to building trust. Yet how can we guarantee that? Clients may want to know with whom we will share the information they provide, yet how do we know what law enforcement agencies may demand? What do we say to give confidence to clients, yet act with integrity?

How do we encourage others to balance their need to exercise integrity with the needs of others who may have different views?

Teamwork, but whose team? And what of the lone maverick?

As a team leader, you have a brilliant team member who delivers the best performance and without whom your overall section performance would suffer. He is a loner who shares little with others, and when he does, he is highly destructive in his interpersonal relationships, adversely affecting team relationships. Training has no effect on him. What do you do?

You have been asked to do an interesting project which would be a development opportunity for a staff member, but time is short, and it would utilise your specific expertise. What do you do?

The team has completed a challenging project, but it would not have been possible without your expertise. You are praised for the result. What do you say?

Community, but at what cost to individual objectives?

One section of the organisation needs the input of several departments to be successful. Each of these departments is very busy and feels under-resourced. They argue that in order to help this department, they might risk not achieving their own objectives. How should this be resolved?

Act, but at the expense of professionalism?

Staff procedures are designed to ensure fairness of treatment to staff, but can slow down operations. You have identified a staff member in another department who would be ideal to fill a vacancy you have. Personnel tell you that it will take several weeks, but you need to get the person on the team for an important project in a week. What do you do?

The second exercise involved participants drawing from their experience of good and bad role models in order to identify the behaviours that supported or undermined these values. They ended up with two lists of good and bad behaviours, and as each course was finished, their contribution was added to a brief that was circulated. It gave a clearer understanding of what was expected to promote and to avoid, as well as gaining buy-in from the involvement of a growing a number of people.

Having circulated this, people were encouraged to challenge people when they saw the values not being lived out in practice and commenting positively when they saw behaviour that promoted them.

TABLE 5.1 Rating my acceptance of organisational values
Rate yourself on the questionnaire below

Level	Behaviours	Where I am	Where I should be
Reacting	Willing to learn the values Accepts that they are good		
Acquiring	Understands and states the values and guiding principles Tries to demonstrate the values		
Adapting	Spontaneously takes action that aligns with stated values Expresses thoughts and feelings honestly and openly		
Anticipating	Walks the talk when it takes effort to do so Demonstrates courage to fight for what is right		
Shaping	Acts as a role model for the values Puts own job at risk to do the right thing		
Building	Empowers others to act as advocates for the values Backs up others who act courageously in support of the values		
Transforming	Changes the organisation to reflect the values Sacrifices short-term goals for work unity in favour of the longer-term good of the organisation		
		Do I exhibit any of these?	What should I do to avoid them?
Derailing	Displays aggressive disrespectful behaviour Hides mistakes Switches allegiances depending upon the audience		

Note: this self-administered questionnaire was developed with Rita McGee, who has given permission for its inclusion here

Finally, and for their own benefit, they were asked to rate themselves on their adherence to the values in the form given in Table 5.1.

CASE STUDY 2 (20): THE CASE FOR ETHICS IN BUSINESS

Johnson & Johnson was originally founded by the Johnson family, which has had a long history of supplying medical products to the world. In 1943, Robert Wood Johnson, the chairman at the time, wrote a document called the Credo, in which he set out the principles by which the company would be managed. It starts by saying: 'we believe our first responsibility is to doctors, nurses and patients, to mothers and fathers and all others who use our products and services'.

In 1975, James Burke, president of the company, felt that the Credo was no longer guiding behaviour. He challenged his management to either make it relevant or scrap it. The debate ended by confirming that it was still relevant, and that effort should be put into ensuring it guided decisions. The test for Johnson & Johnson came in 1982, when one of its premier products, Tylenol, found in most American bathroom cabinets, was found to have killed people. Some had been laced with cyanide. In a matter of hours, panic ensued across America as people were told not to use it or even flush it down the toilet in case the sewer was poisoned.

A war cabinet was formed that wrestled with the myriad of decisions. A crucial meeting was held in Washington DC with the FBI and the Food and Drug Administration (FDA) to discuss what to do next. These two bodies recommended that the company should recall the product, but only in the Chicago area as there had been no reported deaths anywhere else. They argued that a national recall would needlessly frighten the public, embolden the poisoner and encourage copycats. Of course, it would also cost millions. However, the Credo was taken seriously and it was decided to recall every Tylenol product – 31 million in all at a cost of $100 million. Industry pundits and advertising gurus opined that Tylenol was dead and nothing could ever be sold under that brand again. Over the coming days, the company mounted a campaign to inform the public, doctors and other agencies, as well as developing tamper-proof packaging. Much to the concern of the company's lawyers, Burke undertook a media tour, explaining to the public what was being done to make things safe and expressing regret at what had happened. The Credo helped the company to make the multitude of decisions because there was no playbook to rely upon.

Much to the pundits' surprise, sales began to recover back to previous levels. Their response has now been taken as a guide to how to handle future corporate disasters. It reinforced the recognition that the Credo had established key principles, namely that the safety and well-being of customers was paramount and more important than profits, and the realisation (something of a revelation to some) that being ethical and doing the right thing builds trust, which is ultimately good for business.

CASE STUDY 3 (21): MEASURING BEHAVIOURAL CHANGE

A national electrical regulatory body wanted to shift its culture and started with the behaviour of the board. The author was invited to interview each member periodically so that they could rate themselves and their colleagues, giving a rating of 1 (meets the required standard) to 5 (improvement required). The data were presented at the monthly meeting and a discussion took place about how they could improve. Over several months the score improved as they all became more conscious of what they had to do. The example in Figure 5.3 showed that individually and they as a team had still more work to do.

Behaviour	How am I doing?	Mean	How is the team doing?	Mean
Work collectively	3 (4), 4 (7)	3.63	2 (2), 3 (6), 4 (3)	3.09
Respect each other's views	4 (11)	4	3 (6), 4 (4), 5 (1)	3.54
Resolve differences of opinion	3 (5), 4 (6)	3.54	3 (8), 4 (3)	3.27
Focus on the issues not personalities	3 (4), 4 (6), 5 (1)	3.73	2 (1), 3 (5), 4 (3), 5 (1)	3.09
Praise each other for good contributions	2 (1), 3 (4), 4 (3), 5 (3)	3.73	2 (4), 3 (4), 4 (3)	2.91
Take courage to speak up	3 (4), 4 (7)	3.63	2 (2), 3 (3), 4 (6)	3.36
Average		3.71		3.21

FIGURE 5.2 Critical meeting behaviours

VALUES AND RELIGION

You might expect that there would be a strong correlation between religious belief and the values that are espoused. In particular, religious leaders in their capacity as role models for their faith might live by their beliefs. For the Christian, the early desert fathers spelt out the seven deadly sins to be avoided (lust, gluttony, greed, sloth, wrath, envy and pride) and the virtues to be embraced (chastity, temperance, charity, diligence, patience, kindness and humility). In the New Testament, the Gospels spell out behaviours that exhibit Christian values in action (love, joy, peace, forbearance, kindness, goodness, faithfulness, gentleness and self-control: Galatians 5:22) and the behaviours to shun (sexual immorality, impurity and debauchery, idolatry and witchcraft, hatred, discord, jealousy, fits of rage, selfish ambition, dissensions, factions and envy, drunkenness, orgies and the like) (Galatians 5:19).

However, the evidence points to the human failings of the clergy being as bad as any. The commissions of inquiry round the world into child sex abuse showed the horrific crimes carried out by priests. There was recently a case of a nun embezzling funds and a report by the Anglican Church pointing to domestic violence being greater than in the population at large (22). A twisting of Paul's teaching about men and women gave the justification for patriarchy, a power imbalance, and a belief in the entitlement of men to abuse women. They confused the cultural norms of the time – patriarchy - with Christ's teaching of love and respect for both genders.

It is a regrettable conclusion that even those who you might expect to be the most committed to living out their values and above reproach fall prey to human failings –lust, greed and fear.

SUMMARY AND CONCLUSIONS

- Values – i.e., what we hold dear – guide our actions and behaviour. However, our espoused values may not been the same as those that actually guide our decisions.
- There are cultural and individual differences in our values and in particular when we are forced to make choices.
- We only know our true values when we have to make choices, especially those where both courses of action might be reasonable. This becomes even more critical when it is a choice of the lesser of two evils.
- Managers face a dilemma between ethical behaviour and high performance when the two conflict.
- Our values are primed early in our lives and can result in a sense of entitlement beyond what is reasonable and fair to others.
- Ethical behaviour has great financial and other benefits to companies and societies.
- Some companies and industries enforce codes of conduct, but these are by no means universal.
- Toxic cultures can easily arise when human failings of lust, greed and fear overtake our high espoused morality.
- There appears to be a renewed emphasis on encouraging more ethical behaviour in business, government and religion. We should applaud these efforts, but not be too optimistic that such worthy efforts can be sustained in the long term.

NOTES

1 There are many definitions of the poverty line. This is a popular one: https://www.novuna.co.uk/news-and-insights. Other definitions are about income levels: https://www.trustforlondon.org.uk/data/poverty-thresholds.

2 In 2021, the policy was changed to allow couples to have three children, though this is a result of a declining birth rate rather than any desire to counter the sense of privilege and entitlement of 'little emperors'.

3 Antonio Gramschi, an Italian Marxist, has argued this point in his books.

4 Let the buyer beware.

5 In France, a man was convicted of giving a job to his wife, while in the USA, a couple were sent to prison for buying a place for their child at a university.

6 A controversial statement made by this author about the impact of woke politics in his book *Woke inc.* on page 21. (Ramaswamy, V. (2021) *Woke, Inc.: Inside Corporate America's Social Justice Scam*. Center street).

REFERENCES

1 I am indebted to my co-researcher Rita McGee for her help in developing this model.

2 Nolte, D.L. (1998) *Children learn what they live*. Workman Publishing.

3 Pruckner, G.J. and Sausgruber, R. (2013) Honesty on the streets: A field study on newspaper purchasing. *Journal of European Economic Association, 3*, 661-679.

4 Lareau, A. (2003) *Unequal childhoods: Class, race, and family life*. University of California Press.

5 Piff, P.K. (2012) On wealth and wrongdoing: How social class influences unethical behaviour. PhD thesis, University of California, Berkeley.

6 "We protect each other at all costs." The full Shore School muck-up day list has been leaked. Retrieved 10 May 2022 from https://www.mamamia.com.au/shore-school-muck-up-day.

7 Baird, J. (2020) *Phosphorescence*. HarperCollins.

8 Caldwell, C. (2020) *The age of entitlement*. Simon & Schuster.

9 Rausch, J. (2020, 17 January) Rights movement go wrong? *New York Times.*

10 Hitlin, S. (2003) Values as the core of personal identity: Drawing links between two theories of self. *Psychology Quarterly, 66*(2), 118-137.

11 Peters, T.J. and Waterman, R.H. (2004) *In search of excellence*. HarperCollins.

12 Australian Securities and Investments Commission (2018) ASIC annual reports. Retrieved 10 May 2022 from https://asic.gov.au/about-asic/corporate-publications/asic-annual-reports.

13 Financial Services Royal Commission (2019) Royal Commission into Misconduct in the Banking, Superannuation and Financial Services Industry.

14 Ang, Y.Y. (2020) China's gilded cage: The paradox of economic boom and vast corruption. Cambridge University Press.

15 The ethical advantage. (2020) *The economic and social benefits of ethics to Australia*. Deloitte Access Economics. https://www2.deloitte.com/au/en/pages/economics/articles/ethical-advantage-economic-social-benefits-ethics-australia.html

16 See https://worldsmostethicalcompanies.com.

17 FASEA (2020) Code of Ethics. Financial Adviser Standards and Ethics Authority (fasea.gov.au)

18 Snowden, E. (2014) No place to hide: Edward Snowden, the NSA, and the U.S. Surveillance State. Metropolitan Books.

19 There is a poem which encapsulates this problem by Reinhold Niebuhr (1892–1971): 'God, grant me the serenity to accept the things I cannot change, courage to change the things I can, and wisdom to know the difference.' Its origins have been variously attributed to an ancient Sanskrit text, Aristotle, St Augustine, St Francis of Assisi and others.

20 I have drawn on a variety of sources for this case, including Johnson & Johnson (1982): Latson, J. (2014, 29 September) How poisoned Tylenol became a crisis-management teaching model. TIME. Retrieved 10 May 2022 from https://time.com/3423136/tylenol-deaths-1982; The Johnson & Johnson's Tylenol controversies. Retrieved 10 May 2022 from https://www.icmrindia.org/free%20resources/casestudies/Business%20Ethics/Johnson%20&%20Johnson's%20Tylenol%20Controversies.htm.

21 NICEIC, the association for electrical contractors in the UK.

22 National Anglican Family Violence Project (NAFVP) (2021) National Anglican Family Violence research report. Retrieved 12 April 2022 from https://anglican.org.au/wp-content/uploads/2021/08/1.-NAFVP-Research-Report.pdf.

Part C
Organisation

CHAPTER 6

Organisational design
The toxic impact of structure and process

INTRODUCTION

One of the primary tasks of management is to organise work to achieve some outcome and to determine whether the right people are in the right jobs doing the right tasks. But what happens when this does not occur in an optimal way? In this chapter we examine how the different facets of organisational design can create tensions and poor outcomes if they are badly constructed or implemented. There is no perfect organisational design, but an important task is to regulate conflicts that might arise and minimise friction between the boundaries. Many factors define the design, and the design often moulds the subsequent culture:

> The next day Moses took his seat to serve as judge for the people, and they stood around him from morning till evening. When his father-in-law saw all that Moses was doing for the people, he said: 'What is this you are doing for the people? Why do you alone sit as judge, while all these people stand around you from morning till evening?'
>
> Moses answered him: 'Because the people come to me to seek God's will. Whenever they have a dispute, it is brought to me, and I decide between the parties and inform them of God's decrees and instructions.' Moses' father-in-law replied: 'What you are doing is not good. You will only wear yourself out. The work is too heavy for you; you cannot handle it alone. Listen now to me and I will give you some advice, and may God be with you … select capable men from all the people - men who fear God, trustworthy men who hate dishonest gain - and appoint them as officials over thousands, hundreds, fifties, and tens. Have them serve as judges for the people at all times, but have them bring every difficult case to you; the simple cases they can decide themselves. That will make your load lighter because they will share it with you. If you do this and God so commands, you will be able to stand the strain, and all these people will go home satisfied.[1]

This is one of the earliest examples of organisational design where the principle of delegation and division of labour in a hierarchy was established. This principle has underpinned organisations of all kinds for millennia. As organisations have become more complex, so specialisation of functions has increased and the potential for conflict between competing objectives and philosophies has encouraged more partisan viewpoints and potential alienation. Governments, armies and organisations of all kinds develop a culture of their own, sometimes regardless of the positive human interventions or failings of those who inhabit them.

DOI: 10.4324/9781003307334-10

In organisations of any significant size, more formalised structures of divisions and departments become common and many writers have historically sought to categorise these organisational forms (1). Wherever there is a boundary between these, the possibility of conflict exists. Another tension that arises is between size, economies of scale and efficiency when flexibility is required. Overcentralised rigid bureaucracies work well when clear direction is required, but do not work effectively when there is imperfect information. In this case local discretion based on local knowledge works better. Where authority for decisions does not match where action occurs, delay is the result. In the film *United 93*, concerning the plane hijack on 9/11, a powerful scene is played out where authority to engage the plane by fighter aircraft was delayed, losing valuable time, because the commander on the ground who had the facts did not have the authority to engage.

ORGANISATIONAL DESIGN

There are many activities in forming a successful design beyond organisation structure:

- Agreeing mission and goals that are universally understood and accepted (at least by the leadership and major stakeholders).
- Determining whether activities to deliver those goals should be grouped by function, process, business unit, technology, geography, etc.
- Establishing boundaries between functions and the degree of formality of these boundaries.
- Defining critical processes and how they relate to the structure when they cross boundaries. The flow of work is key to efficiency.
- Determining the levels of hierarchy and what denotes them (symbols), and how far informality will override formal work roles.
- Establishing policies and rules that will support the mission in a legal, ethical and fair way.

However, as Cummings and Worley (2) state when discussing equifinality (similar outcomes can come from many different designs), 'there is no universal best way to design an organisation'. The evidence lies in the constant restructuring that goes on in many organisations. The impact of these restructurings is sometimes in doubt. In one instance a manager remarked after a reorganisation: 'My department has changed, my title has changed, my reporting relationship has changed, but I am still doing the same job.' The way in which organisations typically resolve these tensions lies in the informal organisation, which we will look at in Chapter 7.

> We trained hard, but it seemed that every time we were beginning to form up into teams we would be reorganised. I was to learn later in life that we tend to meet any new situation by reorganising and a wonderful method it can be for creating the illusion of progress while producing confusion, inefficiency and demoralisation. (Caius Petronius, AD 86)

How decisions are to be made and who makes them depends on personal relationships as much as on formal job descriptions and reporting relationships. If you ask anyone in an organisation how things get done, they will invariably talk about the people with whom they communicate. So, ultimately organisations have to create a common language for technical terms and abbreviations. Drawing the patterns of those interactions in a similar form to a mind map, it is apparent that they rarely conform to the formal organisation structure. Paradoxically, if they do, this is often a sign of a dysfunctional organisation, because it implies that there are only formal channels for communication and approval, and these invariably slow things down. Fast decision making becomes hindered, encouraging more informal corridor conversations which can come unstuck when decisions are not recorded or when key people have not been involved and not all the facts have been considered. Of course, formal structures have other purposes to ensure clear account-abilities which are avoided by friendly chats across organisational boundaries. Former UK Prime Minister Tony Blair was criticised for his informal style as it left people unclear as to what was required and by whom.

Design has elements of structure and process, and it is the latter which is often seen as secondary once structure is in place. This can so easily become a source of dysfunction and frustration. There is an inevitable tension between clear lines of accountability which often demands a chain of command from top to bottom and processes which can cut across the organisation.

Of the many organisation forms that have emerged to address the problems of size and complex-ity, a relatively recent form is the complex matrix or network form. Examples include clusters of separate specialised manufacturing units with varying types of ownership from owners to divisions of conglomerates, but they all share some common purpose (such as munitions during wartime) or have trading arrangements which bind them together in longer-term relationships (Toyota city in Japan). They are all characterised by multiple transactions over a long period and as a consequence encourage more flexibility in reaching their individual goals in the short term in return for maintain-ing the relationship. These forms can be unstable over time, but are more capable of adjusting and adapting to changed circumstances compared to monolithic structures. They rely on relationships and mutual interest. Johnsons, a producer of cashmere in Scotland, has sourced wool from many suppliers, amongst which is the same family of Mongolian herders for six generations. Price is less important than a steady supply of quality wool - a relationship built on trust.

Toyota pioneered a system of organisation known as *Lean* Manufacturing, based on the work of Taiichi Ohno (3). In this system the focus was on flow and continuous learning and away from command-and-control systems. Ohno realised that organisations have a huge burden of 'failure demand' – activity which is about remedying some failure in the organisation. For example, qual-ity control picks up mistakes that require rework, while customer service centres deal with cus-tomer complaints and failure in the delivery of the product or service to the right quality or to a specified deadline. It is this burden which also creates tensions and turf wars between the checkers and the checked. His solution was to build responsibility and learning into the place where the work was originally done.

The case study below provides an example of a company that set out to improve quality in its repair business:

A repair shop mended electrical goods and was plagued with customer complaints. Management targets were set on the cost of a repair based on speed of completion of a repair, but the true cost was much more when taking account of dealing with customer queries and rework. The shop abandoned the time metric, focusing on total cost of repair. Each repair carried a card saying 'this repair was carried out by John. Any queries come back to me'. Customer complaints dropped and costs per repair dropped. The repair engineers felt responsible and learnt more about customer needs. Management focus was in ensuring the flow of work and supply of spare parts was as efficient as possible.

Organisation structures are about dividing work into meaningful groups and every time a division happens, there is a boundary which demands communication and can be the source of misunderstanding and confusion. The hand-offs between functions and especially boundaries between divisions who might have different priorities are the major source of error, as we saw in Chapter 1.

ASSESSING THE ORGANISATIONAL DESIGN: TESTS OF ORGANISATIONAL DESIGN

Does the design do the following?:

1. Focus resources and attention on what is critical for success and ensures that other activities do not inhibit or slowdown that work. Where, for example, the strategy calls for a highly responsive entrepreneurial culture, rules, legal constraints and checking procedures can negate any advantage that might be possible from people with those talents.

    Focusing resources where it will have the most effect is shown in the example below:

    > *During the Second World War, planes returning from missions were analysed for the bullet holes they sustained with the intention of strengthening the aircraft for the future. However, it was pointed out that these planes were the ones that survived. Focus should be on the areas where there were no holes as they were more likely to be the places where planes did not survive...*

2. Ensure that the design of roles and the process of making appointments to them do not create conflicts of interest. In one example, a prison director reported to a non-executive board, the chairman of which was chosen by the director. Their closeness and unwillingness for the board to challenge the director resulted in a feeling of frustration amongst staff and only came to a head when the director showed signs of mental illness.

3. Ensure that the different (and may be competing) needs of the different stakeholders are met. Jared Diamond in his book *Collapse* (4) describes the culture of the Plum Creek Timber company derived from locals' comments: 'Plum Creek cares only about the bottom line', 'Plum Creek earns money in whatever way it can from the land'. Attitudes are shifting, and sustainability and environmental protection are occupying a higher position in people's concerns. This poses a real difficulty for corporate owners in terms of how to balance these competing pressures.

4. Identify a staffing plan with the skills that are critical to success. Are those skills available and, if not, is their sufficient capacity within the organisation to develop them? As Winston Churchill is reputed to have said: 'However grand the strategy, you should occasionally look at the results.' Is this mission possible? In Chapter 3 we identified the problems of psychopathic and narcissistic leaders. Similar problems arise with leaders who do not have the capability or capacity to lead and make the tough decisions required. In one case an incompetent leader was described as 'a rabbit in the headlights incapable of making a decision and an embarrassment to watch'.[2]

5. Respond easily to change. A tension that exists is the balance between constancy and change. In order to achieve outcomes of all kinds, organisations establish structures and routines. The biblical quote given above illustrates the underlying desire of groups to establish hierarchy and specialisation, to push work down the hierarchy and to divide work into prescribed roles. The assumption is that routine work is going to be more efficiently managed if it is divided up. And given the nature of much work, which is routine, systematic and dependent on hierarchy for direction, order and control, this approach has worked successfully much of the time. This became the mainstream paradigm in the 19th century with the emergence of 'scientific management' and bureaucracy. However, bureaucracies are less capable of handling dramatic change.

6. Have the capacity to facilitate creativity and innovation. The process of creativity and innovation to solve problems and develop new products and services relies less on formal roles and expertise, and more on ideas and insight.

7. Allow freedom between divisions to develop their own norms and behaviours suited to their circumstances, and determine the appropriate balance between freedom and control.

8. Anticipate the friction points that arise because of a stressed hierarchy or a power imbalance between divisions and with customers. This imbalance is often apparent in state-run bureaucracies which are funded through taxation. Citizens may need to wait for a service of some kind far longer than if the service was paid for directly by customers. A variety of experiments to address this problem have been conducted (e.g. the Driver and Vehicle Licensing Agency in the UK) where departments have become semi-autonomous business units.

9. Add value in each role and at each level. A trend in recent years is to flatten structures. Technology has enabled many middle-management functions to be avoided, allowing easier communication and faster processing of information and decision making.

10. Anticipate likely changes that might occur in the future. One of the more successful tools organisations deploy is scenario planning, when they look at all the warning signs of future events, use 'red teams'[3] to challenge assumptions and 'skunk works'[4] on new projects, with the aim of breaking out of conventional thinking and organisational controls.

11. Ensure there is a clear chain of command where it is easily determined who is accountable for what and to whom (5).

THE INFLUENCE CURVE

The intuitive assumption is that influence over events in an organisation increases with seniority. However, this does not appear to be universally true. A more likely pattern is given in Figure 6.1. Those at the top are too remote from everyday events to control everything, whilst those at the bottom don't have the authority or visibility over the whole organisation to make substantive changes. It is the people in the middle – the mighty middle - who are most in touch with the top and the bottom, but have the unenviable job of translating top direction into meaningful action at the bottom and mediating negative reactions from below. No wonder middle managers report being the 'meat in the sandwich' and are seen as resisting change by the top. In their legitimate need to keep both ends on side, it is understandable that compromises are made, blind eyes are turned and not every instruction is carried out to the letter.

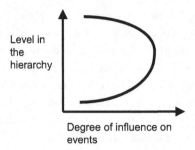

Level in
the
hierarchy

Degree of influence on
events

FIGURE 6.1 The influence on events by level of hierarchy

INNOVATION

In Gary Klein's book on seeing what others don't (6), he describes two traps that organisations fall into: predictability and perfection. These stem from the desire to avoid errors and to deliver plans. One might add that shareholders want predictability of dividends and customers want continuity of supply to defined standards. The remarkable achievement of many manufacturers to produce the same product year in year out to the same quality (most of the time) often goes without saying and unnoticed. Chaos and confusion emerge when someone says 'I have an idea – let's change this to improve it'. Indeed, it might be an improvement, but if it derails the existing plans and cost estimates, then every fibre of the organisation will resist. Mueller (7) found that 'if an idea is novel, people automatically assume it isn't practical, reliable or error free. Novel ideas are associated with failure'.

Many examples of innovation come from spotting an opportunity in the midst of normal business. Indeed, there has been a shift in the area of organisational development towards engaging the widest constituency in order to harvest ideas for improvement and harnessing that involvement and contribution towards bringing about change. We can no longer leave improvement to the new products division or the improvement expert.

Creativity and innovation have become major issues as businesses struggle with dramatic market shifts fuelled by global politics, pandemics and technological change. Yet the design of many organisations inhibits innovation because it is focused on doing what it has done in the past efficiently rather than positioning itself to take advantage of change. 'If you continue to do what you have always done, you will get what you have always got.'

There are some six features of organisations which inhibit creativity:

- Where the freedom to experiment or test new products, processes or ways of working is limited. This is often a result of a tight budget or strict timelines for delivery of existing products with little spare capacity to experiment. This may be further reinforced by sanctions. The example of Hewlett-Packard and the story of the development of the occiliscope (8), which encouraged a culture of freedom to pursue new products and ideas, was in sharp contrast to a case described by Susy Wetlaufer, where employees were fired for developing new products without authority (9).
- In Figure 6.2 (10) the ideal time for innovation activity appears to be at the beginning of the shaded area. This ensures that when the new product is launched, its contribution will

compensate for the decline in the existing product. However, it is uncertain at that point whether the new product might work, especially when the existing products are doing so well. The result then is a conflict over the allocation of resources and extra work for everyone. However, if innovation only starts when decline is occurring, the problem becomes worse, as there will be even fewer resources to power new innovations.

- Where organisation structure places strict demarcation lines between functions such as marketing and new product development, turf wars can emerge about the ownership of new ideas. New ideas know no boundaries and limiting the opportunities for them to emerge inhibits their creation.

- Management style which tends towards command and control, enforcing existing rules and processes, and subordinating individual ideas to the authorised view of the management hierarchy, rather than empowering and supporting those ideas from wherever they might come. What happens when a new idea emerges? A feature which differentiates organisations in this regard is the degree of support. Is it 'not invented here', 'no budget for development', 'not your job', etc., or is it 'how can we support you' (11)?

    Clearly in some instances command and control is an entirely appropriate way of managing, but has as its consequence the necessity for management to always have the 'right' answer.

- Situations that present major challenges (war, pandemics) are often a great stimulus to innovation. When the only challenge is to work harder following increased targets or tougher budgets, there is little incentive to work smarter. Crafting the challenge presented to the organisation and individual employees is a key to encouraging motivation and capacity to innovate.

- In recent years there has been much talk about the 'learning organisation'. At its simplest, it means picking up mistakes fast – 'failing fast' and quickly applying the lessons learnt. It requires a culture of willingness to expose mistakes when things go wrong and a preparedness to reinforce that courageous behaviour by demonstrating a desire to listen and understand. As Eric Hoffer said: 'We must produce not learned but learning people … in times of change learners inherit the earth while the learned find themselves beautifully equipped for a world that no longer exists' (12).

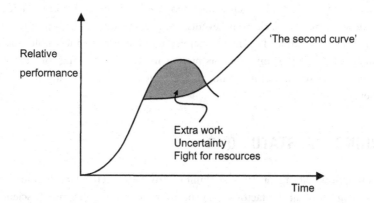

FIGURE 6.2 The challenges of change

Yet we know that trial and error is one of the most important aspects of the creative process. When criticised for failing, Thomas Edison replied that 'I now know what doesn't work' and Henry Ford remarked that he loves failure because it creates the opportunity to start again more intelligently. Nevertheless, organisational philosophy has a bias towards error elimination, whether it be total quality control and Six Sigma or the legal consequences when there are defects in products. The Japanese philosophy of Kaizen (continuous improvement) moves away from a focus on error towards an infinite journey of improvement. In this regard, it has been highly successful and Japanese business success has demonstrated the efficacy of this approach. 'Show me a craftsman and I will show you someone permanently dissatisfied' is an old Japanese saying. It is that constructive dissatisfaction that is the hallmark of achieving superior performance.

The automatic response to finding errors is to increase checks, controls and documentation. These actions often do reduce errors, but at the expense of increased bureaucracy, slower decision making and greater caution. A plethora of support jobs are also focused on minimising errors rather than improving things for the future. Security is about keeping people out, lawyers are about avoiding litigation and HR is often about keeping out of employment tribunals. The problem with checklists is that they cannot determine every possible situation because they are based on historical cases rather than seeking to anticipate future problems. One wit suggested that you don't drive a car by looking in the rear-view mirror. A downside of checklists is that they become routine rather than causing people to think. The person checking no longer feels any responsibility for the process, especially when something is not on the checklist.

Nevertheless, some checks are essential and can be effective in reducing errors. After a plane had a serious failure, it was found that an engineer had left a tool in the engine bay which had fouled the engine. They resolved this by producing a toolkit where there was a defined place for every tool, so it was an easy check to see if every tool was back in the box.

Another consequence of an over-emphasis on error reduction is that when errors do occur, there is a temptation to suppress it, thus inhibiting the action to identify what went wrong and to find new fixes to solve them. After 9/11, it emerged that Kenneth Williams, a CIA agent in Phoenix, was concerned why some people were enrolling at a flying school and did not seem interested in practising take-off and landing. He wrote a memo ('the Phoenix memo') about his concerns and recommended a series of follow-up investigations. But this seemed so beyond anyone's thinking that no one acted on it and the memo was suppressed. Organisations in particular find it difficult to imagine and plan for 'black swan'[5] events. So, a bias towards error minimisation and safety, etc., whilst good in itself, can lead to the unintended consequence of a less agile organisation able to take advantage of the opportunities errors present in terms of looking for improvements. We will explore this further when looking at norms and beliefs and how threatened people feel when they are challenged.

CHALLENGING THE STATUS QUO

There is an assumption that organisations are built on truth – objective facts, rational argument and deliberate weighing up of all the factors - and no more so than in the case of science. Yet every scientific endeavour is riddled with potential biases. Kuhn (13) identified many sources of bias and prejudice. In the academic world, the pressure to publish or perish encourages limited studies of variable quality. Even the peer-review process can get derailed when experimental results hide anomalies or data that does not fit the conclusions. Pet theories drive much endeavour and the desire to prove the theory right encourages a bias against results that proved it wrong. Studies that are successful tend to get published more, though studies that show the reverse are just as useful in the pursuit of knowledge – so we are back to Thomas Edison seeing the value of what *doesn't* work.

The literature on the positive role of conflict and struggle in the development of innovation and as a facilitator of change is widespread (14). The Catholic Church in establishing a commission to consider sainthood appoints a devil's advocate to argue the case against. This legitimate role ensures a careful review of all the evidence in a critical light and reduces any personal animosity. 3i, a venture capital company, tried a similar approach. Whenever there was a proposal to invest, a person was appointed in the review team to advance the case and someone else to point out all the risks. These two were listened to before a general debate occurred with the rest. This simple approach greatly improved the company's decision making.

Organisational theorists of various persuasions have located conflict in the tussle between labour and capital. It has been described as a continuing kaleidoscope of action and reaction, collaborative in good times and competitive in others, with the negative outcomes demonstrable in the forms of turnover and absence, and with sabotage, corruption, loss of discretionary effort, dissatisfaction and low motivation in the worst cases. Whilst these somewhat Marxist theories have largely been discredited, the search still goes on to find organisational forms that harmoniously balance the needs and desires of the different stakeholders in an enterprise. Whilst profit maximisation and/or cost reduction drives much of this search, new drivers continue to come on to the stage – environmental pressures, minority groups asserting their rights, the continuing demands of consumer lobby groups and demands for ethical trading.

Traditional views of management hierarchies and the power vested in them have been whittled down over the years, initially by strong unions, but in the waning of the union movement, by the mobility of an educated workforce who demand a much more even relationship than the old master-servant relationship. Organisations who still cling to those more adversarial ways of managing tend to be where staff have more limited opportunities to leave. Some industries such as transport, and to some extent health in some countries, still have vestiges of a heavily unionised adversarial system, leading to a less than productive culture. However, such a system has been successful in some instances in terms of delivering a fairer division of rewards.

PHYSICAL DESIGN

One aspect that is rarely considered in organisational design is the physical design of the workspace. Yet the layout of buildings can have many effects. Encouraging helpful encounters between people lies at the heart of generating effective cultures. Architects have sometimes built this idea into their buildings – for example, the 'Waterside' office for British Airways at Heathrow Airport, London, and AstraZeneca's office in Oslo. Conferences and problem-solving groups are all about engaging people's minds and their emotions to encourage a sense of belonging and being part of something. Facilitators of problem-solving groups will deliberately design the space to involve participants and maximise creative interactions. Whilst technology has meant the death of distance, physical proximity at some points gives more than is possible through just a screen.

However, close proximity can have negative consequences for performance, as the case below illustrates:

In one factory a series of stoppages for petty reasons began to cripple production. A survey revealed that it was a very noisy environment, and was stressful and disorientating to many. On examining the noise, the hard surfaces and low roof meant that the reverberation count was very high and the resulting sound waves caused tiredness, which was manifest in the stoppages – anything to stop the noise, and a silent protest against working conditions. Sound deadening and clever acoustic engineering reduced the noise and subsequent industrial disputes.

A pharmaceutical company in Switzerland had built a new head office employing a world-renowned architect and the resulting structure was beautiful, but the layout was not easy for collaborative working. Without any overt reason, morale went down, absence increased and departmental friction increased.

CONTROL

It seems almost inevitable that organisations become more complex over time. The evidence comes from many examples of companies periodically having to get back to basics in order to cut the bureaucracy, simplify their systems and improve control.

In the example below, a company found that increased control could be achieved by fewer checks:

A manufacturing company wanted to control capital expenditure and approval for any project required the signature of some 12 people. The result was little control as each of them assumed that someone else on the list would check the detail. On reducing it to three (the manager requesting the capital and who was responsible for delivering the result, the accountant to check the maths, and the business unit manager), demands for capital went down, more cost-effective projects were delivered and less time was taken up by needless paperwork.

In the latter part of the 20th century the banking industry launched a series of new exotic products. Derivatives[6] were a major development in finance. As one wit described them, 'half the people don't understand them, and the other half are bluffing'. In another area, complexity in currency trading and the need for speed left more discretion with traders and greater difficulties in terms of oversight. Nick Leeson, the man who brought down Barings Bank, is a case in point. His trades against the Japanese yen went bad and he tried to bet his way out, without success. In the ensuing post-mortem, his supervisors did not really understand what was going on and the compliance systems could be easily subverted to hide the problem. It was an example of when high rewards are possible and discretion is given, control systems and surveillance systems need to match the tasks. Where they are seen as flexible and 'negotiable', the incentive is great to get round them rather than fear them.

Conflict of interests is a major driver of a toxic culture when individuals have to choose between 'doing the right thing by the customer' and their own interests. Where 'independent' advice is compromised by the advisor gaining some financial reward for a specific course of action, such as one product compared to others, then the temptation to be anything other than independent is great. Conflict arises over bonuses and strong sales commissions where there is no counterbalance to ensure customers are serviced well. This is further compounded when information systems lack transparency as to what is really happening. When individuals have tough targets or their organisations demand excessive loyalty such that misdemeanours are not reported due to a desire to preserve their reputation, individuals are faced with moral dilemmas. Reputation and image are powerful incentives to hide things. There needs to be a balance of power between the consumer and the service/product provider. Where regulatory bodies lack teeth, strong sales cultures over time can gain the upper hand. Paradoxically, in tight management systems, employees who may feel unfairly treated are more likely to take it out on the company through sabotage, pilfering or low levels of cooperation.

Trust is at the heart of the relationship between customer and provider. In Europe and Australia, when you go to a service station, you fill up with petrol and then go to the pay desk. In some parts of America, you pay first and then fill up and get a refund if you have paid too much. The latter indicates a low trust culture.

ORGANISATIONAL DESIGNS THAT WORK (AND THEIR PROBLEMS)

A study by Baron and Hannan (15) found that technology start-ups in Silicon Valley used one of three organisational models: the star model focused on finding the brightest people, the professional model focused on building the group around specific skill sets, and the commitment model focused on developing a group with shared values and strong emotional bonds. It was the last model that ensured higher levels of survival and success.

One key principle of organisational design in terms of both structure and process is to have a clear line of sight down the transmission system. When instructions are given, is it clear who is doing what, who is accountable for what and does everyone know? In the recent pandemic in Victoria, Australia, the premier of the state admitted to a public inquiry that he did not know who was responsible for fatal decisions to appoint security contractors to supervise quarantine in hotels. Because of poor training and unclear rules, a massive outbreak of COVID-19 occurred, resulting in many deaths in aged care and an economy that was shut down for weeks. There was 'a creeping assumption' that someone is accountable, but no one knew who. This highlights that transparency and communications about who does what are fundamental, especially in a fast-changing world where yesterday's assumptions might no longer be applicable today.

A good organisational design delivers appropriate outcomes to all stakeholders. This is often difficult to achieve in the short term in highly competitive businesses because the demands of sales and profit tend to dominate. In industries where selling is 'sell and forget', it matters less if customers feel aggrieved than in those where longer-term relationships are key to survival. However, in the former, poor experience quickly spreads, especially on social media, and businesses can be easily destroyed. Gerald Ratner was the MD of a chain of jewellery stores in the UK. The products were moderately priced but not of the best quality. However, people wanted to believe they were buying something of value. The illusion was destroyed and the business was soon lost when Ratner announced that: 'We also do cut-glass sherry decanters complete with six glasses on a silver-plated tray that your butler can serve you drinks on, all for £4.95. People say, "How can you sell this for such a low price?", I say, "because it's total crap".' The company lost huge value, and was eventually sold and renamed to restore its reputation (16).

One consequence of organisation growth is that more time has to be spent on the overhead activities of organisational maintenance. These tasks absorb time and resources such that decision making slows (because of the need to consult a wider range of people). Change becomes more difficult to achieve smoothly because of the greater disruptions and the greater sense of alienation that those not directly connected to the decision might feel at being left out. Growth therefore drives the need for more delegated authority if agility is to be maintained. The greater degree of independence granted to organisation units increases the probability of differences becoming sources of friction and challenges approaches to control. Management of diverse units is a continuing process of negotiation, with a range of approaches emerging, from tight operational control to separation where the only link to the centre/owner is through a financial transaction with the independent division.

One of the curious features of toxic cultures brought about by narcissistic and psychopathic leaders is the capacity of others to collude with them, even though they are fully aware of the leaders' appalling behaviour. The self-talk to justify silence takes many forms – 'It's not my place', 'no one would listen to me', 'I'm too junior'. Underlying these statements may be fears of being dismissed, ostracised or ridiculed. It requires courage to tell the emperor that he has no clothes. Nevertheless, most organisations of any size have several policing roles – HR, Audit, Security, etc. - whose job is to call out those who break the rules. But what happens when it's their boss who is doing it? Donald Trump's behaviour provided many examples of those who had stood up to him or criticised him being either dismissed or made extremely uncomfortable in their role.

The role of an independent judiciary, an independent regulator or an non-executive director on the remuneration committee are all vital devices to provide checks on poor behaviour.

HR PRACTICES THAT IMPACT CULTURE

Of the many essential processes in organisations, hiring practices are all subject to bias, even those that go beyond an interview, a CV and maybe a reference check. CVs can be massaged to go beyond a positive description of their achievements (which is common in all CVs) to a more elaborate creation of a fictitious career. The outplacement industry at its best helps people to present themselves at their best, but at its worst encourages falsehoods to be expressed. Interviews are subject to many biases, as it's a test of agreeableness and connection rather than ability.

There is always unconscious bias, however hard you try to avoid it. Nevertheless, there are tactics that companies try, including multiple interviews, panel interviews, tests, presentations about a key issue, which are all designed to get beyond one-person subjective judgement. The ability to make sound decisions when there are multiple factors, assessors and candidates becomes more difficult as the number of each of these elements increase. The consequence is poor decision making borne out of frustration and a pressure to decide.

It is often difficult to prove bias, yet the experience of women and minority groups is that they frequently experience it in subtle ways. If you are an older, unattractive (however defined) women of colour, you stand a lower chance of being hired in many jobs compared to a younger, white male, even with comparable qualifications and experience.

People get hired for their backgrounds and experience on paper, but usually fired for their behaviour and attitude – something that is not picked up in interviews. Off-course nepotism also plays a part and can result in hiring clones. The rationale for cloning existing staff is that it makes for an easier life when 'everyone is like me'. However, mounting evidence of the benefits of diversity in terms of breadth of experience, differing approaches and more creative problem solving points to the limitations of cloning.

When a manager has no responsibility for hiring their staff, ownership of performance management is reduced. This might occur when HR or some other body hires and fires, though their role is often to check that staff meet certain minimum standards before hiring them. In government departments, a staffing committee sometimes decides who works for whom and controls transfers and promotions. This leaves a lack of clear accountability, especially when dealing with cases of poor performance or discipline.

Committees are another area where toxic cultures take root. There is a tension between getting a few decision makers in a room (which is easier to organise and get a decision) and ensuring that there is participation from all potential stakeholders (which takes longer and is more likely to be stalled). The larger and more formal the meeting, the greater the inhibition to speak out, especially to disagree, and the lower the probability of good decisions being made. Where responsibility may seem to rest with the committee, in effect no one individual is accountable. The real decisions are then made by a small group of key influential people outside any meeting. Northcote Parkinson in his classic book *Parkinson's law* suggests, based on experience of government cabinets and committees, that no useful work is done (17) once the number of participants exceeds around 20. Other views from a psychological perspective indicate rather different numbers: less than 5 and there may not be the diversity of views to encourage sufficient debate; more than 8 or 9 and people begin to feel inhibited, as well as being limited in the time available for making any particular contribution (18).

The author once had the experience of chairing a big international meeting where a contentious issue was the budget. After some debate, an agreement appeared to have been made and in order to secure it, I asked each person to state their agreement (known as gaining behaviourally committed speaking). Receiving total commitment, I assumed that that would be that. However, after the meeting, I was ambushed by two people who started renegotiating the terms. Having had a difficult time closing the conversation, I learnt how large meetings to some people are merely rituals and the real agreements are 'taken offline' for the key individuals to really make the decision. On one board, there was one woman amongst several men. She complained bitterly that she was never party to these offline discussions as they usually took place in the men's toilet after the meeting.

A legacy of the ancient Greeks is the idea of democracy being the result of a debate amongst peers (no slaves allowed). The German philosopher Hegel suggested the dialectic – thesis, antithesis, synthesis. And it is these ideas which suffuse our governing assemblies, courts and, indeed, science. It rests upon the assumption of (reasonably) civilised behaviour and a willingness to concede when your side has lost through some agreed process (voting or decisions by an accepted judge or some arbitration group). Where this goes wrong is when these assumptions are violated and/or when the voter, jury and people don't consider the issue, but merely decide on the basis of prejudice or affiliation to some party or team. Sport is an area where violence can easily erupt as passions run high and the referee is vital but often (unfairly) criticised.

BOUNDARY MANAGEMENT

A major decision in the structural design of organisations is where to place the boundaries between activities. Whether activities are clustered by location, function or business unit (or personal fiefdom), as the numbers of employees grows, boundaries have to be established. In times of change these boundaries may need to be flexible. At the level of the team, 'team flex' (19) is a way that organisations can deal with changes in capability and competence as well as external demands on the business unit. It is rare that these boundaries are perfectly aligned to the needs of the organisation, let alone every wish or preference of those involved. It is as a result of these tensions that conflict arises, and toxicity can emerge. The most common conflict is where legitimate debate about how to link functions becomes a turf war fuelled by power grabs. These in turn are encouraged by job evaluation schemes that reward managers based on size of unit (number of staff, budget, etc.). One tactic that is deployed in turf wars is the withholding of information from the other party – information is power – which at best may wrong-foot the other, but at worst may result in loss of business or even life (see the example of the Boeing 737 Max, which we will examine in Chapter 8).

RULES AND POLICIES

Rules are tools – a guide for the wise, the blind obedience of fools (20).

The following story may be apocryphal, but it illustrates the all-too-common conflict between rules and the needs of the moment - a case where inflexible rules created without regard to local conditions proved fatal:

> *One day in the Midwest of America, a steam train was crossing a wooden trestle bridge which caught fire. The driver radioed his controller to report the incident and was instructed on no account to move the train. Whilst the driver protested that he needed to move off the bridge to save the train, the rules were clear that the train should not be moved. The bridge collapsed soon afterwards, taking the train with it.*

This case highlights the need for flexibility in interpretation of the rules, but begs the question of who should interpret the rules and what freedom they have. The problem with a local deviation to a rule is that it creates a precedent for future occasions.

Rule systems arise for several reasons. The primary ones are to regulate behaviour so that society in all its forms can function. Any social grouping establishes rules early on in their forming. Whilst it may give rise to subsequent 'storming' where rules are disputed, in due course they are accepted. They enable priorities to be set in dealing with constraints in non-crisis situations and for turf wars to be avoided. Rules that are formally stated override individual whims and their circumstances, and legitimise any sanctions that may be applied when they are broken. In time, there is a belief that they are permanent and cannot be changed. Rules to create fairness and support people doing the right thing can become ends in themselves. 'Jobsworth' has become a catchphrase for those who see the rules as paramount regardless of their impact on others or even the success of the enterprise.

THE ROLE OF RULES

In order to be fulfilled, rules and policies require four characteristics:

- To be important for efficient operation and for achieving what is required.
- To be achievable by reasonable (and legal) behaviour.

- To be congruent with accepted norms of behaviour and ideally with the values of those charged with carrying them out.
- To avoid conflict with reward policies.

Rules need to be administered by those who understand the intended as well as the likely unintended effects. An example is the COVID-19 vaccination debacle in Europe, where the European Commission took on the task of negotiating a European-wide agreement which was given to a department whose previous concerns had been food labelling!

RULES AS A RESPONSE TO CRISIS

When things go wrong – a mistake is made or a disaster occurs - the familiar response is to enact a new rule. Governments are forever generating more controls and bureaucratic procedures in an effort to establish fairness and to avoid fraud. However, rules stifle innovation and enterprise, and as frustration grows, so the pendulum swings to cut the red tape.

Cultures, where there is a bias towards action, often give tacit approval to find ways round the rules when they no longer fit. Indeed, some will argue that rules invariably fit only a proportion of the situations they are designed to control. One of the powerful ways in which unions bring organisations to their knees is by working-to- rule - a strange paradox(!), but illustrative of the fact that rigid adherence to rules often results in a loss of output. So, there is a conflict here between the outcomes desired by the rules (fairness, safety, control, etc.) and output (production, easier ways of working, time savings, etc.). To resolve this dilemma, many have focused less on rules and more on values in the belief that if people know what the right thing to do is, then they will interpret the situation better than any rule or policy might predict, as we saw in Chapter 5.

The legitimacy of rules is particularly apparent when mistakes are made. If the rules have been broken, then the response is punishment. But if the person responded in accordance with the values but a mistake was still made, then the response is to look more deeply at how we do business (assuming we still share this value).

CASE STUDY: EMPOWERING STAFF TO ACT

One evening in a depot in the Midwest of America, a storm brought down a communication tower. The company held strong values about how customers were important and it would go the extra mile to satisfy requirements. At this time, though, there was a recession and cost control was tight, with strict authorisations required for expenditure. The security guard who saw the tower collapse was faced with a dilemma: to call out a repair crew at night would cost money for which he had no authority, yet if the tower was not operational, customer orders would suffer. He went ahead and brought in the crew.

In the morning, as they started up again, the manager's first response was one of annoyance that money had been spent with no authorisation and by someone who would never have that level of discretion. On further reflection, he realised that the guard had done the right thing and in front of the staff he deliberately praised him for doing it. Whilst it reinforced the value of customer service being paramount and raised a strong show of support for more junior staff doing the right thing, it also provided a platform for discussing how they dealt with competing values. The outcome was a review of all aspects where money could be saved without compromising customer service and in which all were involved and felt engaged.[7]

A byproduct of this was that employees felt more empowered to take decisions, being mindful of serving customers as well as saving money. But it could have gone the other way if the guard had been disciplined for exceeding his authority, as was a case in an airline which is described in Chapter 9.

Earlier in the introduction, I mentioned a TV show entitled *Back to the floor.*[8] which demonstrated how surprised senior executives were when faced with the tasks more junior staff had to endure each day. Rules and policies that made eminent sense in the board room sometimes did not work on the shop floor. The author, when a board member of a UK retailer, ran a competition for the best branch. The prize was a trip to a holiday resort for a week for all members of the winning branch with their partners. The author naively suggested that the board run the branch in the staff's absence. Not only had we never worked so hard, but it also proved to be the best training course in the practical application of retailing theory. In the following week, we changed many policies and practices in light of what we had learnt.

FIDDLING THE RULES

Rules are only complied with if the sticks and carrots show that compliance is the best option. In the recent pandemic, social distancing and limited exceptions for leaving the house were enforced, with fines for non-compliance. However, where there was a necessity to go out, people manufactured an excuse to do so. In one example, a mother went to her daughter to help with home schooling, a reason that was not considered to be officially legitimate. So, she took a doctor's prescription with her, so that if stopped, she would fall within the allowed categories for medical supplies.

Individuals typically seek to make life easier for themselves by cutting corners or ignoring rules. Safety officers continually have to remind workers of the consequences for safety if rules are not followed involving equipment, protective guards and checks, as these inhibit speedy working and so are often discarded or avoided. Some groups deride such rules ('too much part of the nanny state') as overprotective and see themselves in a positive light for avoiding them.

Several examples will illustrate how when rules are compromised or become impossible to follow, deviant behaviour emerges to the detriment of the organisation's culture and customers.

CASE STUDY: THE MILK DELIVERY SERVICE

Several years ago, the Tavistock Institute in London was asked by a dairy that delivered milk to investigate the labour turnover of milkmen. It was a difficult job to recruit for, as it required an exceedingly early start: 4 am was the usual time for milkmen to come to the depot to collect the load for the day. The job involved increasing complexity as more lines were carried, from different types of milk to a range of groceries. The real difficulty was keeping track of customer needs and payment required, as customers would change their mind about their order, leave notes on the doors step or go on holiday. Keeping track of it all in order to collect the money was a challenge. The dairy, realising that there were plenty of opportunities for milkmen to play the system had set up systems to identify what left the depot, what returned and what money was collected, and if there was a shortfall, the milkmen had to make it up themselves. Those who could not handle it left quickly. Yet some milkmen seemed to manage. So how did they do so? Well, the study identified that those milkmen who survived had been introduced to a successful fiddle. Basically, they made up the orders, adding the cost of a carton here and there to a person's bill. If the customer disputed it, they rectified it, but basically on average they were ahead and at the end of the month when they tallied it up, they pocketed the excess over what the dairy management said.

When the management read the Tavistock report, they accepted it as the norm and filed the report. By condoning it, the fiddle spread as the vast majority of the milkmen now did it, believing this was totally acceptable. Such fiddling then became the norm in other areas, including periodically cheating the farmers in terms of the price they set for their milk. The culture had become corrupted. When word of this got out to customers, arguments ensued and sales went down. A new manager was installed who felt he couldn't condone such behaviour and clamped down even further, demanding customers report any discrepancies direct to the dairy. The milkmen staged a walk-out, saying the job was impossible. Management relented and asked them not to fiddle, but they were given an allowance of a 10% disparity. However, the fiddling culture persisted, and it was some time before more ethical practices became the norm (21).

It is interesting to speculate how much fiddling is condoned in other businesses. In one example, salespeople often gave small kickbacks to the purchaser in return for orders upon which they would earn commission. This was largely ignored as whilst it was unethical, no one lost out. However, it again created an impression that fiddling was OK. This reached a breaking point when salespeople were adding additional loadings to the prices, citing 'administrative fees' and siphoning off such fees to their own private account. Management stepped in and people were dismissed. However, whilst fiddling stopped for a while, it had become such a part of the culture that it crept back in, albeit at a lower level.

Where there is a high level of disaffection, a range of forms of sabotage might occur from minor instances, such as not bothering to clear the jam in the photocopier, to major instances, like deliberately breaking a piece of equipment. The following list gives some examples:

- A disgruntled group of workers in a seaside rock factory, rather than putting in the name of the town in the rock, put in various rude words and phrases. It must have been an unpleasant shock to a parent to discover their child was licking a stick that said 'fuck off'.
- A computer programmer was disciplined for complaining about insecure systems, so he altered the payroll programme to delete the whole company record if his name was deleted. Eventually he was fired and the following month no one got paid.
- A disaffected employee emptied a packet of tacks in the executive car park. Rather than condemnation of the individual's actions, there was widespread support, indicating that this was not the result of one disaffected person, but was rather symptomatic of wider anger.
- Teams or work gangs in manufacturing develop certain norms, which may range from limiting speed and duration of work to an allowance for breaks (or as compensation for perceived lack of other rewards), to more organised crime. In one example in a manufacturer, a computer programmer, a storeman in the warehouse and a trucking company worked together to alter stock records so that products could get past security at the gate, where they were then delivered to street markets for disposal without trace.

As we discussed in Chapter 4, the psychopath is not bound by external rules, because they are less amenable to social pressure or the need for affiliation to be part of a team. They are often good at mimicking the behaviours that are valued and that may be used as a reason for being more tolerant of a lack of adherence to rules, standards and key performance indicators (KPIs). Finding a protective umbrella or sponsor (sometimes called the 'pawn patron' strategy) is the way in which individuals who are masters at managing corporate politics ensure an easier ride than those subject to the bare rules. The application of tools such as 360-degree feedback expose such people who are good at manipulating upwards ('brown-nosing' as it is somewhat crudely described). Whilst the manipulative psychopath might exploit this 'pawn patron' for their own ends, they might just as well be used by people wanting to get the work done where the rules are getting in the way. The wedge in the door, which self-closes for safety and fire reasons, gets left there when it becomes irksome and inefficient to get the key every time for people using the door.

SUMMARY AND CONCLUSIONS

- Organisational design aims to group functions, establish processes, and set policies and rules that fulfil the organisation's mission and goals.
- Design encompasses many elements and provides many opportunities for a toxic and unproductive culture to develop, especially when the elements do not connect or are not in balance. Friction caused by poor design and poor boundary management is a key cause of poor performance.
- Structure and process are essential elements in determining how people act and may help or hinder unproductive practices. The physical design of workspace and workflow are also contributory factors.
- The informal organisation (which will be considered in Chapter 7) mediates structure and process, and is influenced by the pattern of communications.
- Designs that facilitate innovation differ from rigid bureaucracies. Innovation requires a more fluid organisation open to ideas and influences from a wide range of sources.
- There are 11 tests to determine whether the design is appropriate for any organisation.
- Of the many processes that HR manage, hiring the right people is critical for success. Bias and prejudice can easily slip into the selection process.
- Rules are an essential part of regulating behaviour, but when irksome or introduced without widespread agreement can become subverted and give rise to a variety of work-arounds and corrupt behaviours.

NOTES

1 Exodus 18:13-23, New International Version.
2 A remark made about a former director of Crown Casinos – for more on this, see Chapter 8.
3 A red team is an independent group that challenges an organisation to improve its effectiveness by assuming an adversarial role or point of view. It originated in the US military.
4 'Skunk works' is a term to describe a group within an organisation that is given a high degree of autonomy and is unhampered by bureaucracy. Its early use was in Lockheed Martin in the development of new planes

5 A black swan is an unpredictable event that is beyond what is normally expected of a situation and has potentially severe consequences. Black swan events are characterised by their extreme rarity, severe impact and the widespread insistence that they were obvious in hindsight.

6 A derivative is a contract that derives its value from the performance of an underlying entity. This underlying entity can be an asset, index or interest rate, and is often simply called the 'underlying asset'.

7 This story was recounted at the British Government leadership programme in 2016.

8 Different titles have been used in different territories, such as *Undercover boss*.

REFERENCES

1 See, for example, Minzberg, H. (1979) *The structuring of organisations.* Pearson.

2 Cummings, T.G. and Worley. C.G. (1997) *Organisation development and change.* Southwestern College.

3 Seddon, J. (2005) *Freedom from Command and Control.* Vanguard Education.

4 Diamond, J. (2011) *Collapse.* Penguin.

5 Cannon, J.A., McGee, R. and Stanford, N. (2010) *Organisation design and capability building.* CIPD.

6 Klein, G. (2014) *Seeing what others don't: The remarkable ways we gain insights.* Nicholas Brealey Publishing.

7 Mueller, J.S., Melwani, S and Goncalo, J.A. (2012) The bias against creativity: Why people desire but reject creative ideas. *Psychological Science, 23*, 13-17.

8 HP Oscilloscope … Not a 'Me Too' product … Retrieved 10 May 2022 from https://www.hpmemory-project.org/wa_pages/wall_a_page_12.htm.

9 Wetlaufer, S. (1994, November–December) The team that wasn't. *Harvard Business Review.*

10 Lynch, D. and Kordis, P.L. (1990) *Strategy of the dolphin.* Arrow Books.

11 Cannon, R. and Cannon, J. (2022) *Aha! A user's guide to creativity.* Austin Macauley (in press).

12 Hoffer, E. (1973) *Reflections on the human condition.* Hopewell Publications.

13 Kuhn, T.S. (2012) *The structure of scientific revolutions.* University of Chicago Press.

14 Cannon, R. and Cannon, J. (2022) *Aha! A user's guide to creativity.* Austin Macauley (in press).

15 Barron, J. and Hannan, M. (2002) Organisational blueprints for success in high tech start-ups: Lessons from the Stanford project on emerging companies. *California Management Review, 44*, 8-36, https://doi.org/10.2307%2F41166130.

16 Address by Gerald Ratner CEO of Ratners, to the IOD conference at the Albert Hall, on 23rd April 1991. Here is one account that appeared in the press: https://thehustle.co/gerald-ratners-billion-dollar-speech/

17 Parkinson, N. (1958) *Parkinson's law.* John Murray.

18 Amir, O., Amir, D., Shahar, Y., Hart, Y. and Gal, K. (2018) The more the merrier? Increasing group size may be detrimental to decision-making performance in nominal groups. https://doi.org/10.1371/journal.pone.0192213.

19 Cannon, R. and Cannon, J. (2022) *Aha! A user's guide to creativity.* Austin Macauley (in press).

20 Variously attributed to Harry Day and Douglas Bader

21 A conversation held some years ago with Don Bryant of the Tavistock Institute. This example mirrors the most recent study by Ditton quoted in Chapter 10.

CHAPTER 7

The informal organisation

INTRODUCTION

The world's rainforests serve as home to many poisonous plants. The poisons of these plants – dispersed in different ways – cause varying reactions in the creatures affected. The stinging bush, native to north-eastern Australian rainforests, uses toxic hairs to poison potential predators. The strychnine tree produces berries with seeds which contain deadly strychnine. The toxin in the curare vine's flowers is so poisonous that indigenous people coat their hunting arrows in their juice. These examples give us a clue as to how organisms react to threats. A useful analogy is to see organisations as organisms that, when faced with threat, develop a range of defensive mechanisms that may seem harmless to their creators, but are toxic to others.

Many of the actions that individuals take in response to their environment are without much thought of how they relate to the reactions of others, let alone the long-term consequences. The events in the USA during the end of 2020 and 2021 following the presidential election show how one individual can start sowing seeds of discontent that then become magnified. Each person acted from their own perspective, but this spread like wildfire and resulted in major disruption. In Chapter 1 we highlighted the role of the beliefs, norms and values, and in this chapter we examine norms in more detail to identify how these become subverted.

NORMS

The informal organisation is determined by the pattern of relationships and, whilst difficult to prove, can be a benefit or a hindrance to achieving effective outcomes. When formal and informal systems are aligned and there is acceptance of the ingredients of good performance (fair pay systems, agreed goals, opportunity to gain mastery in the role, appropriate job aids such as equipment, etc.), the outcomes can be beneficial. When elements are missing, the informal organisation can work to limit output, to sabotage workflow and to cause disruption at the boundaries between work groups. Organisations work through relationships that both serve the business needs of each role as well as the social needs for connection. Nevertheless, there are limits to destructive behaviour, and two factors emerge: individual desire for reward and the tolerance of a manager about practices not directly related to work.

A dilemma for management is how much slack to afford to employees: too much and over time, these practices become institutionalised and difficult to change; too little and both creativity and initiative become stifled, and more hidden ways to subvert the situation are likely to become

DOI: 10.4324/9781003307334-11

found. The need to obtain cooperation and maximum effort is balanced with tolerance of rule breaking and behaviour that is not helpful to achieving outcomes. Few would challenge employee using an office pen to write their shopping list, but it is a slippery slope towards larger 'theft' – using an office computer for your own business, 'borrowing' equipment, etc.

There is a cycle of acceptance which gives rise to new norms. For example: a member of a team comes back from a long lunch clearly drunk. There are no specific rules about drinking at lunchtime other than it being frowned upon, so the manager asks him to desist from this in future, but takes no action. Others see that there are no consequences to this behaviour and when next there is a cause for some celebration, the team head off for a merry lunch. When the manager remonstrates, they say that it was OK for X and so nothing happens. It increasingly becomes confirmed that drinking at lunchtime is permitted and there are no consequences other than a reprimand. In time, other less attractive behaviours start emerging (called the 4 Ds – drink, dares, devilment and dumbness). Once behaviour becomes established as a cultural norm, it becomes harder to change.

The higher the degree of social cohesion, often associated with strong group affiliation such as a club or union, the greater the likelihood of conformity to agreed norms. Where an individual's career capital is tied up with a particular organisation, they are less likely to go against prevailing norms as they run a greater risk of not finding alternative work if they have to leave. Individuals with more transferable skills are less concerned with group norms and more with their wider employability. This might be manifest in professional ethics, reputation and competency.

THE PSYCHOLOGICAL CONTRACT

The creation of rules and policies may be based on seeking to improve performance. However, the nature of non-custodial organisational life means that performance is the result of an implicit contract between the benefit of working (pay and intrinsic benefits of doing enjoyable work) and the demand for contribution according to the requirements of the hirer. As such rule systems are based on a philosophy of how performance is to be achieved and assumptions about the extent to which individuals are prepared to comply with the rules.

The psychological contract describes the often-unwritten expectations an employee/contractor/supplier has of an employer and vice versa. These expectations are shaped by many factors, including the prior experience of both parties, which in turn is influenced by knowledge of others' experience and norms prevailing in the cultural milieu in which the parties are engaging. This changes over time and is different for each individual. Being largely unwritten, it relies on trust. Organisations are patterns of conversation and reciprocity: I ask you to do something and you do something in return. Reciprocity is based on trust which underpins these interactions, ensuring we don't have to negotiate every time we need something. There are concentric circles of trust: the closer people are to you, the greater the trust, so people may trust their colleagues, less so the boss and even less so the CEO. Even in wartime, sufficient trust can be built up to allow the sides to move beyond conflict, even if only for a time (for example, the famous football match during the First World War between German and English forces in no man's land). People trust their Member of Parliament more than they trust the government on the same principle that you can have a more direct relationship with an individual and are more likely to trust them (until contrary evidence emerges in this respect) than the amorphous government.

'Low trust management is conventionally described as strong management, bureaucratised, rule bound, introspective and a slave to its history' (1). The old supervisory ratios of the past that were low and as a consequence resulted in multiple layers of management had an overhead cost and often slowed down decision making. The move to de-layering involves increasing trust so that cost reduction comes with lower levels of supervision and an increased likelihood of more variable performance outcomes.

One significant shift is when a relationship moves from a long-term relationship, where there may be many interactions over time, to a more transitory relationship, such as casual working in the gig economy. In the former case, where trust has developed, both parties may be willing to tolerate a greater imbalance in the contract in the short term in order to preserve the longer-term relationship. The latter is less resilient to short-term imbalances. The long-term employee who has a bad day may get the day off; the contractor may never get used again. The more transitory psychological contract certainly suits some as it gives freedom to pick and choose, to move to new pastures and to no longer feel a sense of loyalty beyond what is contractually required ('if you want loyalty, get a dog' said a disgruntled employee). The danger of the old contract where in exchange for loyalty you are given long-term employment and suitable benefits is a reluctance to sacrifice that (often illusory) security when asked to engage in new, perhaps more uncertain ventures. Given the rate of obsolescence of skills, staying with one employer may limit your employability in terms of acquiring a wider range of experience and expertise from a number of employers.

> I have worked for this company for 24 years and done everything they asked of me, to sometimes great inconvenience to my family. They now have made me redundant, and I don't have any other experience. I think I am unemployable. What did I do wrong? (A redundant worker of a manufacturer facing competition from China)

TWO MANAGEMENT PHILOSOPHIES

There have been two streams of thought running through the management literature for over a century. The first was articulated most strongly by F.W. Taylor and scientific management, with the assumption that precise design of jobs and work rates was the key to success. Work study and business process re-engineering are products of this stream. The other has been labelled as the human relations school, whereby enlightened management treats people well and seeks to empower them to become the best expression of themselves. The move towards autonomy and individualism through individual rather than collective contracts aims to satisfy the search for identity in a more liberal age.

The early experiments by Roethlisberger and Dickson at the Hawthorne Works (2) highlighted the role of the informal organisation in determining productivity. They demonstrated how attention and a feeling of significance were important and more so than formal methods of work organisation. They further identified how norms develop to protect the group from what they saw as unfair managerial treatment. Norms developed about a fair work rate, not 'squealing to the foreman' and not being too bossy when you took on a supervisory role. Sanctions of varying kinds imposed upon those breaking the norms ultimately led to ostracism from the group. They also showed that solidarity exerted a powerful force on limiting performance, even to the seemingly illogical act of reducing their pay. The dominant desire was job security, and this was a more successful strategy, as maximising pay would be as a result of increasing output, which they believed would lead to some of them losing their jobs.

Whilst many organisations may espouse moral polices and rules, the hidden informal behaviour rarely becomes public. Misbehaviour, however defined, emanates from different assumptions about each management philosophy. The first might be that avoiding instructions might be wilful rebellion by subverting the prescriptions of management, whilst the second might be that freedom encourages work not related to the task at hand, but more about personal interest. The tension then becomes most manifest when looking at creativity and innovation, and the belief by some companies that a proportion of time should be spent on personal projects, whilst other companies might reject this as a misuse of company time. The argument for the first proposition is that motivation to work on employees' interests will have spin-offs including greater engagement and loyalty to the organisation, as well as the possibility that an innovation might result that will benefit the company.

STATUS

Status in a group can come from several sources, which can be both helpful and unhelpful to group performance. It comes from respect shown, particularly by a reference group. In professional groups, status might be enhanced by reference to external qualifications and professional accolades rather than internal position or even reputation. In some traditional societies, external status indicators such as the position you occupy in your tribe will be more important than the position you occupy in an organisation hierarchy.[1] When status is conferred on those who are highly skilled or have a strong buy-in to the organisation's values and goals, this can be helpful. The barrack room lawyer who is subversive, on the other hand, can be destructive to morale and can limit opportunities for improvement or innovation.

Informal organisation, especially where it results in considerable autonomy, runs the risk of being hijacked by individuals with their own agenda. The history of militant industrial relations is littered with such leaders – for example, 'Red Robbo' in the British car industry, who had communist sympathies and saw industrial action as being as much about his politics as about representing employees.

The informal ways of organising and working can become formalised, with mixed results. The skilled craftsman has honed his craft over many years and has developed routines that work for him. The danger of the apprentice is to follow too slavishly what is observed. As someone once said, you cannot learn to juggle just by watching a juggler; you have to feel it for yourself and develop the eyes and hand coordination that works for you. The informal organisation will develop over time as relationships deepen and familiarity with the formal, rules, policies and processes become second nature. More work-rounds and tacit rule breaking occur as people become more confident about what they do and knowledgeable about what they can get away with. This may be for the best of reasons, as prescribed policies and procedures rarely work effectively in every situation. As an individual's status increases, so they are likely to exercise more freedom from following strict norms as they are less likely to be challenged – and if they are, then they are in a stronger position to argue their case.

Organisational behaviour is difficult to easily categorise as good or bad, partly because each organisation will define practices in different ways, but also because the context often determines whether it is helpful or not. These contexts can result in positive responses, from innovation that can increase when rigid job descriptions and rule books are relaxed, to finding more efficient ways of working by team-based problem solving. Negative responses can arise when innovation that requires large organised and integrated work teams cannot be organised and sustained over time in these more fast-moving and flexible approaches to organisation.

ORGANISATIONAL CHANGE

With increasing numbers of knowledge workers, traditional methods of measuring work rate and output no longer apply. This has in part meant that old systems of work study are no longer applicable and new methods have been devised, notably cost control. This places pressure on employees to deliver using few resources as possible. Technology has also created its own drivers, with the speed of response to the blizzard of emails and demands for time and attention, the major determinants of work rate and performance. Striking, working to rule and other ways of limiting output have become less prevalent with the decline in trade unions and rule books. Nevertheless, we should not be beguiled into believing that all is sweetness and light, as both management and employees of all kinds are in a shifting power balance, which results in constant negotiation and indeed manipulation of that relationship to achieve each role's interests.

Rigid work practices limit the capacity of the organisation to be flexible in tough times, which reduces its resilience. If ever there was a capacity in great demand in all organisations today, it is to change rapidly, and this capacity becomes limited when there is insufficient commitment to the goals of the organisation and the effort that may be required. When the relationship is transitory, there is a greater likelihood of working to contract rather than doing whatever is required in the circumstances. In an accelerating world of change, the leader's skill set must embrace the drive and pace to accomplish change, whilst avoiding the bullying that often characterises the manager out of their depth and lacking in the social and motivational skills to bring people with them. Organisations have become more 'psychopath-friendly' in recent years, and when the drive for change is vital for survival, the hard-driving psychopath who gets things done but thinks nothing of the collateral damage to staff around them may seem like a knight in shining armour!

Change gives ample opportunity for those who get a buzz out of politicking as there may be jockeying for new positions and manipulation of rumours to promote fake stories or to play on people's fears of uncertainty. Managing change often involves some secrecy whilst plans are being properly prepared. Given the difficulty of communications in times like this, there are those who claim to have the inside story which confers some status and power upon them. The opportunity to exercise impression management provides a field day for the game player.

The impact of organisational change is to disrupt social networks and thus the informal organisation. This drag on organisational performance is rarely considered and adds a burden to effective performance until new relationships are established. For those who survive by manipulation and sweet talking, such change is a boon, as it takes time for new colleagues to expose their flaws.

In times of reorganisation, managers may take the opportunity to get rid of those who no longer fit. They may collude by encouraging the poor performer to apply for a role in another department and giving them a good reference. It is easier to palm someone off elsewhere than to go through disciplinary and dismissal processes. Change impacts people differently and provides plenty of opportunities for inconsistency and unfairness to emerge. A cost-cutting exercise involving significant restructuring might leave people demoralised for several reasons, as is shown in the following case study.

> *The company had been generous with the redundancy packages, and in the leaving parties the leavers were delighted, as many of them had found new work and were contemplating a nice holiday or a new car with their termination payments. Those who were left felt put upon as they were told they were lucky to have a job, but had to work harder for a frozen pay packet. Voluntary turnover from this group increased afterwards. They certainly didn't feel like the lucky ones.*

In another example, executives were still flying business class, yet they had scrapped the free coffee scheme for staff. Restructuring (even if there is no loss of jobs) involves change and it is often the trivial things that trigger a negative reaction. David Rock (3) has researched the neuroscience behind stress and found that many of the triggers are related to these scenarios. An individual's status is at risk both in terms of their position in the hierarchy and in their own perception of their competence, especially if this requires moving to a new job where they feel unable to fully master it. Times of change are associated with uncertainty, which is often a source of stress, and a loss of autonomy. Lack of freedom is perceived when others are making decisions that affect you and you have no power to change them.

Organisations are social structures where collaboration is essential to achieve outcomes. Yet they are also places of competition – for reward from performance, the favour of those in power or influence on events. Change disrupts these patterns and leaves uncertainty about who has influence and power in the future. When some win and some lose in the jostle involved in organisational change, especially when driven by external events, it can seem deeply unfair, as if the rules of natural justice are upended.

TOXIC GAMES AND PASSIVE-AGGRESSIVE BEHAVIOUR

In Soviet times there was a Russian story that 'workers pretended to work, and the management pretended to pay them'. One pretence is to work on your personal projects in company time, possibly using company materials. Theft is described by various euphemisms – shrinkage, product leakage or user testing. Those who sell electronic time recording badge decoders and other sophisticated devices sell their wares based on the fear that staff are time thieves and are eroding their contribution if not properly checked. Surveillance of telephone calls, etc. is a response to cultures that are far from compliant, instead encouraging work limitation to control their contribution. The reaction to clocking can range from excuses about the need to be out of the office to sabotage of the system. Clocking-in other people (a serious offence) is a widespread practice.

If you have had someone standing over you whilst you are working, you will know that it can be off-putting. In one mine, the supervisor was universally disliked and so every time he came to inspect the work, the miners stopped until he had gone. Some typical passive aggressive-behaviours include the following:

- Avoiding any communication.
- Saying only what is expected rather than giving a truthful response.
- Gossiping behind people's backs in a critical way.
- Behaving like a victim who has been unfairly treated.
- Displacement of their failings onto others.
- Intentional procrastination to frustrate others.
- Every event is interpreted in a negative way and more positive initiatives are dismissed as naïve.
- Criticism is cynical and sarcastic (4).

Passive-aggressive behaviour is often subtle and not overt even to the person affected, and may cause them to question their sanity, perception of reality or memories. People experiencing 'gaslighting' often feel confused, anxious and unable to trust themselves. Even when such behaviour is clearly apparent to the victim, persuading others of its veracity and obtaining suitable redress can be problematic.

HUMOUR

Joking has always been part of any social grouping. Satire and indeed humour of all kinds can hide many layers of meaning and innuendo. Shared jokes are a way of social bonding and of breaking down barriers. Laughter creates an informality and eases tensions. However, humour can be far from innocuous in its effect on others. Sexual innuendo is a form of harassment that many women find distasteful. Even amongst members of the same gender, sexual references can be resented, especially when they generate laughter at someone else's expense. Where humour about an idea or situation turns nasty is when it becomes focused on someone. Where that person is a member of the group, it becomes a source of harassment; where outside it increases potential conflict, though often binding group members together more closely.

Humour can create a sense of identity. Some groups have shared jokes, in-jokes or line of joking – the pun, the crude joke or jokes against other groups (especially races) – that all serve to reinforce identity. Being allowed and accepted into the banter regime is a mark of passage into the inner group – you are no longer an outsider. The benefit of being on the inside of a group can be seen as beneficial to many, even to the extent of tolerating considerable personal teasing or abuse.

Humour can be seen as allowing people to express their feelings and attitudes more freely. Joking has been a way of expressing things that normally would be seen as subversive or offensive. In questions of race, religion, sexuality, etc., humour tests out whether others have similar attitudes and prejudices, without great commitment, allowing face to be saved and the relationship to be maintained if they disagree. Humour also allows a get-out – 'I was only joking'. It also allows mistakes to be laughed off.

Humour can be a stress reducer. In the ambulance service in London, some of the humour would seem very black to an outsider, but to the ambulance workers, it is a form of tension release.

Jokes have targets and audiences - sometimes they are the same when people can laugh at themselves but are often different. Teasing as a form of joking at the expense of others is also a borderline activity between fun and harassment. In some relationships, it is one-way. Where it is reciprocal, it can strengthen the relationship through in-jokes, although it excludes others. When reciprocity is denied in teasing, it is seen as very unfair. 'He gives it out but won't take it back' was a typical comment. Once this behaviour triggers resentment, it can produce freezing-out, feuds and a breakdown in civil communication that is vital for the interests of the organisation. It requires a degree of sensitivity amongst group members as to where the boundaries lie between fun and causing real offence. There is a degree of calculation about being a teaser, a critic or a joker – in effect a non-conformist – with the risk of being labelled as a troublemaker or an outsider, resulting in managerial sanction or ostracism.

When self-organisation flourishes and creates more informal networks of communication, efficiency is often enhanced, but it can so easily be subverted when participants overstep the acceptable limits by badinage that then becomes cruel. When it occurs across the formal structure, it limits the chain of command's capacity to intervene without destroying the benefits of the informal organisation, because it results in a formalising of relationships between departments. Cruel behaviour often only comes to light when someone 'snaps' and raises an official complaint. The situation then moves into a different type of problem, the solution to which relies more on policies and rules and thus a formalising of acceptable behaviour. Whilst sanctions may be applied – even legal redress - it invariably does not end well for the complainant and relations become more formal and strained. The aftermath of an unproven claim of sexual harassment was described as 'everyone walking on eggshells'.

Clowning around and rituals such as hazing are rites of passage. Crossing the equator on ships traditionally involved rituals which were good humoured as long as the poor victim took it in good heart. Clowning around involving pranks can easily go awry, resulting in physical harm and emotional damage. At the very least, such behaviour takes time and sometimes resources away from actual work of the organisation. At worst, it becomes a subculture where such pranks are planned and involve considerable effort, and may even cause damage. Organisations often turn a blind eye to these, concluding that they are part of the norms and history of the place, and to disturb them would undermine the distinctive culture. However, attitudes change and what was once acceptable to men and (rarely) women is now deemed very inappropriate to both. Wolf whistles at and bottom pinching of women was once seen as fun by some men, although barely tolerated by women who believed they had little or no redress at the time.

Clowns in the workplace may be driven by their own need for attention, possibly substituting for more serious approval of their actual work. It can create a relaxed atmosphere, but equally can become a regular show. Condoning it by ignoring it based on the argument of 'let sleeping dogs lie' might result in it becoming less prevalent as the clown no longer has an audience. However, it places a manager in a dilemma, in that tolerance may imply that such behaviour of the clown is condoned, resulting in an inability to confront performance issues. This arises from a fear that the audience may see it as sour grapes or evidence that the manager can't take a joke. Clowning is also a form of rebellion, asserting individuality in organisations where conformity to norms (dress, behaviour, rules, etc.) denies any distinctions. In this situation, the clown can become the hero, seemingly less threatening than the out-and-out rebel, but insidiously effective in mobilising resistance or resentment at the organisation. 'Ironic, sardonic, and satirical commentary on management initiatives which has been endemic in Britain have become, in the current context, significant forms of misbehaviour' (5).

Satire is another form of joking intended to poke fun and expose the ridiculous side of individuals or organisations. Arcane rules, pompous behaviour and unfathomable instructions are all the stuff of satire and when directed at the organisation can be highly subversive, especially when it becomes institutionalised such that any managerial announcement is met with cynicism and satire. This is the time for the clowns to get to work, which is illustrated in the satirical Dilbert cartoon strip. This extraordinarily successful cartoon exposes the real consequences of many management fads and initiatives. The reason why jokes work is that they mimic inconsistencies in the world and exploit them by bringing them to the surface in a novel way. One cartoon read: 'there will be a 10% cut across the board. That is except for the Board'.

Humour as entertainment is also tolerated politically. In parts of the world, protest songs and agitprop have been acceptable forms of protest because of the (mistaken?) belief that they have little effect on public discourse, yet their underground spreading and widespread knowledge indicate they have more effect than might be recognised.

POWER RELATIONS AND CULTURAL LEGACY

> 'Cultural legacies are powerful forces. They have deep roots and long lives ... and play such a role in directing attitudes and behaviour that we cannot make sense of our world without them' (6).

Employees tend to follow the behaviour of their boss and if it is abusive, it sets a pattern to be followed through the organisation. We look to see what is behaved as a guide, not what is said. From our first day in an organisation, we are looking for clues as to how things are done and, once identified, these become copied. Over time, they form our beliefs, which stem from our past experiences and the inferences (7) we draw from them. These start from our observation and selection of what is significant, based on the meaning we attribute to it, and, depending on the conclusions we draw, we decide on some response. Those beliefs then form a filter and frame the assumptions we make about the world (try the listening exercise given in Chapter 9).

TOXIC TEAM CULTURE

Social systems seem to have a mind of their own. Effective teams are more than the sum of the parts and in particular have a strong sense of solidarity, which is helpful in getting work done. A clear sign of a toxic culture is when the natural solidarity that good teams experience becomes a weapon to play politics and attack other teams. Collaboration turns to competition and efforts to discredit others. However, one of the consequences of this is that in a desire for unity, people go along too easily with this toxic behaviour, even when they might feel something different. The Abilene paradox is an example of this phenomenon.[2] When team culture turns critically toxic, cohesion declines and grandstanding increases. This occurs when individuals distance themselves from others to display their own moral rectitude.

Lencioni analysed dysfunctional teams (8) and identified several features:

- Inattention to results where the pursuit of individual goals and personal status erodes the focus on collective success. This is manifest in team behaviours that ignore the purpose of the team.
- Others feel excluded from a group that exclusively socialises. When they are included, this is expressed in a condescending manner. This marginalisation can result in splinter groups that further limit the effectiveness of the workflow. The group deliberately do not invite others to

meetings. The 'silent treatment' given to these unfortunate individuals causes bad feelings and results in a range of unhelpful behaviours, including revenge and an unwillingness to engage in other areas of possible connection.

- Projects are often offered to a particular group, regardless of their talent or experience. Favouritism replaces evidence-based promotions.
- Large parts of the working day are spent whispering or chatting on messaging platforms.
- General outward disinterest from the group in anyone else – unless it involves gossip or 'drama'.
- Pranks and general clowning around are common.
- Avoidance of accountability where the need to avoid interpersonal discomfort prevents team members from holding one another accountable. In an alternative scenario where the consequences of failure are high, blame is passed to others (sometimes described as 'sloping shoulders').
- Lack of commitment where a lack of clarity or buy-in prevents team members from making decisions they will stick to.
- Fear of conflict where the desire to preserve artificial harmony stifles the occurrence of productive conflict. Vigorous debate based on alternative viewpoints and information can lead to better outcomes. When it becomes derailed by personal conflicts, then it becomes unproductive.
- Absence of trust where the fear of being vulnerable with team members prevents the building of trust within the team.

Such selfish behaviour, which is only concerned about personal interests, makes people blind to the unintended consequences. Ultimately it comes down to trust that others will be honest in their views, but have other team members' best interests at heart. It is an important distinguishing feature of teams that exhibit discretionary effort and their toxic opposites. In contrast, Pentlands (9) summarised the characteristics of good team behaviour using five factors:

- People talk and listen in equal measures.
- They maintain a high level of eye contact.
- Communication is direct, not hub and spoke through the leader.
- Conversations occur outside team settings between members (note: back channels are useful, but when members become unwilling to be open, they can become subversive).
- External exploration outside to find new information is encouraged.

In the race to develop software to link an internet search item to the delivery of suitable ads, Overture and Google battled it out. Overture was more bureaucratic and process-driven, whereas Google was more freewheeling. Coyle (10) quotes *Wired* magazine: 'Google didn't win because it was smarter, it won because it was safer'. The behaviour that children learn from an early age is about how to survive and gain affection from parents and significant others, and it patterns our behaviour for life. Teams that provide that safety and warm recognition mirror that early desire.

One of the characteristics of poor-performing teams is their lack of interdependency. However well roles are structured, effective teams rely on using each other's skills and capacities for the most efficient work to be done. When trust is low, there is a greater tendency for people to feel they have to do it themselves or, more disastrously, let tasks slip between roles. Interdependency was shown in the following case.

> *In London, there is an Italian sandwich bar which epitomises a good team. There are three generations behind the counter and a huge variety of fillings in the cabinets. Behind them are a wide variety of rolls and breads. There are usually three or four queues and as you reach the front, you give your order. One filling might be at one end and the second filling at the other. A ballet then ensues as a roll is buttered and fillings are passed down from either end, because other family members have heard what is required. They each have their own queues and customers and are doing the same, but they each rely on each other to listen out for their needs and pass the appropriate filling. Perfect teamwork! When this doesn't happen, then chaos ensues, as when a new employee does not understand the cues, merely focusing on their own tasks.*

This is not say that competition cannot occur between team members, provided it does not threaten the stability of the team. A powerful motivator is the opportunity to achieve mastery in one's skill set and that can lead to both helpful mentoring and advice to those less skilled, and recognition of the experts in the group, but also a degree of professional rivalry. Where this rivalry leads to avoiding helping those who might be a threat to their status as an expert, team performance suffers. Cohesion in a team which leads to a performance in which they take pride can be enormously motivating, leading to discretionary effort to ensure the team continues to perform well. It can be a damaging time for management if the rewards from improved performance are not in line with the team's expectations and beliefs about fairness. This typically occurs when targets for the future are unreasonably raised, or expected rewards – monetary and otherwise - are not given.

Unifying a group against some external threat is another strategy sometimes deployed to overcome individual differences and enhance cooperation towards a common goal that demands overcoming individual reservations. However, when the 'external threat' is seen as management, then that strong team culture can become subversive.

THE WORKING CLIMATE

So how do we shift climate to reduce recalcitrant behaviour? The first point is to distinguish between the influence of individual attitudes and behaviour from the constraints resulting from group values and norms established over time. In a historical study in the 1960s, Blau (11) found that where an individual's attitudes and values were congruent with historical group norms, the climate was enhanced, though when they were incongruent, the effect was more difficult to predict as it depended on the strength of the individual's beliefs and their ability to influence the group. We might conclude that one strategy is to select individuals for teams on their attitudes as much as their skills and experience, as it is certainly easier to enhance skills compared to changing underlying values and beliefs.

SEXUAL BEHAVIOUR IN THE WORKPLACE

The shifts towards greater gender equality, the reduced segregation of personal and public roles, and the fluidity of working locations and hours all point to greater opportunities for bringing personal relations into the workplace. When women enter traditionally male preserves, both genders behave differently together than in single-gender groups, and there seems to be an increased incidence of harassment, showing off and power plays. It is difficult for managers to define the boundary between work and where private life affects work negatively, though codes and laws to regulate sexual behaviour in organisations have been increasing over a long period. 'In the Middle Ages Bishops received a punishment of eight years' fasting for fornicating with cattle' (12).

One of the arguments in the past for segregating the sexes in some workplaces such as factories and mines was the belief that sexual contact would arise. This was considered both inappropriate and potentially unsafe if attention was not focused on the work being under-taken, but on more amorous pursuits. The growing breakdown of traditional gender lines, such as in the navy, has resulted in protests from navy wives, indicating that the threat of a liaison initiated from either sex is seen as real.

One area that has been a consistent aspect of all organisational life is 'mating manoeuvres on company time' (13). Anecdotal evidence points to many a marriage starting with dating a person from work, and many affairs will also occur because of the amount of time staff spend together. Working life brings people into close contact for many hours and indeed, for some who spend more time at work than at home, it is hardly surprising that relationships turn romantic. Once a relationship becomes known, many organisations will take steps to deal with the situation because of fears that this relationship may cut across the formal communication and management channels. In cases where it is the boss and his secretary, cliché as it is, many organisations will require one to either leave or move to a position where there is no conflict of interest. As a result, there are often attempts by the parties to keep any relationship secret, though it is rare that it can be kept secret from sensitive watchers:

> Work environments characterised by sexual comments and overtures are the same ones that frown on dating among employees, whereas sex integrated environments that have no regula-tions about employed dating also have relatively little overt expression of sexuality (14).

There is also a (probably unwarranted) fear that people who are emotionally involved might not be rational in their decision making, and their desire to keep their relationship hidden may lead to them making wrong choices, including whether they take unwarranted absences during the day. The assumption of rational organisation theory and the concept of professional conduct demand that people leave their sexual life outside the workplace. The belief that strong libidos can be easily set aside is naïve, and a more open approach is required towards recognising that relationships at work will sometimes take on a romantic connotation.

Despite years of legal and moral opprobrium of sexist language and behaviour towards women, there still exists a high degree of covert pressure on women to be attractive in terms of their dress and appearance, even in roles that are not public-facing. This sexualising of the work-place all contributes to an undercurrent that is subversive. The 'Me Too' movement has shown the consequences of male dominance and the way in which women have been forced to accept the incorrect belief that they have no other options. Women have often reported that they must adopt a male persona in their style and body language if they want to progress managerially. Yet to become too aggressive creates a threat to men that might well backfire. Of course, women may choose to accept the male requirements of dress, etc. as a quid pro quo for an opportunity to gain greater influence than might otherwise might have occurred. For women, this can result in con-siderable emotional effort, often mentioned in the context of flight attendants and other intensive customer-facing roles, but also to varying degrees in every job where a woman has to go beyond being a human being and to use her femininity to influence others.

The question remains: are men manipulating women or is it the other way round? When does an arrangement that suits both parties (however distasteful it may seem to others) become abusive or even criminal? Is harassment of women by men a response to a perceived threat? Men may interpret legitimate aspirations of women as a push for power, influence or status. Or, is it a crude exertion of male power? Naomi Wolf has argued that power feminism is 'unapologetically sexual' (15). For some, the image of the passive woman in these relationships is to deny the strength that women can deploy and their ability to exercise choice about how they present themselves.

In an Australian report entitled *Respect at work* (16) Kate Jenkins, the Sex Discrimination Commissioner, pointed out that harassment of women is more prevalent in organisations that are male-dominated and hierarchical in nature, as the power dynamic is emphasised. These organisations have also been found to have a higher prevalence of sexual harassment than the rate across all industries of 31%.

> Underpinning this aggregate figure is an equally shocking reflection of the gendered and intersectional nature of workplace sexual harassment. As the 2018 National Survey revealed, almost two in five women (39%) and just over one in four men (26%) have experienced sexual harassment in the workplace in the past five years. Aboriginal and Torres Strait Islander people were more likely to have experienced workplace sexual harassment than people who are non-Indigenous (53% and 32% respectively).

Features of these male-dominated cultures (for example, the construction and mining industries) that contributed to harassment were as follows:

* The gender ratio.
* The overrepresentation of men in senior leadership roles.
* The nature of the work being considered 'non-traditional' for women.
* The masculine workplace culture.
* These cultures are typically organised according to a hierarchical structure (for example, in police organisations, the Australian Defence Force, and the medical and legal professions).

Power imbalance between the genders, as we have seen with the 'Me Too' movement, have become entrenched in many companies and industries. Where this relationship is unwanted by either party, it can lead to harassment and manipulative behaviour. A power imbalance with sexual overtones has recently been disclosed in professional swimming where young women with minimal clothing have experienced body shaming by coaches. These coaches – usually men - are eager for success, as is the swimmer, but their dominant position has meant pushing the swimmer beyond reasonable limits in the interests of winning.

A recent case in Australia has revealed how a senior judge Dyson Heydon harassed some six women (and maybe others), causing several of these junior staff to give up on their careers. His behaviour resulted in a toxic environment for women at work. In the course of the investigation, it transpired that he had a reputation, being known as 'Dirty Dyson' and 'Handsy Heydon', information which was passed on amongst women to protect themselves. In a hierarchical environment where the boss had power over employees' future career prospects, there was a conspiracy of silence. The significant power imbalance – a major factor in both cases of harassment and the secrecy surrounding them - is further exacerbated when the actions are conducted by someone in a position of power and age that discourages those who might bring that person to account.

from doing so When your future career rests on the patronage of a judge and, by virtue of the organisational structure of a judge's chambers, you are beholden to them, it is difficult to object to the actions of a senior individual. The victim is likely to anticipate the problems that might occur in their career – loss of skill and experience, scandal, and loss of reputation for the institution. An institution like the law is difficult to bring to account when it sits in judgment on others and when such deference is shown to judges by everyone else.

Another factor confounding gender relations is cultural norms. For men in Islamic countries who have been used to seeing women dressed in a certain way, Western women's styles may seem highly provocative. In one case in a Middle Eastern country, a man who had sexually assaulted a woman was freed after he claimed that only a prostitute would wear such a short skirt and have such a plunging neckline, and he claimed that he had not met any moral and modest woman dressed in this way.

WHAT CHANGING TOXIC CULTURES REQUIRES

Here is a checklist of points that have emerged from press and academic reports following numerous examples of toxic cultures, particularly involving sexual harassment:

1. An independent body to deal carefully with complaints of all kinds and the power to impose sanctions and remedies. Systems of complaint, reward and discipline need to reflect respect of all parties.
2. Once identified, behaviour should be called out without fear of sanction, though steps should need to be taken to avoid malicious or untruthful accounts. Suitable redress should be available. Public campaigns should be promoted. Nudge psychology has been used in public campaigns to encourage change (paying tax and reducing littering). In one legal firm, it became a duty to report any sexual harassment and sanctions in terms of appropriate disciplinary action were invoked if it was not reported.
3. Protection of whistleblowers. A total of 81% in a survey supported whistleblowers in Australia (17). Companies that sanction legitimate protest should be prevented from such action. Considerable public criticism was levelled at Amazon, which dismissed two IT workers who gave technical assistance to a group of employees in a warehouse who were protesting about inadequate COVID-19 precautions.
4. In the Dyson case, the Chief Justice Susan Kiefel apologised and used language that was heartfelt and genuine, not management speak. The result was greater confidence that future occurrences would not be brushed aside and is a guide to how others should respond.
5. Education of boys about respect for women and sufficient social opprobrium to keep their testosterone in check should be mandatory. This should start at primary school and at an appropriate stage, both genders need to learn how to negotiate consent to any sexual behaviour.
6. There is a simple test that any man should use: if such behaviour were done to a daughter or partner, would it be acceptable? Put yourself in their shoes. Is there also a test of common decency that should cover any activity?
7. Change the language to address the perpetrator rather than to focus on the victim.
8. The workplace language has to be more respectful of anyone, regardless of their race, gender, age or sexual orientation.

SUMMARY AND CONCLUSIONS

- Human groups of all kinds can be seen as organisms that are in constant flux, as individuals and groups respond to the real and perceived challenges they face.
- The informal organisation, arising from the norms, beliefs and values that are shared, can have a powerful influence on the performance of the organisation, whether for good or ill.
- There are many ways in which passive-aggressive behaviour and toxic games can create a poor working climate. Humour can be entertaining, but can easily become subversive and turn to resentment.
- Behavioural norms that are unhelpful can arise when poor behaviour is condoned. Over time, these norms become embedded in the culture and the practices are then followed by others.
- In recent times, sexual misbehaviour has become more reported, especially when power imbalances between the genders have resulted in harassment and assault. Norms have shifted in public discourse against such behaviour.
- The psychological contract is at the heart of the relationship between people and the organisation, and is affected by expectations of what is seen as reasonable by both parties. In times of change, this balance becomes disturbed and can lead to a decline in performance and a toxic culture.

NOTES

1 The author had this experience in Nigeria working in a Western oil company where a junior employee had higher status and received greater deference compared to the manager because he was a chief in a local minor tribe.
2 In the Abilene paradox, a group of people collectively decide on a course of action that is counter to the preferences of many or all of the individuals in the group.

REFERENCES

1 Ackroyd, S. and Thompson, P. (1999) *Organisational misbehaviour.* Sage.
2 Roethlisberger, F.J. and Dickson, W.L. (1964) *Management and the worker.* Harvard University Press.
3 Rock, D. (2007) *Quiet leadership.* HarperCollins.
4 9 toxic behaviors passive-aggressive people share. Retrieved 19 May 2022 from http://blog.baysideonline. com/2017/06/9-toxic-behaviors-passive-aggressive-people-share-and-why-passive-aggression-is-a-spiritual-problem.
5 Ackroyd, S. and Thompson, P. (1999) *Organisational misbehaviour.* Sage.
6 Gladwell, M. (2008) *Tipping point.* Little Brown and Company. See also Gladwell, M. (2008) *Outliers: The story of success.* Penguin.
7 Argyris, C. (1990) *Overcoming organisational defences: Facilitating organisational learning.* Pearson Education.
8 Lencioni, P. (2002) *The five dysfunctions of a team.* Jossey-Bass.
9 Pentland, A. and Curhan, J. (2007) Thin slices of negotiation: Predicting outcomes from conversational dynamics within the first five minutes. *Journal of Applied Psychology, 92,* 802–811.
10 Coyle, D. (2108) *The culture code.* New York: Bantam Books.
11 Blau, P.M. (1977) A macrosociological theory of social structure. *American Journal of Sociology, 83*(1), 26–54
12 Ackroyd, S. and Thompson, P. (1999) *Organisational misbehaviour.* Sage.

13 Roy, D. (1974) Sex in the factory: Informal heterosexual relations between supervisors and workgroups. In Bryant, C.D. (Ed.), *Deviant behaviour*. Rand McNally

14 Gutek, B. (1985) *Sex and the workplace*. Jossey-Bass.

15 Wolf, N. (1993) *Fire with fire: The new female power and how it will change the 21st century*. Chatto & Windus.

16 Jenkins, K. (2020) *Respect at work*. Australian Human Rights Commission. Retrieved 19 May 2021 from https://humanrights.gov.au/our-work/sex-discrimination/publications/respectwork-sexual-harassment-national-inquiry-report.

17 Brown, A.J., Dozo, N. and Roberts, P. (2016) *Whistleblowing processes & procedures: An Australian & New Zealand snapshot. Preliminary results of the Whistling While They Work 2 project*. Griffith University.

CHAPTER 8

Relations with the external environment

INTRODUCTION

In this chapter we examine the interaction of organisations with their environment and external stakeholders. How can external agencies cause the relationship with an organisation to become toxic and vice versa? There are several areas that we will explore here and the sources of toxicity can be classified into three major categories:

1 Unbalanced power relationships.
2 Ill-defined legal and regulatory frameworks.
3 Tragedy of the commons'.

These causes in turn lead to specific undesirable and in some cases illegal activity:

• Bribery to obtain and retain business.
• Compromising values to achieve business or to survive.
• Hiding transactions from legal and tax authorities.
• Bullying suppliers, which in turn becomes the norm internally.

The interface between the organisation and the outside world of different stakeholders – customers, suppliers, regulators, shareholders, voters, etc. - offers choices to the organisation in terms of how they could be conducted. Some activities can be done in-house or contracted out. Sales, accounts, customer service and logistics are all examples of activities which have been managed by independent organisations. Other activities lie at the core of the organisation's mission.

Many activities have a point of contact with the customer at some time, some of which might be overlooked, as in the following case study:

> *A retailer surveyed their customers on its service. The company had just launched a major training programme to improve in-store service, but the survey showed that it was the delivery service and after-sales service (which it had contracted out thinking these were less important) which was letting it down.*

This case suggests that there are many touch points that might influence the outside world's perception and that in organisations where customer service is critical to success, a culture of good service has to run throughout the organisation. The old maxim 'if you don't serve the customer,

DOI: 10.4324/9781003307334-12

you had better serve your internal customer as you would an external customer' illustrates this. It adds a further dimension to selection and training of staff that might be an occasional touch point (like accounts) but doesn't ordinarily get included in customer service training. One retailer shifted its recruitment of store staff towards people who had some experience of the caring professions (health and social service) as these individuals were more inclined by virtue of their personality and earlier career choices to be people-orientated.

Where organisations are heavily embedded in local communities, such as mining or manufacturing, families might be employed, and company relationships are intertwined with external networks of personal relationships. Working culture will be greatly influenced by the history of these relationships, for good or ill. Change might be more difficult where personal relationships outside the workplace could be adversely affected. Even though there may be strong friendship bonds, there is still the expectation that business will be conducted as if those involved were strangers. In many parts of the world, establishing a personal relationship before discussing business is expected. An old Arabic saying suggests that business cannot be discussed 'until the third cup of coffee'.

Strong trade union traditions that were established in earlier times might be more difficult to change in a different world. Corruption and nepotism are more likely in these situations as appointments and business are more prone to be guided by personal relationships.

UNBALANCED POWER RELATIONSHIPS

In Chapter 3 we explored the role that power and, in particular, imbalances play in toxic cultures. The growth of businesses begins to pose dilemmas for governments of all persuasions – whether to impose restrictions on their power to ensure that undue market dominance does not distort the marketplace, or whether to acquiesce to their demands in the light of the employment that they create and the tax revenue they generate. The debate became real when during the global financial crisis, the discussion about whether the banks should be allowed to fail centred on the question of moral hazard: if the banks were to be financially supported, it might encourage undue risk taking in the future. If banks were allowed to fail, then the economy might suffer great damage. Whilst some banks failed (such as Lehman Brothers), the majority were bailed out and the question remains as to whether the banks have truly learnt their lesson or whether similar disasters might occur in the future when the global financial crisis fades into history.

In the public sector, the power imbalance is of a different nature: governments control many levers of power, and citizens, even in a liberal democracy, can only ultimately exercise power at the ballot box periodically. The aged care sector has attracted investors because of the ageing populations in many countries, but there is a key tension between the cost and delivery of care. During the recent COVID-19 pandemic, residents suffered particularly badly with higher death rates in care homes. The 'asymmetric geometry' of power relationships between the government (which provides the money either directly or through commercial providers), the service deliverer, which has to cover its costs and, in some instances, make a profit, the resident, who is usually in no position to challenge the service level, and relatives, who only have tangential power, is a system that does not favour the resident (the ultimate customer). The relative can only complain based on hearsay from the resident, but usually has few choices other than moving the resident to another facility that may not be as convenient.

A typical scenario goes like this:

Mary is increasingly concerned about her elderly mother, who is showing signs of dementia and has recently had several falls in her home. Mary has two school-age children, is divorced and works full time. Her life is a constant juggling of responsibilities. She believes that her mother should come and live with her, as her grandmother did whilst she was growing up. But she has no space for a granny flat and could not cope with an additional person to look after. Reluctantly she looks for a home and is shocked at the cost. Eventually she finds somewhere, but her mother's room is small, and she is concerned by the smells and cleanliness of the place. A few months later, on visiting, she notices some bruises on her mother's arm. Her mother never seems to have any money, even though Mary ensures she has a little money for toiletries, etc. She never sees the same staff twice as they are casual staff and work across multiple jobs.

COVID-19 strikes and despite some precautions being taken, many residents become ill and die. Her mother (just) survives and Mary wonders what to do next.

This is not an uncommon scenario (Australia recently had a Royal Commission into the aged care sector, which exposed many of the bad practices that had flourished).

At the root of the problem is a business model that sees this as like any other service industry from which a profit can be made (or, when state-run, where costs can be minimised). However, decision makers like Mary are often desperate to find somewhere and are faced with limited choice in terms of what is close enough to visit. The resident (Mary's mother), who has little agency in the situation, is in no position to demand another home. The casual staff are often low-paid and working shifts, so build up no relationship with the residents and have little emotional connection with them. This is in contrast to some full-time staff, who are dedicated and well trained, but the financial model does not allow for these staff to be the sole complement.

COVID-19 has shown that casual staff moving from job to job are prime carriers of the virus - and, of course, once they have caught it, infect other workplaces and their families.

The Royal Commission has recommended minimum staffing levels to ensure adequate time for each resident, training to increase levels of skill, a registered nurse on-site and better oversight. This all costs money and it remains to be seen whether this power imbalance might be alleviated by money alone. The history of Royal Commission findings being implemented is not encouraging.

In the three case studies given at the end of this chapter, there are examples of unbalanced power relationships. In the case of Crown Resorts, the regulators were unable to operate successfully because they had been 'leaned on'. In the case of the American healthcare industries, patients have little opportunity to shop around for care as the health insurers have their preferred suppliers and in some cases the patient does not know the cost until the bill is presented to them. In the case of Boeing, the nature of the industry means that buyers caused the company to take action that in the end was disastrous, and a regulatory agency that could have been a countervailing force was not totally independent.

ILL-DEFINED LEGAL AND REGULATORY FRAMEWORKS

The lack of clear rules in aged care on staffing and qualifications is one example of where a relaxed approach leads to major harm. Another lies in current Australian competition laws. The

Competition & Consumer Commission has no jurisdiction over monopoly ports such as Newcastle, which is controlled by China. This creates a potential stranglehold on the coal export business for both profit and political reasons.

An opposite problem occurs in the USA, where under the Administrative Procedure Act (APA), which was enacted in 1946, Congress allowed agencies to fill in the gaps caused by vaguely worded laws when deciding how they should be implemented. Today, the vast majority of laws governing the USA are not passed by Congress, but are issued as regulations. One study found that in 2007, Congress enacted 138 public laws, while federal agencies finalised 2,926 rules, bodies that had little or no public oversight (1).

In an age of spin and fake news, it is to be expected that corporate communications will never tell the unvarnished truth (though what is truth?). Instead, the PR spin will be at the forefront and will have plenty of incentive to hide bad news. Transparency is a major contributor to cleaning up toxic cultures. However, when individuals have proven to be doing wrong, the incentive is to let them go quietly in case the media assume that it shows a weakness in the business and might encourage others to have a go. Transparency International is an organisation whose purpose is to hold governments and agencies of all kinds to account (2).

A recent debate has emerged as a result of the move by corporations to espouse social concerns from equality and race relations and to embrace activist movements such as 'Me Too' and 'Black Lives Matter'. Some argue that there has always been an implied social contract; in return for limited liability, corporations are expected to be socially responsible. Others argue (3) that corporations are using their power for their own ends, and such matters of social values and polices should be debated in the public sphere. Clearly, where rich and powerful corporations are misusing their power and resources to support some causes that they prefer and not others, there is a layer of distortion which undermines the traditional democratic process.

TRAGEDY OF THE COMMONS[1]

In market economies the role of self-interest, as was first shown by Adam Smith, is seen as fundamental to the dynamics of making markets work efficiently. Whilst we have described the causes of toxic cultures in terms of individual bad behaviour arising from narcissism and psychopathy, it can also arise from purely rational behaviour to pursue individual interests. In Wall Street the 'remorseless logic of predatory trading' (4), whereby investors in distress are pursued for profit, is well known and is accepted as the norm for that marketplace, where *caveat emptor* is the rule.

Untrammelled self-interest leads to the 'tragedy of the commons', which is not unlike what occurs in organisations when some toxic event may have triggered a series of actions that ultimately result in a dysfunctional organisation. Jared Diamond (5) describes self-absorbed leaders who seek power or wealth that led to toxic cultures. Enron executives pursued money in a very rational way. Easter Islanders cut down trees to enable the moving of large statues and trojans opened the gates to introduce a horse to Troy. These short-term decisions that are perfectly rational and reasonable in the circumstances ultimately led to disaster. Indeed, many acts of war may seem rational to the aggressor, but as the result of the First and Second World Wars has shown, they led to disaster for Germany and Japan.

A recent example is the case of the Dead Sea in Israel, which is shrinking, causing considerable environmental damage. The cause is the extraction of water for industry and agriculture further north; each industry is acting in its own self-interest, but collectively they are causing harm downstream for which they have no concern or accountability.

THE RESULTING UNDESIRABLE ACTIVITIES

Bribery

Between the 1950s and 1970s in the USA, a bribery scandal erupted concerning the Lockheed aircraft company. Company officials bribed people with influence in order to win aircraft orders. The legacy of this was the Foreign Corrupt Practices Act and the requirement of executives in American companies round the world to sign a declaration each year that they had not received gifts of more than a few dollars. Such events have been replicated in many territories. In the UK there was a similar scandal with BAE Systems. Bribery can appear in many forms and under many euphemisms. Amongst intermediaries in commercial transactions, commissions, payments for introductions, administrative charges, legal services or even gifts are all common. These may well be legitimate in many cases, but it is a fine line.

Compromising values to achieve business or to survive

The dilemma for many organisations doing business in some parts of the world – the Middle East and Africa in particular – is that if bribes are not paid, then the business is not obtained, as there will be other less scrupulous companies and countries that would pay the bribes in order to get the business. Recently, there has been exposure of the abuses suffered by the Uighurs in Xinjiang. The undercover BBC film and the recent leak of Chinese Communist Party documents to the *New York Times* revealed that a million Muslim minorities are now detained in a Chinese operation that uses forced labour in 're-education' camps. We see alternative responses to this revelation. The H&M and Nike companies have criticised this and have stopped sourcing their products, particularly those made with cotton grown there. They have suffered some reprisals in China. On the other hand, it has been reported in the press (6) that Apple suppliers have used forced labour in China. Apple has denied this assertion.

Tax

Avoiding tax, a legal activity, as opposed to evading it has been going on for as long as societies have sought to tax its citizens. Much effort is expended by citizens and companies to minimise their tax bill. National institutions have a fundamental role in maintaining an ethical culture in a nation and none more so than the tax authorities. Not only do they have to be scrupulously fair, following the letter of the law and measured in any interpretation of legislation, but they also have to be seen to be acting in that way.

A recent case study concerns the tax authorities in Australia:

Mr Boyle became an internal whistleblower in 2017 when he made a disclosure under the provisions of the Public Interest Disclosure (PID) Act 2013 to the Australian Tax Office (ATO). His allegations were investigated by a senior ATO investigator and dismissed.

He alleged that some ATO staff were instructed to use an aggressive debt collection practice known as garnishee notices, which allows the ATO to seize funds from the bank accounts of Australian taxpayers without notice or consideration of their circumstances.

> *The ATO offered him a settlement over an alleged breach of the Public Service Code of Conduct, offering him a payout and a statement of service, with no admission of liability, on the proviso that he signed a gag order. He declined and went public in a joint media investigation with the ABC. His home in Edwardstown (south-west of Adelaide) was raided and his laptop and phone were seized. At the time, the ATO said protecting taxpayer confidentiality was critical for the integrity of Australia's tax and super systems. 'From the raid, I have been in a state of anxiety wondering what was going to come next', he said. But he said if people did not speak up, 'how are we going to change things?'*

Subsequently, the ATO, in what some have described as a highly cynical move, launched a new policy: 'From 1 July 2019, individuals are now better protected under the law when they disclose tax avoidance behaviour and other tax issues to us about an entity (including an individual) they are, or have been, in a relationship with.' Despite this policy, the ATO is still pursuing a legal case against Mr Boyle. Regardless of the precise legalities, the credibility of the ATO as a trustworthy public institution has been severely dented (7).

Hiding transactions from legal and tax authorities

When EMI, a music company, was acquired by an investment company, an early exercise was to go through the books to carefully consider all the costs. One item was labelled 'fruit and flowers', which seemed an odd category, especially when it ran into a considerable sum. This turned out to be a slush fund for the senior managers to have a good time – 'wine, women and song', as one insider described it. By way of contrast, Black+Decker, an American tool company, had strict ethical standards. In Italy in the post-war period, corruption and tax evasion flourished, and companies had two sets of books: one for the tax authorities and one for their own reckoning. Black+Decker only had one set of books, which the tax authorities did not believe that was the case, and invariably when they investigated, they demanded to see the 'real books'.

As a result of modern technology (such as big data and AI), the chance of getting caught has increased, causing a subsequent increase in even more elaborate schemes to hide transactions. Regardless of whether these are successful or not, the consequence is to corrupt the organisation by drawing more people into the web of deceit. The case of Volkswagen and what became known as 'Dieselgate' is a case in point, where an overarching drive to sell diesel cars led to software being altered to hide excess emissions when testing was undertaken by the regulatory authorities. The cost to the company's sales and reputation was estimated at $30 billion (8).

Bullying suppliers, which in turn becomes the norm internally

Tough negotiations with suppliers are part and parcel of commercial life. However, when there is a power imbalance and bullying occurs, several consequences occur. The first is that the pool of suppliers might diminish, shifting power back to the supplier, but a persistent power imbalance also breeds a certain arrogance and sense of superiority. This in turn can result in the same attitudes pervading internal transactions. In one example, an airline purchasing group set out to tighten suppliers' contracts:

> *The success of the group led to it gaining considerable prestige. This showed if you wanted something from a supplier or another department, you had to use rough tactics. Over time, relations between departments suffered, as they took the lead from purchasing. Departments which relied on each other and hitherto had more informal relations now became more formal, and flexibility suffered. One tactic used by the purchasing department internally was to limit specifications to the bare minimum and demanding cost-benefit justification for anything over and above this. Some products and services that the airline required were more intangible – speed of response, flexibility, and quality of service – and these didn't figure in the purchasing department's assessment, so suppliers who offered these were ruled out. Rather than using the purchasing department, other departments in the airline began to purchase items outside, limiting the opportunity for better deals for the company.*

Human differences, racism and gender

Our views about those who are different were often formed in our early years from parents and family. They were absorbed at a time when we had undeveloped critical faculties to determine the rights and wrongs of such labelling. So, these attitudes become hard-wired and difficult to shift later in life. When groups and organisations, especially those with strong in-group solidarity, see those outside as something different, prejudice can arise. This is further exacerbated when these differences relate to race and colour.

In 1987-1991, a Royal Commission in Australia examined the causes of excessive deaths in custody of Indigenous people – particularly young men (9). In 2020 the killing of George Floyd in the USA by a policeman sparked riots across the world and forced into public consciousness the #blacklivesmatter hashtag, which had been coined in 2013. Whilst nothing can excuse the excessive use of force by any policemen, when faced with a threat, even the best-trained officer will on occasion react unpredictably. The police are expected to act in a calm and professional manner regardless of provocation, and this is the standard to which they should be held accountable. The challenge for all police forces is to use the minimum of force to uphold the law and when on those occasions human failings of prejudice, stress and resentment cause excessive force, lessons are learnt and behaviour is improved. The police may on occasions be the instrument through which unpopular policies are implemented. In South Africa, separate development (apartheid) grew out of a desire to protect white supremacy, but also recognising that different cultures may need to pursue different paths to achieve their fulfilment. This became the justification for apartheid and suppression.

So where does racial discrimination come from and how does it become so embedded in an organisation's culture that it becomes acceptable?

In many countries there have been laws against discrimination for some years on various grounds - race, gender, sexual orientation, faith, etc. Yet many who are not white still suffer discrimination and in an institutional form. It is normal to want to spend time with people who have the same interests, background, culture and language. It creates a sense of belonging that is important. The downside is that it can also set up differences between other groups and, over time, this might lead to thinking that one group is better than others. Discrimination in all its forms has deep psychological roots. The scanning for threat is a continuing necessary process that emanates in the amygdala and is particularly aroused when noticing difference.

Differences of whatever form excite a range of emotions: curiosity, horror, fear and rejection. The body reacts by increased vigilance and there is often a release of adrenaline if there is any hint of danger. The reaction is solidified when evidence from elsewhere such as the media or our prior experience enters our consciousness. When we are uncertain about this difference, we rely upon prior knowledge to inform our opinion, which in turn becomes a filter through which we view events.

Early explorers and colonialists in Africa and Australia encountered people that they saw and labelled as primitive, because of dress and customs. In the 19th century, Europe was advanced technologically, and this was another reason why the 'natives' were labelled as 'backward'. As we now know, Indigenous people in Australia were sophisticated, with extraordinarily complex social structures across the many nations, and survival skills in harsh environments far in excess of those of Westerners. Race, skin colour and culture are frequently assumed to be one and the same, yet many people of colour born and raised in white societies have adopted the culture of their home. Nevertheless, their skin colour still forms the basis of discrimination because of centuries of historical attribution that black equals 'backward'.

Fear is a powerful force in people's lives because it limits our capacity and willingness to explore the world. Universities have traditionally aspired to be places where there is the opportunity to express and debate views and ideas that are controversial without fear or favour. Freedom of expression in academia has always been highly prized. But a new battleground is emerging between those who champion the right of free expression (at the extreme, without consideration of the impact on others) and those who are championing respect and consideration of the impact on others as a more important responsibility. This conflict is played out in many aspects of cultural life – politics, religion, gender relations (10) and several academic disciplines – and has found its ways into the lexicon with terms such as 'cancel culture' and 'wokeism'. Fear of engaging in the controversy has the potential to stifle debate and cause a conformity to certain norms defined at the time by dominant voices. Organisations, particularly universities that cause such a limiting of views, are potentially going to suffer in terms of their ability to take on board new ideas and to prompt innovation. Yet there is a pressing need to find ways of reconciling these views in a world where respect for those who are different is fundamental to a harmonious society.

THREE CASE STUDIES

The emergence of toxic organisations and indeed industries has much to do with their interaction with their environment. The following case studies of Crown Resorts, the US health industry and Boeing illustrate the major points in this chapter:

- Unbalanced power relationships (all three).
- Ill-defined legal and regulatory frameworks (Crown Resorts and Boeing).
- Tragedy of the commons' (the US health industry),
- Bribery to obtain and retain business (Crown Resorts).
- Compromising values to achieve business or to survive (Boeing).
- Hiding transactions from legal and tax authorities (Crown Resorts).
- Bullying suppliers that in turn becomes the norm internally (the US health industry).

Case study 1: Crown Resorts (11)

A recent corporate fall from grace is Crown Resorts, the gambling and leisure company controlled until recently by billionaire James Packer. The trigger was the denial of a gambling licence for the company's new $2.2 billion complex at Barangaroo on Sydney Harbour. In the report by the special inquiry by Patricia Bergin, a former NSW Supreme Court judge, into Crown's casino business, she found that the company – through its subsidiary Crown Sydney Gaming – was not suitable to hold the licence for the second Sydney casino.

The inquiry was set up on the back of reports by the press (*The Age, Sydney Morning Herald* and *60 Minutes*), which raised allegations that Crown 'breached gambling laws'. The investigations also claimed that Crown had links with drug traffickers, money launderers through shell accounts linked to its Perth and Melbourne casinos, and human traffickers. The investigation alleged that they disregarded the welfare of its China-based staff who were arrested in 2016 for contravening China's laws on gambling. In her final report, Ms Bergin described Crown's slow and grudging response to the allegations – some of which were discussed internally six years ago - as 'corporate arrogance'.

It emerged that a combination of factors had led to this outcome. Gambling has always been an industry that has been on the edge of illegal behaviour. The nature of gambling, the large sums of money involved and its proneness to compulsive behaviour have led to exploitation of gamblers in various ways. Even though it is well known that the odds of winning are low and the probability is always stacked in favour of the house, people persist in the belief that one day they will strike it lucky. Gambling has also attracted large cash flows, often gained from illegal activities such as drug dealing and organised crime, including protection money and money laundering.

In the case of James Packer (who was described as 'deeply flawed' and whose influence had 'disastrous consequences' by distorting proper corporate governance) his diagnosis of bipolar disorder affected his performance. Managers at Crown claimed that Packer created a culture of avoiding bad news, resulting in managers not telling him what was going on. This climate of secrecy facilitated shady transactions, and management was unresponsive to calls for change to tighten controls on illegal activities. When the rewards from gambling are so good, there is little incentive to change and a 'greed is good' culture prevailed. Success, as we have mentioned, before breeds arrogance and a belief that others do not really understand their business, let alone how to make such profits – so, these 'amateurs' should be disregarded.

Crown's Board, particularly under its previous chairman, showed loyalty to the Packer family and thus was reluctant to challenge any cultural practices. The chairman was 'either blind to the reality or lacking in candour' in confronting serious problems such as 'infiltration of criminal elements'. The lack of proper oversight and approval processes led the organisation to become compromised. The chief executive also came in for heavy criticism (being described as 'unimpressive' in the Bergin report) when it was apparent that he was ignorant of the money laundering and did nothing about it when he did find out, implying that he was not up to the job of dealing with such a culture, let alone changing it. The regulatory agency did not have the power or backing to challenge these practices.

A further issue is the involvement of the state; the licence for Crown was granted following a meeting between Barry O'Farrell, the state premier at the time, and James Packer in 2012, with no tendering process. The state is interested in gambling for the revenue it generates and the employment it offers, but avoiding public tendering processes creates further opportunities for, at best, rules to be bent and, at worst, further corruption.

So, we have an example of a culture particularly prone to being subverted for criminal purposes and run by individuals who were both flawed and incapable of running a legal and ethical operation, especially one where processes had been compromised and where reporting of problems did not surface. 'The culture that allowed it to be blind to the risks of money laundering and the infiltration of organised crime appears embedded in its DNA' (12).

Cleaning up Crown: making improvements

In the wake of the report, Crown's board resigned (some reluctantly), which provided the opportunity to rebuild the working culture, though merely changing the top team is only the start of that process as it is likely that there will be many processes and practices that will need to change. A start has been made by recruiting a former police chief to tighten controls on money laundering and counter terrorism funding and to improve staff training. The company has terminated agreements with junket operators who have alleged links to organised crime. Careful vetting of key staff and their subsequent oversight will be crucial to rebuilding confidence in a defence against crime.

A useful example here is Singapore, which correctly perceived the need for tight control if organised crime were to be prevented from moving in on gambling operations. By focusing on gambling as part of integrated resorts, the aim is to position gambling as one of a number of entertainment options at the resort, rather than gambling being the sole purpose of the visit. These resorts operate with annual entry fees and external oversight that has considerable powers. The regulatory authority focuses only on casinos funded by industry levies, and vets employees and processes to ensure their integrity. It is free to act and investigate at any time and its tough prescriptive approach, especially towards junket operators, has kept crime to a minimum.

Case study 2: the US health industry (13)

An industry that has acquired considerable opprobrium is healthcare in America. Marty Makry, a surgeon at the Johns Hopkins Hospital in Baltimore, began to research the state of healthcare and, in particular, its costs. What he found were shocking examples of where vulnerable people were being grossly exploited due to huge medical bills. In his book *The price we pay*, he documents dozens of examples of where money has created a system that whilst on the surface delivers a quality service to the patient, in reality creates a huge industry for companies and middlemen to make a fortune. He details a number of practices:

- Delivering tests and procedures which at best are unnecessary, but at worst might lay the patient open to some risk. 'Predatory screening' is apparent in testing for peripheral vascular disease, a condition that rarely requires a surgical procedure. He suggests that '21% of procedures are unnecessary'.
- The 'mark-up and discount game'. Medical bills for the same procedure vary widely between providers. There is a large mark-up that is then discounted following negotiations, creating the illusion that the patient has got a good deal. Insurers also negotiate big discounts with providers, ensuring their profits increase, but leaving the patient with a large deductible.
- Secrecy is so important to this practice that California has passed a law banning insurers from bullying hospitals that disclose prices. These practices fall heavily on the low paid, for whom medical bills are a big expense. A study by the Kaiser Family Foundation found that 70% of Americans are cutting back on the basics to pay for medical bills.

Other practices

- Patients who need an air ambulance are usually in no position to argue, let alone shop around, and are billed separately, but are subject to 'out of network price gouging'. Medical staff are incentivised by the helicopter companies to put business their way.
- More caesarean section births are conducted than are necessary in order to avoid medical staff being called out of hours.
- The insistence of insurance companies on using a certain provider. In one case the inferior treatment of a woman led to complications and the procedure had to be redone by a more competent specialist.
- Pharmacy benefit managers (PBMs) have an incentive to favour high-priced drugs over drugs that are more cost-effective, because they often receive rebates that are calculated as a percentage of the manufacturer's list price. As such, they make money from the spread between what is paid to a pharmacy and what is charged to an employer.

Reforming the system

Medicine in America is highly political, as the battles over the Affordable Care Act showed. Makry argues (14) that several ingredients are required to improve the system regardless of the politics:

- Data disaggregated in order to establish patterns and comparisons between different physicians' practice in doing the same procedures.
- Data to identify the rogue employer and peer benchmarking with usable data to create a culture of accountability.
- Designing charge programmes that involve people and using peer-to-peer data sharing which encourages a desire to do the right thing.
- Breaking up procedures to itemise billing and instituting transparency on pricing.

Case study 3: the Boeing 737 MAX story (15)

In 2018 and 2019, two Boeing aircraft crashed[2] involving two different airlines and a new aircraft: the 737 MAX. Amongst the reports and investigations, several issues emerged relating to the relationship between the company and the Federal Aviation Administration (FAA), the relationship with customers, a culture which did not take notice of employees' safety concerns and the assumptions made about the changing skills of their customers.

The background to the decision to develop the 737 MAX

W. James McNerney, Jr., Boeing's CEO at the time, received a call from American Airlines' chief executive, Gerard Arpey. Arpey reportedly said that his airline was close to a deal for hundreds of Airbus narrow-body aircraft, warning that Boeing had to be more aggressive and timelier in order to win its business. Until that point, American Airlines had exclusively purchased from Boeing for more than a decade. Desperate to win the order, Boeing ditched the idea of designing a whole new plane — which could take up to ten years to get in the air — and instead pivoted to placing new engines on the 737 to create another new generation. It took a few months to finalise the design, but it wasn't quite fast enough to prevent American Airlines from ordering 130 A320 Neo jets. It also said that it would order 100 of Boeing's new 737s when it was ready.

The advantage to airlines was that the 737 MAX retained a great degree of commonality with its predecessors, meaning that one pool of pilots and ground staff could work on both planes, with some supplementary training, rather than having to be certified on a new aircraft type. Pilots were ultimately only required to take a brief tablet-based course rather than new training in a simulator.

The assumptions

The engines on the 737 MAX were larger, positioned further forward and higher up on the wing than the engines on the earlier 737. This caused the plane to behave differently. To compensate for that, Boeing designed automated software called the Manoeuvring Control Augmentation System (MCAS), which would automatically activate to stabilise the pitch and nudge the aircraft's nose back down 'so that it feels and flies like other 737s', which have been flying for many years. Notably, however, Boeing did not include training on MCAS in the pilots' manual, reasoning that the software would work in the background.

In a private meeting with the pilots' union of American Airlines that was secretly recorded by the union's president, Boeing said it had decided not to reveal the existence of the MCAS in the 737 MAX flight manual on the grounds that it didn't want to inundate pilots with unnecessary information. 'That enraged us', Captain Tajer said. 'Boeing always gives you the information, they don't parcel it out.' Investigators were surprised to learn that Boeing had installed a flight control software program that could force the plane into a dive without the pilots' knowledge.

Crucially, the MCAS was designed to take effect when just a single sensor showed that the angle of attack was high. This meant that if one of the two sensors was damaged or faulty, it could activate. The MCAS was accidentally triggered on both Lion Air flights because a defective angle of attack (AOA) sensor had transmitted incorrect information about the position of the plane's nose. Although there are two AOA sensors on the 737 MAX, the MCAS was only connected to one of them. 'It's a lack of redundancy that appears to me to be unacceptable in airplane design', said aviation journalist Christine Negroni, author of the book *The Crash Detectives*.

Following the two crashes in 2019, regulators around the world grounded their 737 MAX planes on 11 March. The US FAA was a lone holdout, initially reaffirming that the plane was airworthy. However, the agency followed its international counterparts and ordered the plane grounded on 13 March. Meanwhile, numerous investigations and lawsuits began, exploring how Boeing allowed it to be possible for the MCAS to activate from a single faulty sensor reading and how the FAA didn't catch the potential flaw.

Cultural indicators

In the hearing on Capitol Hill about the plane's certification, it was revealed that an internal FAA analysis showed a high likelihood of future crashes - as many as 15 over the 30–40 year life of the jet. However, the FAA let the plane keep flying. Boeing's critics said this was evidence of a systemic problem with both the company culture and the plane, and a consequence of the FAA delegating oversight.

'This aeroplane is designed by clowns who in turn are supervised by monkeys', one employee wrote, while another noted in 2018 that 'I still haven't been forgiven by God for the covering up I did last year'. Meanwhile, foreign object debris was found in stored 737 MAX planes, indicating a major quality control problem. The investigation uncovered internal Boeing emails that showed some employees had raised concerns about the 737 MAX while it was still in development and that they had questioned the safety culture of the company as well. A recent film (16) pointed to a change in culture when Boeing and McDonnell Douglas merged, with the latter being more focused on cost-cutting.

The aftermath

Over 100 victims' families filed a lawsuit against Boeing, alleging that the 737 MAX had a defective design and that Boeing issued an inadequate warning about the aircraft. Boeing denied the allegations. The FAA was forced to retreat from its initial defence of the plane, and Boeing had to accept a public onslaught, including congressional hearings, federal investigations, calls for the criminal prosecution of Boeing executives, revelations by whistleblowers, attacks in the news media, the exploitation of personal tragedy and perceptions of the company's liability. 'This is going to go down as one of the most callous, deliberate efforts to keep a product in the public domain for the wrong reasons', said Robert Clifford, of Clifford Law Offices, who is one of the attorneys suing Boeing.

In its final report, released in September 2020, an investigation by the House of Representatives concluded that Boeing had placed the safety of the flying public in jeopardy for competitive reasons.

Airline and pilot problems

After the loss of Lion Air 610, the company suggested that the 737 MAX was as safe as its predecessors. The company seemed hesitant to point the finger at a prickly customer, Lion Air, which had several billion dollars' worth of orders on the table and could withdraw them at any time. The dilemma is familiar to manufacturers after major accidents in which it is usually a pilot and not an plane that has been the cause. Nonetheless, Boeing's reticence allowed a narrative to emerge that the company had developed the system to elude regulators, that it was all about shortcuts and greed, that it had cynically gambled with the lives of the flying public, that the Lion Air pilots were overwhelmed by the failures of a hidden system they could not reasonably have been expected to resist, and that the design of the MCAS was unquestionably the cause of the accident. But none of this was quite true. The rush to lay blame was based in part on a poor understanding not just of the technicalities, but also of Boeing's commercial aviation culture. The MAX's creation took place in suburban Seattle among engineers and pilots of integrity, including supervising officials from the FAA. Although Boeing's designers were aware of timetables and competitive pressures, the mistakes they made were not a result of an intentional sacrifice of safety for gain. As always, there was a problem with like-mindedness (groupthink) and a reluctance by team players to stand out from the crowd. Even more pernicious was the FAA's longstanding delegation of regulatory authority to Boeing employees, which may indeed have been related to the configuration of the troublesome system as it was installed. Nevertheless, there was no implication of systematic corruption.

Boeing had a history of working with airlines in developing countries, notably China, and ten years ago when it decided to intervene with Lion Air. Despite the efforts of Boeing, it was not good enough and Lion Air continued to suffer crashes. The Indonesian authorities lacked the political will to prevent this and it is no secret that Rusdi Kirana, co-founder of Lion Air, prioritised efficiency over regulation. Recently he made it clear that he also resented Boeing for being presumptuous and typically condescending: 'They look down on my airline and my country', he told *Reuters*. 'They treat us as third-world' (17)

Boeing had a philosophy of relying on pilots' skills and experience as aviators inherited from the days of mechanical failures and needing pilots to think on the spot. As more automation came into the cockpit, newer pilots flew by the checklist and did not necessarily have the experienced airmanship to intervene when things did go wrong. In the face of these changes, Boeing clung resolutely to its pilot-centric designs, but in Toulouse, Airbus decided to take on Boeing by creating a robotic new plane that would address the accelerating decline in airmanship and require minimal piloting skills largely by using digital flight controls to reduce pilot workload, iron out undesirable handling characteristics and build in pilot-proof protections against errors like aerodynamic stalls, excessive banks and spiral dives.

Summary of the key points

- There was a hurry to introduce an aircraft to compete with the Airbus A320 Neo which Boeing's major customer American Airlines had ordered. This resulted in the decision to update the 737, which for many years had been a highly successful aircraft. The advantage lay in not requiring a whole new certification, savings in pilot training and simulations, and speed of development.
- Assumptions were made about how pilots would react if a new piece of technology called the MCAS failed. This proved to be wrong in the case of inexperienced pilots learning about it from a tablet. The interaction of different cultures led to wrong assumptions on all sides.
- Several failings, largely drawn from internal emails, indicated a culture of downplaying engineering in the interests of speed. Some have also argued that the pressure from Wall Street for dividends placed an emphasis on cost-cutting and cutting corners. Investigations took place that in turn revealed a series of changes in the way of operating that moved the fine balance from safety and engineering being dominant towards financial performance. The independence of the FAA was potentially compromised by the delegation of its duties and authorities to Boeing staff.
- Whilst the focus was on Boeing, the two airlines also came in for criticism over their pilot training practices and pilots' inabilities to go beyond the checklist learnt by rote, towards 'airmanship' and the capacity to think in a crisis beyond the standard routines. The wider issue is raised of human vigilance and the ability to override increasingly sophisticated and complex technology when human intervention is required. This is an issue that will become critical in the future on the subject of driverless cars.

POWER MAP

In Chapter 3 we suggested that a map of power relationships was a useful way of summarising the power imbalances that lead to toxic cultures. Using Tang's two axes – influence (most to least) and support (support to oppose), we can apply an analysis that summarises and illuminates these three cases and the role that power imbalances played in their cultural evolution.

In Figure 8.1, the apparent power/influence imbalance is plain. Those sources of power that might be expected to maintain standards: FAA for Boeing with safety, ILGA for Crown Resorts with probity, and patients in getting choice of practitioner at a fair price in US healthcare, all had low influence compared to the power of managers and corporate customers. American airlines who wanted a new airplane from Boeing, the NSW government, which wanted revenue and jobs

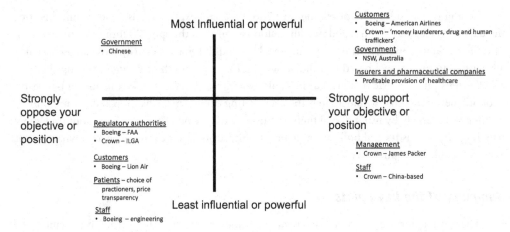

FIGURE 8.1 Power map summary of key drivers in the above cases

from Crown, and insurers and pharmaceutical companies, which wanted a profitable business all had greater power. In the case of Lion Air, Boeing's influence was comparatively weak and was insufficient to ensure adequate pilot competence. The Chinese government exerted their power by expelling Crown staff from China, but this was insufficient to prompt cultural change.

SUMMARY AND CONCLUSIONS

- Organisations of all kinds have choices about how they manage their services, whether in-house or contracted out. There are many touch points with the outside world and each of these has the potential to be managed well or the source of conflict and corruption.
- Stressful situations are liable to bring out hidden biases and prejudices, in particular about race and gender. They have the potential for exacerbating relations with stakeholders of all kinds.
- In market economies, there will always be the need for some supervisory body and legislation to deal with power imbalances that distort relationships and encourage abuse. Ill-defined legal and regulatory frameworks drive debate about the degree and extent of control.
- Transparency and protection for those who expose abuse should be enhanced.
- The unintended consequences of action taken without fully understanding the ramifications, known as the tragedy of the commons, is always likely in complex and fast-changing situations.
- In a mixed economy there is constant debate about where national services should be located and funded.
- Human desires, especially for wealth, influence and control, and the avoidance of things we fear will often override the most well-intentioned values, leading to:
  o   bribery to obtain and retain business;
  o   compromising values to achieve business or to survive;
  o   hiding transactions from legal and tax authorities.
- The role of commissions and kickbacks in industries which rely on intermediaries is especially prone to bad practices. In situations where clients are hoping for best advice, but the intermediary is tempted by what pays best commission, there is an inevitable conflict of interest.
- A power map is a useful way of explaining the causes of the culture that emerges in the three cases in this chapter.

NOTES

1 The 'tragedy of the commons' refers to how self-interest can cause greater hardship than collaboration. The concept originated in an essay written in 1833 by the British economist William Forster
Lloyd, who used a hypothetical example of the effects of unregulated grazing on common land.

2 Lion Air Flight 610 from Jakarta on 29 October 2018 and the Ethiopian Airlines Flight 302 from Addis
Ababa on 10 March 2019,

REFERENCES

1 Turley, J. (2013, 24 May) The rise of the fourth branch of government. *Washington Post*. Retrieved
9 June 2022 from https://www.washingtonpost.com/opinions/the-rise-of-the-fourth-branch-of-
government/2013/05/24/c7faaad0-c2ed-11e2-9fe2-6ee52d0eb7c1_story.html.

2 https://www.transparency.org/en.

3 Ramaswamy, V. (2021) *Woke Inc. Inside the social justice scam*. Swift.

4 Why the Wall Street bets crowd are able to profit from predatory trading. *The Economist* (4 February 2021).

5 Diamond, J. (2011) *Collapse*. Penguin.

6 Canales, K. (2021, 10 May) 7 Apple suppliers in China have links to forced labor programs, including the use of Uyghur Muslims from Xinjiang, according to a new report. *Business Insider*. Retrieved
22 May 2022 from https://www.businessinsider.com/apple-china-suppliers-uyghur-muslims-forced-
labor-report-2021-5?r=US&IR=T.

7 Khadem, N. (2021, 29 April) Prosecutors proceed with case against ATO whistle-blower Richard Boyle. *ABC News*. Retrieved 22 May 2022 from https://www.abc.net.au/news/2021-04-29/
prosecutors-proceed-case-against-ato-whistleblower-richard-boyle/100105710.

8 Coldwell, D.A.L. (2021) Toxic behaviour in organisations and organisational entropy: A 4th Industrial
Revolution phenomenon? *SN Business Economics*, 1(5), 1-7.

9 Australian Human Rights Commission (2020) *Royal Commission into Aboriginal Deaths in Custody*. Retrieved
22 May 2022 from https://humanrights.gov.au/our-work/indigenous-deaths-custody-chapter-3-
comparison-indigenous-and-non-indigenous-deaths.

10 Watson, S. (2021, 5 June) A backlash against gender ideology is starting in universities. *The Economist*.

11 The sources of this case study are the press reports principally on ABC Television in programmes such as
Four corners, in *Guardian Australia* and the *Sydney Morning Herald* in February 2021.

12 Knight, E. (2021, 13 December) A 'reformed' Crown bets big on a Sydney revival. Retrieved 9 June 2022
from https://www.smh.com.au/business/companies/a-reformed-crown-bets-big-on-a-sydney-revival-
20211213-p59h2h.html.

13 I consulted a number of sources for this case, including Makary, M. (2019) *The price we pay*. Bloomsbury;
Why the US healthcare system is failing, and what might rescue it. NCBI Bookshelf (2020). Retrieved
22 May 2022 from https://www.ncbi.nlm.nih.gov/books/NBK61963.

14 Makary, M. (2019) *The price we pay*. Bloomsbury.

15 I have used a number of sources for this case, including Robinson, P. (2021) *Flying blind: The 737 MAX
tragedy and the fall of Boeing*. Doubleday; Negroni, C. (2016) *The crash detectives: Investigating the world's most
mysterious air disasters*. Penguin; Slotnick, D. (2020, 29 October) The first Boeing 737 Max crash was 2
years ago today. *Business Insider*. Retrieved 9 June 2022 from https://www.businessinsider.com/boeing-
737-max-timeline-history-full-details-2019-9?r=US&IR=T; Langewiesche, W. (2019, 18 September)
What really brought down the Boeing 737 Max? *New York Times*.

16 *Downfall: The case against Boeing*. Netflix (2022).

17 Rusdi Kirana, Lion Air co-founder: Boeing sees me as its piggy bank. *Reuters* (16 April 2019).
Retrieved 22 May 2022 from https://www.ndtv.com/world-news/rusdi-kirana-lion-air-co-founder-
boeing-sees-me-as-its-piggy-bank-2023633.

Part D
The individual

CHAPTER 9

Motivation and communication

INTRODUCTION

An early sign of a toxic culture is low motivation with employees 'going through the motions' rather than being keen to achieve organisational and maybe personal goals. The consequence is that the organisation does not achieve its maximum potential, and forward momentum is lacking. In this chapter we explore the role that motivation and communications play in both enhancing and debilitating culture. The effect on motivation of an array of approaches from fear and punishment to encouragement and a sense of achievement when coupled with different methods of reward lies at the heart of performance management. The product of this mix defines the difference between organisations bursting with energy and creativity, and those toxic cultures we dread. We will cover the subject of reward in the next chapter.

MOTIVATION

One of the earliest theories of motivation was described by Maslow in 1943, who suggested five levels. Later, in 1959, Herzberg proposed a two-factor model and McClelland outlined his two-factor needs and achievement model in 1961.

To bring Maslow's need hierarchy theory of motivation into synchronisation with empirical research, Clayton Alderfer described the ERG theory of motivation. He recategorised Maslow's hierarchy of needs into three simpler and broader classes of needs:

- Existence needs: these include the need for basic material necessities and an individual's physiological and physical safety.
- Relatedness needs: these include the aspirations that individuals have for maintaining significant interpersonal relationships (be it with family, peers or superiors) and receiving public fame and recognition.
- Growth needs: these include the need for self-development, personal growth and advancement. Maslow's self-actualisation and esteem needs fall under this heading.
- More recently, Dan Pink has proposed a refined theory, synthesising earlier ideas.

Each of these theories indicates possible impacts on culture, as shown in Table 9.1.

Other theories include McGregor's participation theory and his concept of theory X and Y, Urwick's theory Z (which is claimed to re-interpret Locke's Goal theory), and Argyris' ideas

DOI: 10.4324/9781003307334-14

TABLE 9.1 Motivational theories

Motivational theorist	Key factors	When these factors are negative	Predicted negative impact on culture
Maslow (1943)	Five levels of need: -Self-actualisation -Self-esteem -Love/belonging -Safety -Physiological	Any of these needs are not met	The full extent of an individual's creativity and discretionary effort may not be realised unless there is some opportunity for self-actualisation
Skinner's reinforcement theory (operant conditioning) (1938/1953)	Conditioning behaviour through reward and punishment	The desired behaviour may not be accomplished without suitable reward	Variability in individual performance depending upon interpretation of what is required and the likely rewards
Herzberg (1959)	Hygiene (i.e., elements of working conditions that are important for functioning and are demotivating if absent, but are not motivational if they are present) and motivators	When no motivating factors are met, only sufficient performance to maintain the job, but no more	Focus only on hygiene factors to the detriment of overall performance achievement
McClelland (1961)	Need for achievement, power and affiliation	Limited opportunity in all three	When affiliation needs are not met, poor teamwork results
Locke (1960s)	Goal setting	When any of the elements are missing (often described as SMART – Specific, Measurable, Achievable, Realistic/ resourced, and Timed)	Unclear goals with greater re-work when wasted work is discovered. Deadlines not achieved
Alderfer (1960s/1970s)	Needs for existence, relatedness, and growth. Sometimes described as a recategorisation of Maslow's theory	'Frustration-regression' theory suggests that if a need is not met, there may be diversion to satisfying other needs	May be difficult to create a coherent motivational programme where all needs are met
Vroom (1964)	Expectancy theory states that an employee's motivation is an outcome of how much an individual wants a reward	Low motivation when reward is not valued	Performance only satisfies individual needs rather than organisational needs
Adams (1965)	Equity between performance and reward.	Imbalance, particularly over an extended period	Higher levels of grievance
Porter and Lawler (1968)	A development of Vroom's theory	When the elements of the relationship between effort, performance, reward and satisfaction are out of balance	As above, but a more complex set of relationships resulting in difficulty in identifying where issues arise
Pink (2011)	Autonomy, mastery and purpose (some overlaps with Alderfer's ERG theory)	Micro-management, prescribed roles and no context for activity	'Jobsworth' attitude. Unwillingness to go beyond prescribed duties

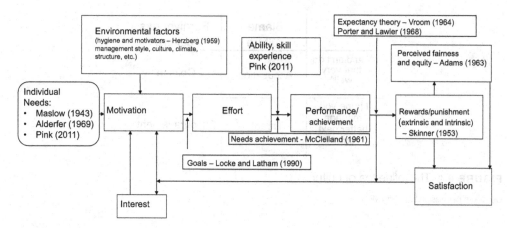

FIGURE 9.1 A motivational map

of how management practices can lead to greater maturity by an employee and hence improve performance.

Figure 9.1 gives a simple model (1) which locates these theories in some of the elements causing motivation and demotivation.

MOTIVATORS

Pink (2) has suggested that the major components of motivation are purpose, autonomy and mastery. These can be described as follows:

- Purpose
  Define an overriding purpose that employees see as meaningful and important in their lives. Some want to change the world, others climb the corporate hierarchy, while others seek new experiences.
- Autonomy
  Give people some freedom to work in the way they want with responsibility for work that is intrinsically satisfying.
- Mastery
  Help them become the best they can be to create a sense of achievement with recognition of good work.

An Indian fable illustrates how purpose can enhance motivation:

> *A man saw three people breaking stones. 'What are you doing?' he asked. The first said, 'I am breaking stones', the second 'I am earning my living' and the third 'I am building a cathedral'.*[1]

Status symbols are also powerful motivators to some, though what denotes high status to one may not be the same for another. Exotic job titles may be greeted with some cynicism. The

	Blame culture	Forgiveness culture
"You didn't do that very well"	Accusation	Opinion
"I hope you manage better next time"	Threat	Encouragement

FIGURE 9.2 The influence of culture

Used with permission from Rita McGee

changing labour market also gives rise to new specialist jobs in sustainability and health, and remote working. This creates new pathways for specialists and professionals whose jobs are marked by growing skills and experience, but do not vary significantly in terms of their activities unless they take on managerial roles. The realisation that some scientists may not make good managers has given rise to titles such as 'chief scientist', a title suggesting greater skill, experience and professional achievement rather than levels of management.

Organisations can be lonely places. Hertz (3) points out that loneliness increases the risk of heart attacks, strokes and dementia. Even in work teams, buffeted by the stresses of job insecurity, work pressures, churning roles and positions, there is little opportunity to create stable relationships, whether professional or otherwise. Stress causes fear, which is one of the most toxic cultural elements. Conversely, organisations can be places of social contagion (4), where attitudes and behaviour, both positive and negative, can spread across the organisation.

Where the culture is already toxic, people are likely to place the worst construction on the message, as shown in Figure 9.2 (5).

THE ROLE OF A BLAME CULTURE VERSUS A LEARNING CULTURE

An airline decided to invest in ramp-handling staff supervisors to encourage more flexible working. These are tough jobs where staff are out in all weathers dealing with docking and unloading the aircraft, often under time pressures. Management delegated more freedom and authority to the supervisors and encouraged them to do whatever was necessary to get the planes turned around as quickly as possible. This airport used a slot system where airlines had to pay for their time slot, which was more expensive at peak times. It was important not to miss the slot. One day a supervisor heard that a bus of schoolchildren was stuck in a traffic jam and were in danger of missing the flight. The supervisor heard this and ordered the bus to come straight to the steps of the aircraft. The children were delighted, the plane took off on time and he understandably felt he had done a good job. However, he broke a few rules and the airline disciplined him. Other supervisors saw this and realised if it was a choice between customers and the rules, the rules won.

The airline realised it had made a mistake and believed that it should have called all the supervisors together and praised the supervisor for his initiative, and then turned the session into a learning forum of how to deal with these difficult situations while following the important safety and security rules. However, the damage had been done.[2]

PRESSURE, FEAR AND THE OPTIMUM POINT

> *In Amnesty international, a policy was instituted called the 'global transition programme', which aimed to move staff from headquarters and closer to the abuses they covered. This caused considerable stress to staff, leading in one case to a suicide. Managers believed that the importance of the NGO's work was so great that they did not need to listen to staff concerns. Senior management seemed to conclude that employees 'should be grateful for being able to work at Amnesty'. Employees also found it difficult to set healthy boundaries on their hours (or on their tolerance of a toxic climate) owing to a deeply held belief in their mission. Even though some support services had been put in place, staff still felt they had been given insufficient support or guidance on how to deal with the very real dilemmas that result from pressured and important work, particularly where an individual's health and well-being was affected. There was a sense – real or imagined – that senior management were not really committed to staff well-being, seeing their important work as overriding any other considerations (6).*

The crux of the issue for all those in management is how to find a point of balance between utilising the positive motivational and cultural benefits of having such an important mission of which employees would be proud to serve, and too much pressure where health and well-being suffers as a result. Such a mission invariably guarantees engagement and loyalty, but runs the risk of giving licence to managers to drive their staff excessively. This behaviour ultimately becomes self-defeating if staff leave or become rebellious.

FEAR

It was President Franklin D. Roosevelt who famously remarked that we have nothing to fear but fear itself. He was alluding to the negative consequences that fear has on our capacity to function. There is the potential for a greater impact when faced with a dangerous and high-stress situation, such as those soldiers and emergency service workers often face. Just at the time when their capacity to respond appropriately to threat should be at its greatest, there is increased stress and potential for dysfunction. Sometimes called the amygdala hijack, (7) the part of our brain that controls fight, flight and freeze becomes dominant and the cortex – the more thinking part of the brain - becomes suppressed. We react first and then think. We see a snake, we freeze, and then we see it is a harmless grass snake and relax. Fear arises from many causes, as we touched on in Chapter 4. Some are instinctive, such as snakes and heights, which nearly everyone has to some degree, while others come from memories of past events that may not even be consciously remembered, but nevertheless leave a legacy of fear when some stimulus arouses the fear associated with that memory.

In the parable of the talents/gold in the Bible,[3] there are many interpretations – spiritual and earthlier - of the problem of delegation and how a master can ensure his employees act responsibly in the way he wants. The successful servant who doubled the money given might well have creamed some off the top for himself – a common problem with high potential rewards and low controls - whereas the third servant acted out of fear. He was cast aside. Fear and greed play a big part in distorting company cultures driven principally by reward and punishment systems. For every company that treats mistakes and poor performance as learning opportunities to do better (a common professed mantra), there are many who work instrumentally, i.e., where they only see the results and then reward or punish staff based solely on these results rather than any consideration of intention[4] or improving learning.

Because fear is such a powerful force and is experienced at some time by everyone, it is hardly surprising that there will be those who exploit it in organisations to bend people to their will. It is the easiest way of exerting power and stems in many instances from some form of inadequacy. This is particularly true of the bully, as we explored in Chapter 3. Fear often achieves compliance but rarely commitment, unless it is accompanied by a destruction of the individual's own identity. In these instances, initiative is limited and it is more likely that blind obedience becomes the norm. In the case of the American military personnel who staffed the minutemen missiles, the punitive culture introduced when things went wrong had a disastrous effect. As one said, 'we don't care if things go properly, we just don't want to get into trouble' (8). Three questions Coyle asks of any team are as follows: 'Are we connected, do we share a future, are we safe?' The answers to all three from the missilemen were negative. It is no wonder errors increased, further compounded by an inappropriate dictatorial regime. 'Missileers' culture is not a result of discipline and character but of an environment custom built to destroy cohesion.'

So, what do we fear in organisational life? Invariably loss of:

- our job and our livelihood;
- our relationships;
- our control over our life;
- our comfort;
- our self-efficacy;
- self-confidence;
- self-respect.

Managers have a prime responsibility for ensuring that unproductive fear is minimised. A consequence of low motivation but a pressured environment is stress and a feeling of burnout.

Some argue that a little pressure gets the best out of us, so it is one of the tasks of good leadership to find the balance point, sometimes called eustress (9), between too little challenge in the work and too much challenge that causes burnout, as shown in Figure 9.3.

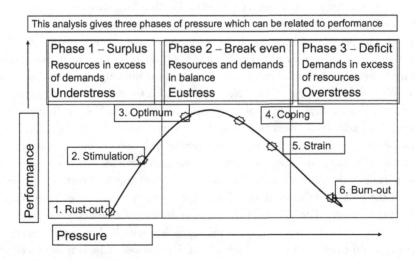

FIGURE 9.3 Finding the optimum pressure point

When people are stressed, there is a fear of speaking up and a feeling that they have no voice, so mistakes and inefficiencies can fester. It can be particularly stressful if people don't know where they stand and are uncertain of their manager's view of them.

Leaders find it difficult to confront toxic behaviour in others because:

- they don't want to rock the boat;
- they might conclude that their subordinate's performance is often good so let's live with the bad behaviour;
- the conversation is too difficult;
- it might make the situation worse;
- they might consider that they have to work with them tomorrow and it's an embarrassing subject to confront, similar to discussing body odour.

Yet many experience less pain from these events than the anticipation of them, as shown in the following case study:

> *A very senior person who lost her job in a corporate power struggle believed that her world had collapsed and that everyone would think that she was incompetent. She soon got another senior job as she was well respected in her industry. She remarked that while it was not as bad as she had feared, and while she didn't want to go through it again, she had learnt a lot, and felt more confident and stronger to face these challenges in the future.*

Fear often causes us to doubt ourselves and our abilities, especially if it is a novel situation. We underestimate our abilities because they come easier to us and so we discount them more. Rita Carter (10) identifies a strategy for managing fear: 'confront the fear, progressively and persistently until the stimuli are associated with positive safe associations.(This can only work when cortically based notions can overcome amygdala-based tenets, but they cannot eradicate them)'. In other words, we have got to get back into the driving seat of our life when self-talk, based on a rational (cortical) assessment, finds the fear irrational and so in time can reduce the emotional fight-or-flight response of the amygdala. Self-talk is a useful strategy to deploy when faced with undesirable situations. We seek to verbalise a more balanced and acceptable description of what is going on and in a way that we can confront. Determining what is the worst that could happen allows us to achieve a more realistic and less emotional viewpoint. Fortunately, most of us in the developed world do not face catastrophic situations every day and we can set our troubles in a broader context – the sun will still rise tomorrow.

So, how do we deal with fear amongst staff? Here are some pointers for managers:

- Engage staff in the mission of your team and their part in it.
- Encourage everyone to demonstrate by their behaviour a tolerance of differences from those around them.
- Give clarity of goals that are achievable, but require some effort.[5]
- Ensure feedback on performance is motivational and designed to improve performance.
- Reinforce learning from mistakes rather than blaming.
- Respect individuals regardless of who they are.

- Recognise the emotional fallout from fearful situations, and move to reassure and mitigate the effects.
- Create strong teams with shared values, a common vision and support for each other.

The conclusion from many incidents is that training, training, training is a must, and it has to be so good that an appropriate response becomes instinctive rather than one purely driven by fear and/ or survival. Of course, fear is our inbuilt survival mechanism and may come into play when we are not conscious of the threat. We feel something that causes us to be wary and on heightened alert. The question for us all in such situations is to reflect on how we take control.

ENGAGEMENT

Allied to motivation (indeed, a precursor) is engagement with the goals and ethos of the organisation. In a Chicago music school project (11), students are invited to write a piece. 'I got my A because…'. They are encouraged to look to that future point when they will have succeeded with that firm goal of high achievement in mind. It is a simple and basic process in any organisation to set goals and excite people with the possibility of getting somewhere better than the present. This might be increased sales and profits (which everyone benefits from in commercial organisations, if only in terms of greater job security), personal achievement or some more altruistic goal of helping others.

When goals become impossible or are not shared, morale suffers, leading to lower levels of engagement. Where people feel disengaged, their performance is invariably not as high as it could be.

An area which is counter-intuitive to many leaders is vulnerability (12). The conventional model is that leaders must be strong and show no doubt or vulnerability. Yet, paradoxically, when they do, they often receive greater support and engagement from their followers. This reinforces the capacity of every individual to contribute, however small this contribution may be, and casts the leader in a more human light.

To enhance engagement, there is nothing so powerful as feeling valued for who you are, what you do and of being heard. One way of achieving this is by asking people what they want! Michael Abrashoff's study of a ship (13) asked his crew of the destroyer *USS Benfold* three things: what do you like about the *Benfold*, what do you like least and what would you change if you were captain? This approach has been used by many businesses with great success. In W.H. Smith the exercise yielded some 5,000 suggestions for improvement which helped to improve the business, but almost more importantly it acknowledged every person's responsibility to look for improvement and bound them into a sense of belonging to the future - a powerful motivator.

FEEDBACK

Feedback has been described as the oxygen of champions. Steve Williams, a key member of the British rowing squad that won gold at both the Athens and Beijing Olympics, described the process after each practice session. Feedback is all focused on how to make the boat go faster and the ground rule was that honest feedback should be given, but with no offence meant and no offence taken. Invariably they would thank each other afterwards, not because it was a pleasant experience (it was often uncomfortable), but because it was an affirmation of their commitment to each other

TABLE 9.2 Feedback and criticism: the difference

Feedback is information designed to change people's behaviour in a positive way	Criticism is venting anger – it is telling people how they should be
Specific	General
Future-oriented	Past-oriented
Descriptive	Evaluative
Tough on the issues	Tough on the person
Seeks solutions	Seeks blame

and their desire to do whatever it took to make the boat go faster. Feedback is different from criticism and is often confused with it. Feedback or criticism is an important determinant of whether the culture becomes more or less motivational. This difference is summarised in Table 9.2.

The legacy of feedback is people walking away more motivated to improve and raise their game, whereas criticism leaves people feeling bruised (and reaching for their lawyer!). When receiving feedback, our antennae are acutely tuned to any sign of rejection, so giving it in a way that allays those fears whilst motivating the person to improve is very skilful, and many managers never learn the art of doing so. Whilst we like praise, it rarely helps us improve, instead reinforcing our view that our performance requires no change. The trick is to demonstrate that we value the person and it is an aspect of their performance that requires change. The most successful approach is to gain agreement on what an excellent performance looks like and help the person identify practical areas that they can improve. A study of schoolchildren showed that most improvement came from praising effort, regardless of the result, rather than intelligence or achievement (14).

HYGIENE CONDITIONS

A study carried out some time ago (15) highlighted the role of hygiene factors (e.g., physical work environment, job security and compensation) in that they may not motivate people, but if they are absent, they cause resentment and demotivation. One company, in its desire to save money, cut out free coffee and biscuits at meetings. People had to buy their own at inferior vending machines. The saving was small, but the impact on morale was huge and signalled that the company didn't really care about its people. The situation was recovered to some extent when the chief executive announced that he was taking a substantial pay cut and he was pitching in to do some of the basic work, demonstrating a knowledge and a desire to see good work done everywhere. It also gave the impression to staff that he was like everyone else in the enterprise and when things needed doing, whoever was able to help should chip in (though without causing role and turf wars).

COMMUNICATIONS

'If I had a dollar for every person who has told me that the problem in their organisation is "communications", I would be a rich man' said a consultant. It is a universal concern, and it is rare to find an example where it has been successfully overcome. Part of the issue lies in a faulty response to a wrong diagnosis of the problem. When 'poor communication' arises in a staff survey, the typical response is to increase 'communication' by another meeting, email, podcast, notice on the notice board, briefing group, etc. But the grumbles remain – why?

First, communication is a two-way process and is the oil that lubricates the wheels of organisations. Many of the traditional approaches to communications in organisational life are about broadcasting because of its efficiency (i.e., giving the same message to everyone) or narrow casting (i.e., giving the message to a specific section in order to make it more personal). Both approaches allow little opportunity for discussion. The dilemma is that discussion is time-consuming and especially on leaders. Indeed, some have pushed back, demanding a 'need to know reset' to limit communication time and overheads. From a managerial viewpoint, no news equals good news, because this relieves them of the time and effort involved in briefing and discussing. From a employee's perspective, no news feels like a blackout. The charge of poor communications results from several worries:

- 'I believe that something is going on that I don't know about and perhaps others do, so why have I been excluded and if I have, it's bound to be something unpleasant.' This form of mild paranoia also underpins many conspiracy theories.
- 'What they are telling me is not what I really want to know – which is I'm doing a good job; it is secure and there is a future which is appealing to me.'

A toxic workplace may have bad communications characterised by the following:

- Constant lack of clarity in relation to projects.
- Different employees receiving different messages.
- Passive-aggressive communication (don'ts, musts, shoulds and highlighting penalties for non-compliance).
- Failure to listen to any feedback.
- Constant 'off-hours' communication (emails at night, weekends and holidays).

So, the solutions lie in engaging and empowering people to ask questions, to seek information that they need and to build trust that no news *is* good news.

One problem that always bedevils organisational communications is interpretation. We each interpret messages according to what we hold to be correct in our circumstances. Common interpretations include the following:

- 'I am sure no one in our section is guilty of this, so this missive does not apply to me.'
- 'I will interpret this policy in a way that works for me.'
- 'I am sure what they really meant to say was…'
- 'I will do nothing right now and wait to see if they are serious.'

Communication is intended to pass on information (which can be some *report*, but equally *rapport* as every communication carries an emotional subtext) in a way that is clearly understood by the recipient. The problem is that we all interpret information through our own frame of reference, and when we don't have complete information, we fill in the gaps with assumptions based on prior knowledge.

A famous historical example is the murder of Thomas Becket in the 12th century, which is reputed to have been caried out by zealous subordinates eager to do the king's will. 'Who will rid me of this troublesome priest?' might have been a throwaway remark by the king, but others interpreted it as an instruction to carry out the deed, probably hoping that they would earn the king's favour (recent examples of the attempted and actual assassination of Alexei Navalny in Russia and Jamal Khashoggi in Turkey show that this still happens in the present day). Remarks become hardened and amplified when there are multiple layers of transmission, each losing some of the context and nuance of the earlier remarks. When the mission to achieve some result (as in military contexts) is critically important, it is easy for ethical behaviour to be suppressed in favour of whatever it takes to win. This is why values are so important to give a steer to even the most junior employee.

'SHERLOCK': A TEST OF LISTENING (16)

Correctly interpreting what people say is crucial to effective communication. The following story illustrates how easy it is to make incorrect assumptions:

A businessman had just turned off the lights in the shop when a man appeared and demanded money. The owner opened a cash register. The contents of the cash register were scooped up and the man sped away. A member of the police was promptly notified.

Statements about the story:

* Put a circle around the 'T' if you think the statement is true.
* Put a circle around the 'F' if you think the statement is false.
* Put a circle around the question mark (?) if the story did not tell you one way or the other.

1. A man appeared after the owner had turned off his shop lights.	T	F?
2. The robber was a man.	T	F?
3. The man did not demand money.	T	F?
4. The man who opened the cash register was the owner.	T	F?
5. The storeowner scooped up the contents of the cash.	T	F?
6. Someone opened a cash register.	T	F?
7. After the man who demanded the money scooped up the contents of the cash register, he ran away.	T	F?
8. Whilst the cash register contained money, the story does not say *how much*.	T	F?
9. The robber demanded money from the owner.	T	F?
10. The story concerns a series of events in which only three persons are referred to: the owner of the store, a man who demanded money and a member of the police force.	T	F?
11. The following events are included in the story: someone demanded money, a cash register was opened, its contents were scooped up and a man dashed out of the store.	T	F?

The answers

Question No.	Answer
1	?
2	?
3	F
4	?
5	?
6	T
7	?
8	?
9	?
10	?
11	?

Very few people get this exercise totally right. Why? Because we make assumptions about what is happening. The story is contrived, but it illustrates how quickly we make assumptions in order to form our opinions. Our assumptions are based on our beliefs about what the story would indicate – i.e., there was a robber rather than a man. Those beliefs are formed from our previous experience.

THE NATURE OF COMMUNICATION AND WHY IT GOES WRONG

How information is structured comes from the mind of the sender. The mindset of the receiver may have difficulty in interpreting it in the way that it was intended because of the following issues:

• Incompatible mental maps between the two and incongruence with existing beliefs and sectional interests, especially when it is novel.
• Incomplete information – too many unanswered questions.
• Irrelevance to the listener.
• Information overload.
• An unpleasant message leading to denial. Emotion has an influence on understanding, so the message gets denied due to the breakdown in rapport.
• A legacy of past poor communication.
• Disbelief because of the source of the information – biases, history and intention.
• The rush to judge, leading to rejection before a complete understanding is gained.

THE TRANSMISSION SYSTEM

The transmission system from top to bottom is a fundamental process that so often goes wrong. Keeping messages simple and relevant is important. When communication ignores what people need and want to hear, but delivers only corporate speak, then engagement is lost.

The vision, mission and goals of the organisation that are conceived at the top somehow have to be transmitted and translated into action that people at all levels of the organisation can understand and apply to their job. What do I have to do as a result of this statement from the board? The following case gives a good example where the message about strategic direction was effectively translated into specific action for an employee:

> *One day a journalist in London attended a briefing by a chief executive of a hotel chain about how they were repositioning the business to a different, more high-value market segment. He wondered how the management language would translate to junior staff, so after the presentation, he went into the bar of one of this hotel chain and asked the barman what the implication of the new strategy was for him. He expected a blank expression. Instead, the barman said that he had to learn to make fancier cocktails. This is a good example of a transmission system working well.*

Where different parts of the organisation work in isolation or in silos, the purpose of the organisation gets fragmented and dissipated and lowers effectiveness. In a review of the Australian federal government (17), the existence of silo thinking was a major cause of the lack of effectiveness of the organisation.

The ancient Greek philosopher Aristotle suggested that we need to communicate along three dimensions if the message is to get across:

- Logos – the appeal of the logic of the argument that provides a compelling reason.
- Pathos – the appeal of the emotional pull of the argument.
- Ethos – the appeal of the credibility of the communicator.

One way to evaluate the transmission system is to examine the degree of distortion as the message goes from top to bottom. A classic example of distortion arising from the grapevine is the children's whispering game 'Send reinforcements. we're going to advance', which was received as: 'Send three and fourpence. We're going to a dance!' Another example was a message sent from the Battle of Waterloo; 'Wellington defeated … (and when the mist cleared) Napoleon'. These famous and maybe apocryphal stories illustrate the challenge of communicating. The first example is typical of the effect of passing information through many hands, whereby the end result is very different from the first information given. The second (supposedly sent from the battle by relays of semaphores) illustrates how only partial information can be so misleading.

Communications of all kinds can become distorted in transmission. The prism model given in Figure 9.4 (18) illustrates some of the factors that result in the received message being different from the message sent. The distortion index is a way of testing it.

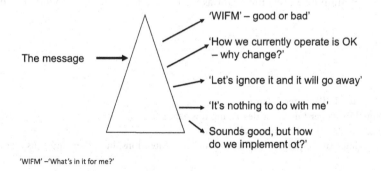

'WIFM' –'What's in it for me?'

FIGURE 9.4 The communication prism

Used by permission of Roger Niven

TABLE 9.3 Measuring distortion

Message intended	Message sent	Interpretation by receivers	High distortion	Medium distortion	Low distortion

MEASURING DISTORTION

Table 9.3 is derived from first identifying the messages you intended to send to the organisation and then asking recipients what messages they received.

Now, make a judgement about the degree of congruence between the messages sent and those received. Where there is low congruence (i.e., high distortion), there is a need to examine what is happening in the transmission system to reduce distortion.

SUMMARY AND CONCLUSIONS

- Motivation and communication are at the heart of performance management and there are many ways for them to become distorted, leading to less desirable outcomes.
- The motivational response to a stimulus is mediated through the cultural lens of blame or forgiveness, with very different results.
- There have been many theories over the last 50 years, and each indicates how demotivation can occur and the result on the prevailing culture. Modern theories emphasise autonomy, mastery and purpose as critical components.
- The results of the stresses and strains of organisational life lead to fear of loss (job, reputation, respect, etc.). There is an optimum point, called eustress, when pressure moves from motivation to lowering performance.
- The challenge of leadership is to find ways of motivating staff without creating unwarranted fear and helping them to become the best they can be.
- Communication is a two-way process to build greater engagement and an essential component in motivation, but it is also important to check that the correct message has been received. The danger of the message being distorted is ever-present.
- How we communicate is as important as what we communicate in building a motivational climate.

NOTES

1 Attributed to the Indian poet Tagore.
2 I am indebted to Roger Niven for describing this example.
3 Matthew 25:14-28, New International Version.
4 There is a saying that we judge ourselves by our good intentions, but others judge us by our words and actions,

5 As illustrated earlier in Table 9.1, a well-used mnemonic in setting goals is SMART, which can be applied to more headings that is traditionally suggested - e.g., S traditionally means Specific, but can also be a reminder of the Strategy to which the goal relates. M stands for Measurable (or at least verifiable), but can also suggest a reminder that all outcomes should be Meaningful. A stands for Achievable, and goals should also be Agreed. R stands for Relevant, Resourced and .Realistic, while T is for Timebound.

REFERENCES

1 Motivational map, developed by the author in a senior management programme for H.M. Government, UK. Theories covered the following:
   a. Maslow, A. (1943) A theory of human motivation. *Psychological Review*, *50*(4), 370–396.
   b. Skinner, B. F. (1938) *The behaviour of organisms: An experimental analysis.* Appleton-Century-Crofts.
   c. Herzberg, F. (1959) One more time: How do you motivate employees? *Harvard Business Review*, *81*(1), 87–96.
   d. McClelland, D. (1961) *The achieving society.* Free Press.
   e. Locke, E.A. and Latham, G.P. (1990) *A theory of goal setting & task performance.* Prentice Hall.
   f. Alderfer, Clayton P. (1969) An empirical test of a new theory of human needs. *Organisational Behaviour and Human Performance*, *4*(2), 142–175.
   g. Adams, J.S. (1965) Inequality in social exchange. *Advanced Experimental Psychology*, *62*, 335–343.
   h. Vroom, V. (1964) *Work and motivation.* John Wiley.
   i. Porter, L. and Lawler, E. (1968) *Managerial attitudes and performance.* Irwin Dorsey.
2 Pink, D. (2011) *Drive: The surprising truth about what motivates.* Penguin.
3 Hertz, N. (2020) *The lonely century: A call to connect.* Sceptre.
4 Effron, D.A., Kakkar, H. and Knowles, E.D. (2018) Group cohesion benefits individuals who express prejudice, but harms their group. *Journal of Experimental Social Psychology, 79*, 239-251.
5 I am indebted to Rita McGee for showing this model to me.
6 Charity begins at work. Toxic workplaces can be found in every sector. The story of Amnesty International. *The Economist* (*8 June* 2019).
7 Rock, D. (2007) *Quiet leadership.* HarperCollins.
8 The Coyle, D. (2108) *The culture code.* Bantam Books.
9 The term 'eustress' was first used by the endocrinologist Hans Selye.
10 Carter, R. (2004) *Mapping the mind.* Phoenix.
11 Zander, R., and B. (2000) *The art of possibility.* Harvard Business Press.
12 Brown, B. (2018) *Dare to lead.* Random House.
13 Abrashoff, M. (2012) *It's your ship: Management techniques from the best damn ship in the Navy.* Little, Brown and Company.
14 Dweck, C.S. and Mueller, C.M. (1998) Praise for intelligence can undermine children's motivation and performance. *Journal of Personality and Social Psychology*, *75*(1), 33-52.
15 Herzberg, F. (2003) One more time: How do you motivate employees? *Harvard Business Review*, *81*(1), 87-96.
16 Described as 'Sherlock' in an exercise quoted by Ohio State University.
17 Select Committee on the effectiveness of the Australian Government's Northern Australia agenda. Retrieved 9 June 2022 from https://www.aph.gov.au/Parliamentary_Business/Committees/Senate/NorthernAustraliaAgenda/NorthernAustraliaAgenda.
18 I am indebted to Roger Niven for sharing this model with me.

Reward

INTRODUCTION

In Chapter 9 we examined motivation; here we examine reward and its relationship with motivation. Whilst we might naturally consider financial rewards first, we can differentiate between extrinsic rewards such as money, holidays, status symbols and other physical and financial benefits, and intrinsic rewards such as job satisfaction arising from work that is valued as being important. Importance comes from a recognition of both effort and result and a feeling of being part of a team who rely on your efforts.

Starting with extrinsic rewards, the 1987 film *Wall Street* sums up the culture of organisations where money has dominated all measures of success, often with unintended but damaging consequences. In the film, Gordon Gekko says: 'The point is ladies and gentlemen, that greed – for lack of a better word – is good. Greed is right. Greed works. Greed clarifies. Cuts through and captures the essence of the evolutionary spirit' (1).

We should be aware that there are cultural differences between national groups and what might appear to be acceptable practices in one area might be seen as toxic in others. This is particularly apparent in incentive schemes.

THE ROYAL COMMISSION INTO THE FINANCIAL SECTOR IN AUSTRALIA

In Australia, the Royal Commission uncovered a catalogue of corruption. Adele Ferguson, an investigative journalist, was at the forefront of bringing many of these egregious cases to the attention of the public, and the resulting furore that the government could no longer ignore led to the Royal Commission being set up to investigate this. In her book *Banking bad*, Ferguson sums up the mood (2):

> Remuneration deals across the sector were restructured to offer incentives to staff with lofty targets set and bonuses paid if targets were met. A culture of profit took hold and risk management became evermore lax.

According to John McLennan,[1] there were no checks and balances, and no quality controls: 'That was the beginning of the end … staff soon learned to flog products to achieve bonuses and, as the saying goes, when profit is the only motive, all forms of corrupt and immoral behaviour can be rationalised.'

DOI: 10.4324/9781003307334-15

The banks were only the latest example in a significant shift that occurred in many industries as the world moved towards deregulation, privatisation and globalisation. A more muscular form of capitalism emerged, focusing on shareholder value and the need to keep increasing it. Andrew Smithers, an economist (3), has 'calculated that the proportion of operating cash flow paid out to shareholders by non-financial American companies was just 19.6% between 1947 and 1999. By the end of that era, share options become popular means of motivating managers. Subsequently the proportion of cash flow paid to shareholders averaged 40.7% between 2000 and 2017, while cash used for investment fell'. Benefiting the owners or shareholders when workers see no benefit is unlikely to be motivational to them.

SHARE SCHEMES

Public companies have often used various share schemes, including offering shares outright, whilst other schemes give options to buy at a certain price at a certain time. These schemes stem from the belief that with hard work, the share price will increase, and a profit can be realised when the shares are sold at the option price. Such schemes reward company performance and benefit employees (or some of them) as well as shareholders. It also aims to bind executives in for a period until the options become payable, in the hope that improved company performance will deliver a profit. However, it does give rise to the suspicion that executive interest becomes centred around the share price rather than the underlying health of the business. Activity becomes focused on reducing costs and boosting profits. In the case of China Merchant Bank (CMB) in Australia, this resulted in reducing the number of compliance and risk assessment staff. The interaction of structures, systems, processes and rewards to reinforce correct behaviour needs to be strong, as self-interest and routine unthinking job behaviour can result in errors or fraud. In times of acquisition, executives may also stand to gain from the boost in the share price as a result of takeover activity and so may be influenced by that rather than what is in the best interests of the business and all its employees. Share schemes are open to manipulation and insider trading.

Profit-sharing schemes fared well in a more altruistic age when a belief that sharing in profits, a form of industrial democracy, would lead to superior performance based on everyone pulling together in a team effort. Over the years, various schemes have been used to overcome the conflict of capital versus labour, such as joint ownership. The John Lewis partnership in the UK is a good example of this, as are supervisory boards in Germany. These seek to deliver fairness in dividing the profits between employees and shareholders.

Traditional industries such as banks, whose primary aim for years has been to provide a service to their community and where probity in their dealings resulted in the bank manager being a trusted pillar of the establishment, became more focused on selling a wide range of products in order to boost profits. The author went in to a branch of his bank in England once to obtain a card reader. When handing it over at the counter, the assistant said: 'I see your car insurance is coming up next month, can we give you a competitive quote compared to what you paid last year?' It was a new development in banking relationships when the bank teller accessed your account, spotted a renewal from examining direct debits, looked at what was paid last year and pitched for the business. Like the banks, life insurance agents felt their prime responsibility was to the company that employed them, not to the customers who bought their products.

The drive towards ever-increasing profits leads to the search for the best talent. Globalisation had led from the 1990s onwards to increased cross-border recruitment. Bob Joss was recruited from Wells Fargo in the USA to head up Westpac in Australia 'and the salary he demanded was more than the combined salaries of the other three major Australian bank CEOs' (4). His appointment set off a wage race with more incentive-based packages of bonuses and options. As we have seen, once someone behaves in a certain way (especially at the top) and it is condoned, it becomes the norm for everyone else, as illustrated in the following case study:

> *A government department in the UK signed a new catering contract. On the first day, a Principal Secretary (PS) held a meeting at which coffee was served. 'No biscuits?' asked the PS. 'Sir, we can provide them' was the answer and they were duly produced. At the end of the year, the contract had overspent by £40,000 due to biscuits. If the PS can have biscuits, it gave the green light to everyone else to do the same.*

MOTIVATION AND REWARD

Recently my wife and I visited two restaurants south of Sydney. They were included in a book of good restaurants and the food was excellent in both. The manager of one engaged us with a smile, asked where we were from and, whilst we dealt with the bill, asked us whether we had enjoyed our time at the restaurant. We left with a warm feeling and a desire to return when we were next in the area. The other restaurant had a wonderful position with great views and comfortable seating. However, the waiter was new and didn't really know about the menu. When we came to pay, the manager had a sour face and was only interested in swiping our card without comment or interest in our experience. No doubt she was having a difficult day, though the restaurant was not full; nevertheless, her impact on us was such that we would not wish to return there in the future.

This experience prompted a consideration of how people in such jobs are rewarded. In the first restaurant, the manager felt rewarded by happy customers who had a good experience. She also knew it was good for business to encourage return custom. The manager in the second restaurant was rewarded only by her wage and clearly felt no responsibility to treat customers well or saw value in doing so.

There are many jobs (which are often not well paid) from which people derive great satisfaction. Winston Churchill is credited with suggesting that you get a living from what you get, while you get a life from what you *give*. An old story is told in India[2] of a film crew filming a nun bathing the wounds of a leper. She overheard the crew talking and one said that he wouldn't do that work for $10,000. She interjected 'and nor would I'. Her reward was in the satisfaction from seeing an ill person gain some comfort from her care and attention, while the film crew's reward was in getting some footage that would please their editor.

These stories prompt a consideration of how and who we hire for what jobs, and what combination of extrinsic and intrinsic rewards will motivate behaviours that are congruent with the organisation's values and purpose, as well as encouraging sustained performance over time.

I recently travelled on the Ghan, a railway that runs for 3,000 kilometres from Darwin to Adelaide through the middle of Australia. It was a luxury train and what made it special was the staff. It is a difficult trick to keep staff on message for four days in an enclosed space when everyone travels together.

TABLE 10.1 Reward needs at different times of life[3]

Possible lifeline	Reward needs
16–25: Start working	Competitive base pay, loan repayment schemes, holidays
20s–30s: Relationships	Time off, weddings, travel, housing mortgages
20s–40s: Children	Time off, flexible working, childcare support, insurances, pensions, financial advice on savings
30s–40s: Larger house	Job security, housing finance, bonuses
30s–50s: Children at school	Flexible working during school holidays
40s–50s: 'Mid- life crisis'	Sabbaticals, counselling/coaching, personal development
50s: Children at college	Loan schemes, financial support for children
50s–60s: Early retirement	Funding
60s–80s: Retirement	Pension, insurance, medical support

They were not particularly well paid and they worked one week on and one week off. They were rewarded by the enjoyment of the passengers, many of whom were taking the trip of a lifetime, and the opportunity to get to know their guests, which was not possible in many other hospitality jobs.

Reward is also tied to a range of other factors, such as what motivates people at different stages in their lives, especially the relationship between cash and benefits. Table 10.1 (5) characterises typical stages people might go through in their lives and how these stages affect their views about reward.

TOXIC REWARDS

So how does reward, both extrinsic and intrinsic, become a source of toxicity in the culture of an organisation? There are several major sources of reward dysfunction:

- Unfairness in relativities between employees and with similar work outside, especially when there are no other compensating sources of reward. There is much talk in the popular press of wage theft, where employers have failed to pay employees' full entitlements and thereby have lost their trust, both in the legal and psychological sense.
- Exploitation of employees when the balance between their needs and rewards is so skewed in the employer's favour that resentment becomes ingrained. This often occurs when employees are required to work long or unsocial hours, or carry out dangerous and dirty work for minimum reward. Whilst bursts of actvity are always possible for most people, in irder to achieve sustained performance over time, some form of work/life balance has to be achieved. Toxic cultures are characterised by a distinct lack of this, which is often caused by leaders with psycopathic tendencies who have little concern for their staff welfare beyond achieving results. Even when the rewards are principally intrinsic, people expect to be fairly rewarded and not exploited.
- Impossible targets that cannot be achieved without superhuman effort. The result of these on subsequent performance is often that employees will give up.
- Unfair distribution of reward between shareholders, owners of other assets such as property, and employees of the enterprise.
- Incentive schemes that target specific behaviours such as sales or production, but run the risk of sacrificing other aspects of good performance, such as quality of work or customer service. Freedom Insurance, an Australian company, has been heavily censored for its unfair practices,

driven by a strong incentive culture to sell and retain customers. Sales agents were incentivised with gift vouchers and holidays, and retention officers received bonuses for each customer they persuaded not to cancel.

- Benefits are given that are little valued by employees as they would have preferred other forms of reward that would have more perceived value to them. Organisations have experimented with 'cafeteria benefits' as a way of matching need more closely to perceived benefit, but these are rare.
- When rewards from the job and environment are not congruent with people's needs, this results in people being in jobs where the rewards provided don't necessarily motivate them.
- The work that gets rewarded gets done, which leads to a strict relationship between activity and reward. Piecework systems of remuneration suffer from this problem.
- Rewards that are focused solely on money rather than any intrinsic elements which are less tangible, such as recognition, a sense of achievement and feeling valued, do not gain the motivational effect that a more holistic package is able to achieve.
- Where companies make attractive consumer products (from chocolates to cars), these can often become part of the perks offered to employees. But in toxic cultures where individuals feel a climate of unfairness, these products may become unofficial perks, as where a blind eye is turned to pilferage.
- Fiddling of expenses becomes the norm when employees feel that they are not adequately compensated or the expenses policy does not (in their view) adequately compensate them. When managers have a degree of sympathy for such behaviour and turn a blind eye, it reinforces a norm that such behaviour, whilst not publicly acceptable, is tolerated.

Such responses may seem deviant and unreasonable, yet they are a reaction against an imperfect relationship between effort and reward. The desire for autonomy and, indeed, the powerful motivational effect of autonomy, especially when coupled with mastery and a clear purpose, will be blunted by inappropriate measures and controls, and can lead to behaviour that is not fully compliant. In extreme cases this becomes theft. We can infer deviance in Table 10.2 from the effect that results from different types of control.

TABLE 10.2 Compliance arising from different types of control

Effects from different types of control	Time	Work	Product	Relationship
Positive effect from clear purpose, opportunity for mastery and autonomy	Time off for a good piece of work that does not get counted towards holiday	Opportunity to use work time/ resources to do a personal project	Free and discounted products, perhaps in return for home testing them	Wears uniform proudly in public
Neutral cooperation with clear rules that are observed to the letter	Strict hours kept by employer and employee	Work specifically prescribed	No perks	Probably changes uniform before travelling in public
Compliance from a disciplined and controlled workplace	Absenteeism only covered by sick pay where available	Bargaining over extra work – overtime or time off in lieu	Some pilferage	Jokes and rituals denigrating the company behind managers' backs
Withdrawal due to harsh and unbending rules and punishments	Labour turnover and possible industrial action	Sabotage or going slow	Theft	Legal or trade union action against the organisation for petty disputes

PERFORMANCE-RELATED PAY

Where pay is tied to performance, the opportunities for abuse are numerous. Selling roles typically use incentive payment schemes, but there is a permanent tension between all the elements that make up a successful sale and, more importantly, subsequent business. Overly generous payments based on a sale may encourage a sell and forget mindset, which can be contrary to what the company desires if after-sales or repeat sales is important. A historical study by Jason Ditton (6) identified that new recruits were trained to rob the customer to hide mistakes in the sales process and avoid any uncertainty that might arise in the measures of sales performance.[4]

A cultural feature of financial institutions is their reliance on bonuses and financial incentives. One UK bank quoted a staff member who claimed she would work 30% less if she was paid only a basic salary (7). For some, earning big money encourages a degree of arrogance, in that it encourages a belief that money equals ability and thus superiority, as we found with Piff's research in Chapter 5. It is easy to be seduced by money.

Reward systems are designed to do several things:

1. To hire the level of skill and experience appropriate for the job at the reward level indicated in the labour market.
2. To motivate performance according to the measures set.
3. To ensure that an individual feels their worth is recognised in the labour market and is competitive with others of similar skill.
4. To give the feeling that the fruits of their labour are being equally shared.

To accomplish all these needs is challenging, which is why reward systems are continually being amended. The first question that arises is what are you paying for: performance or potential? In particular, how do you reward those who have high potential, but as yet are not performing to their potential? The options are shown in Figure 10.1.

The linking of reward to performance has been an aspiration of nearly all organisations, yet is fraught with difficulties in practice. Here are some of the major examples:

1. Performance assessments are rarely totally consistent, despite often complex schemes of metric scales and multiple judgements. This in turn breeds a belief in the inherent unfairness of such systems. They lose their motivational effect because of a range of unhelpful attitudes – 'it's

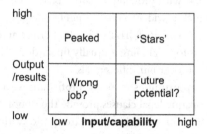

FIGURE 10.1 What are we assessing?

Note: compare this chart with Figure 5.1 in Chapter 5, where output is assessed against adherence to established values.

about sucking up to the boss', 'it's just the luck of the draw', etc. Once the rules become too onerous, more effort is put into getting round the rules rather than following them. A crackdown can trigger claims of harassment when it becomes a legal issue. The difficulty all organisations face is where to draw the line between acceptable and unacceptable performance, especially when seeking to improve performance. These standards may be reinforced by metrics and the eternal quest for the ideal mix of Key Performance Indicators (KPIs). However, where they are more nebulous, these standards are often influenced by the social relationships with greater tolerance for the 'good guys' who get along well with everyone (one of the Big Five personality factors is 'agreeableness' and is sometimes tested in selection situations).

2. Performance is rarely down to a single person's efforts. We all rely on many others for our workplace performance. This is often the cause of resentment when the salesperson is rewarded, but the back office employee processing the sale is not. Pay is not necessarily related to performance. If pay is not competitive, staff may leave, but are unlikely to vary their performance with pay levels. As a doctor remarked: 'I don't get a bonus for doing my job, why should people in the financial services sector?' It is somewhat far-fetched to believe that a doctor, pastor or politician would work harder if they were offered a bonus.

3. The level of reward and its sustainability over time are variable. A bonus one year which might be welcomed as a recognition of good work in the past may become assumed for the future for the same level rather than raising the performance level even higher in the future. When targets become raised each year to obtain a reward, it reaches the point where it no longer sustains improvement because people feel that it becomes increasingly unlikely that they can reach the ever-higher levels of achievement.

4. Bonus schemes that only recognise results fail to take account of effort. When market conditions are good, it is easier to show increased performance than when times are tough, a situation which requires greater effort even to achieve the same results.

5. Large organisations often have formal salary structures determined by job evaluation schemes that set pay scales for particular grades. There is frequently a tension between the market rate for a particular skill and the position in the hierarchy. When skills are in short supply (e.g., technical and IT roles), market rates go up, but in hierarchical terms, they may be low in the grading system. Paying people more than their manager or others on a comparable pay grade in other departments creates resentment and charges of unfairness. Ways round this dilemma invariably involve some compromise which rarely satisfies everyone and adds further fuel to critics that the company is out of touch, doesn't value certain skills or is not committed to treating staff fairly.

6. The differentials between the top and bottom (known as the Gini coefficient[5] between nations) are generally getting wider. Work carried out by Frank Stilwell (8) shows that greater inequality within a society is associated with growing social problems and conflict. Contrast murder and gun crime in the USA, which is widely seen as a highly unequal society and where inequality is getting worse, with Scandinavia, which has low levels of crime and less inequality.

7. Over time, pressure mounts for regrading – usually upwards until there is bunching at the top, further exacerbating friction over fair differentials.

8. Insurance has plenty of opportunities to boost profits and so individual rewards. Complex insurance contracts with opaque legal clauses provide the opportunity to avoid claims. Where sales cultures are heavily incentivised, there is a strong motivation to avoid being fully open with clients about the risks and exclusions. The financial services industry as a whole has made an art form of multiple administrative fees which eat away at the true cost benefit for insurance for customers and enhance bonuses for sales staff.

Cohen Brown, a motivational consultancy, was widely associated with shifting the culture in National Australia Bank (NAB). This bank showed that when sales targets become all-consuming and jobs and income rest on it, there would be some who bend the rules, and in time this would lead to fraud and forgery. The incentive scheme to open new accounts led to creating false accounts, fees for no service, and aggressive selling, which led to poor advice that lacked what was best for the customer. Signatures were forged to expedite the processing of documents. Sales targets measured by income resulted in downgraded service to customers, which led to undesirable consequences in the long term, including reduced renewals of insurance contracts. Apart from the criminal and unethical behaviour, the effect of these practices on morale and work/life balance resulted in mistakes, stress, absenteeism and turnover. Of course, advocates of such a pressured environment would argue that it weeds out the weak and ensures the survival of the fittest.

Some former Commonwealth Bank of Australia (CBA) employees later reported that when staff didn't achieve their targets, they were belittled in front of colleagues. 'Managers patrolled the work area like storm troopers to make sure staff were pushing products to customers at every opportunity. Some bank staff felt the training was a form of brainwashing' (9).

Checks and balances are vital in any business, especially in a high-pressure sales environment where incomes depend on meeting targets. Organisations stand to gain from increased revenues and so how they treat with employees who break the rules says much about their culture. If star performers are let off for infringements, this provides a green light to others. When a star performer is given a second chance instead of being disciplined, it sends a powerful message, because the assumption will be that the organisation is biased towards performance at any cost (see the example of Bo Pahari at AMP in Chapter 4). In one case in the financial sector, even when serious misconduct was found only a marginal reduction of 5% in the bonus was applied. Salary systems that have a low base but considerable opportunity for higher reward based on commissions and bonuses are common in many industries and run the risk of rule bending. Such schemes are often accompanied by published league tables and extra benefits such as trips for star performers. This encourages a culture of greed.

In general, target-based incentives in a culture of low control, dubious morality and opaqueness in fees drive a sale-at-any-cost mentality and are at the root of many cultural problems. However, a study by Xavier Baeten, a professor at Vlerick Business School in Belgium, looked at the relationship between reward and performance of chief executives and found that cash incentives may have some positive effect in the short term, but soon dissipate over several years. This is one of the reasons why there is inflation in the level of bonuses to motivate higher levels of performance (10).

When employees are unaware of the consequences of their actions or have no strong belief in servicing the customer well, indifference can become the attitude, fuelled by senior managers who turn a blind eye or whose focus is on other aspects of the business. 'Too often the answer seems to be greed – the pursuit of short-term profit at the expense of basic standards of honesty … Why do staff (whether customer facing or not) need incentives to do their job unless the incentive is directed towards maximising revenue and profit?' (11) Commissioner Hayne concluded that conflicts cannot be managed by saying 'be good - do the right thing' because people quickly persuade themselves that what is good for them is 'the right thing', even to the detriment of the person they are serving. In extreme cases this can become arrogance or 'I know best'.

The challenge is to adjust such instrumental behaviour without destroying motivation. Some have tried to introduce new lower pay schemes with new employees, reasoning that they will have lower expectations than current employees; however, once the differential is known, a sense of unfairness soon supersedes any other reaction.

As we explored in Chapter 9, traditions can quickly become the norm and what was seen as a privilege soon becomes a right.

Financial incentives are not the only cause of bad behaviour. Medical, legal and financial professions are full of cases of malfeasance where practitioners believed that their expert knowledge gave them an almost moral superiority and a licence to treat customers as ignorant or incapable of taking an alternative view of their expert opinion. Language can confuse and demean by asserting superiority.

When the possibility of significant reward is coupled with little or no ethical consideration, toxic outcomes ensue.

CASE STUDY: INSYS THERAPEUTICS

Insys Therapeutics is an American speciality pharmaceutical company based in Chandler, Arizona. Its main product is Subsys, a sublingual liquid form of fentanyl. The drug fentanyl is a very fast-acting and powerful opioid used to relieve peaks of pain in cancer patients.

Founded in 1990, the company experienced spectacular growth and became a favoured stock in the market. Its fundamental sales model was to recruit doctors to speak on their behalf at medical meetings for which they were paid and rewarded when they prescribed fentanyl. Rewards increased with higher dosages such that patients became addicted, and a number died. Alec Burlakoff, the VP of sales, recruited salesmen with little or no experience of selling medical products, but were attracted by the high bonus culture. He remarked (12) that he looked for people with 'no conscience' who would be unperturbed by the tales of addiction and death that were emerging. The law eventually caught up with them and Dr Kapoor (the founder) and several other executives have gone to jail. One sales representative described how she became compartmentalised and saw the job as 'selling widgets' and not thinking about the impact on the user.

Other cases of deception and poor behaviour that have emerged may not be so egregious as Subsys, but are equally shocking. Domain is an internet platform used in real estate which is an occupation that historically has a tarnished reputation, from overhyping property features to being less than transparent concerning the flaws. But the revelation that a Domain employee made up articles purporting to quote Melbourne-based clinical psychologist Dr Sarah Barker (13) including fictitious quotes, plumbed new depths. In two articles, published on 18 July and 23 August, Dr Barker was quoted. Domain apologised[6] and said Barker was 'not interviewed for these articles and the quotes in these articles were not provided by Dr Barker'. Invariably the motivation may be a reward of some kind, but not necessarily a financial one. Here the reward was more related to recognition (probably coupled with laziness to go and get the truth).

SUMMARY AND CONCLUSIONS

- Reward systems are designed to do many things: reward individual performance, share the profits of collective effort equitably and retain the best people. They are also a major contributing factor to a toxic culture.
- Lack of clear accountabilities for the whole basket of performance measures instead of one narrow metric distorts behaviour.

- Poor calibrated performance and remuneration plans – not paying for the right behaviours - encourages bad behaviour. Complex arrangements that so few understood (if at all)[7] provide greater opportunity for abuse.
- Slowness to identify and fix systemic issues before they become so institutionalised that they become unnoticed are hard to fix. This is in part due to a lack of encouragement and control systems that flag up problems, especially around compliance. Technology with errors and distorting metrics compound the problem.
- A sole focus on personal reward results in a low priority to recompense customers. It is seen as a distraction from generating profits.

NOTES

1 John McLennan had been a senior auditor at Westpac and became important in helping people affected by the bank's poor behaviour and in exposing the many bad practices.
2 Repeated in Stephen Covey's book *The 7 habits of highly effective people*.
3 This table was originally developed by Rita McGee, who has given permission for its inclusion here.
4 See the case study of the dairy given in Chapter 6.
5 The Gini coefficient (named after Corrado Gini) is a measure of statistical dispersion intended to represent the income inequality or the wealth inequality within a nation or a social group. It first appeared in a paper in 1912.
6 The apology was made to Sarah Barker (https://www.domain.com.au/news/apology-to-sarah-barker-983110/).
7 As was found in the case of Nick Leeson, who brought down Barings Bank in 1995.

REFERENCES

1 The character of Gordon Gekko is based on a composite of a number of characters. A more recent film, *The Wolf of Wall Street* (2013), is based on the biography of Jordan Belfort.
2 Ferguson, A. (2019) *Banking bad*. HarperCollins.
3 The real revolution on Wall Street. *The Economist* (6 February 2021).
4 Ferguson, A. (2019) *Banking bad*. HarperCollins.
5 I am indebted to Rita McGee for this graphical presentation.
6 Ditton, J. (1977) Learning to 'fiddle' customers: An essay on the organised production of part-time theft. https://doi.org/10.1177/003803857700400403.
7 Arsalidou, D. (2015) *Rethinking corporate governance in financial institutions*. Routledge.
8 Stilwell, F. (2018) *The political economy of inequality*. Polity. He is referring to work carried out in Wilkinson, R. and Pickett, K. (2018) *The spirit level: Why more equal societies almost always do better*. Allen Lane.
9 Ferguson, A. (2019) *Banking bad*. HarperCollins.
10 Baeten, X. (2021) Giving CEOs financial-based incentives actually damages long-term firm profits. *Business Money*. Retrieved 9 June 2022 from https://bdaily.co.uk/articles/2021/01/06/giving-ceos-financial-based-incentives-actually-damages-long-term-firm-profits.
11 Hayne, K. (2018) *The Royal Commission into Misconduct in the Banking, Superannuation and Financial Services Industry*.
12 Eaton, J. (2020, 24 January) How a drugmaker bribed doctors and helped fuel the opioid epidemic. Retrieved 15 May 2022 from https://www.aarp.org/health/drugs-supplements/info-2019/insys-opioid-bribery-case.html. See also ABC, *4 corners programme*, 5 September 2020.
13 *Domain* published articles, 18 July and 23 August 2020.

Part E
Solutions

CHAPTER 11

Fixing toxic cultures
A strategy for change

INTRODUCTION

> There is no more delicate matter to take in hand, nor more dangerous to conduct, nor more doubtful in its success, than to be a leader in the introduction of changes. For he who innovates will have for enemies all those who are well off under the old order of things, and only lukewarm supporters in those who might be better off under the new. This lukewarm temper arises partly through the fear of adversaries who have the law on their side, and partly from the incredulity of mankind, who will never accept anything new until they have seen it proved by the event (1).

By now I am sure that many readers will be asking in exasperation: 'So how do I fix a toxic culture?' In this chapter a series of actions will be laid out that will in time change cultures, but first let's review what might be the causes of toxic cultures.

From our cases studies, there appear to be numerous causes:

- Amongst the banks 'greed is good' had become a prime motivator, with little regard for how profits were made.
- In aged care a model of partial privatisation had meant that the consumer was powerless to complain about standards, and a combination of lax government standards and the profit motive had caused a casualisation of the workforce.
- In the Australian Parliament the toxic mix of powerful egos away from their families, high stress, young women anxious to get on in their career and alcohol often created opportunities for sexual harassment. In the film industry, similar factors resulted in the 'Me Too' movement.
- In the UK Parliament, a culture of entitlement emerged with no clear rules about expenses that could be reclaimed.
- In the armed forces, wilful blindness shown by some to rogue units in Afghanistan gave free rein to aggression and animal instincts.
- In Crown Casinos, weak management in a tough environment were unable to resist infiltration by organised crime.
- In the American healthcare system, a bias towards exploiting vulnerable sick people for profit became accepted.
- In Boeing, a desperate desire to get a competitive plane in the air resulted in corners being cut and wrong assumptions being made about the changing competence of its customers' pilots.

DOI: 10.4324/9781003307334-17

- In many examples, an imbalance in power between stakeholders was a primary cause of exploitation to the detriment of some of these stakeholders and ultimately to society as a whole.

So, what can we conclude from this? Toxic cultures stem from a set of systemic issues and the consequence is that to fix it requires systemic solutions. Culture is indivisible – you have got to get all the pieces working together.

SO WHAT DO WE WANT TO CHANGE TO?

Several countries periodically survey people to find the 100 best companies to work for (2). The factors that emerge from these surveys are as follows:

- Leadership behaviour and values - can I follow this person?
- Well-being – is there an acceptable level of stress, pressure and work/life balance?
- My manager – does he/she support, trust and care for me?
- My team – do I have good relationships with my colleagues?
- My company – do I feel proud to be part of it? Is it operating ethically and in compliance with laws and regulations?
- Personal growth – is there some challenge and opportunities for the development of skills, variety and advancement?
- Fair compensation – am I compensated fairly in relation to my peers and what I am expected to do?
- Community – is my company giving something back?

WHY IS IT SO DIFFICULT TO CHANGE CULTURES?

There are 11 myths about the strategies to accomplish cultural change, which are often used but rarely work in isolation:

1. Change the organisational chart rather than the dynamics of the patterns of interactions. Organisations can be characterised by a myriad of conversations.
2. Change the chairman rather than key influencers.
3. Invite a prestigious person to the board.
4. Accept the environment in which it operates rather than redefine external relations for mutual benefit.
5. Change the bonus scheme rather than what is rewarded.
6. Focus on measurable performance rather than how people behave.
7. Telling people what the 'new culture' is to be rather than involvement and engagement. Culture is changed through relationships - one conversation at a time.
8. Change the logo, name and stationery. You don't change culture through emails and memos.
9. Run a social engagement programme, but without any clear vision of the way forward.
10. Run a staff survey, but avoid any follow-up action.
11. Accurately predict how the changes will impact culture, but be surprised when the actual outcomes bear little relation to what was intended.

THE LEVERS OF CHANGE

Can culture be changed? It is more likely that culture is the product of all the changes that are made, both planned and unplanned. Fundamentally, unless beliefs and attitudes are changed, behavioural change tends to be short-lived.

Change is an emotional experience and so *how* change is brought about is as important as *what* is changed. Figure 11.1 identifies a sample of the activities that are more likely to engage people in the change and allay some of the emotional fallout.

In the list below, we set out some of the ingredients that, when changed, can have an impact on the resulting culture (3):

- Key people.
- Organisation structure – flat versus pyramidal.
- Task allocation – simple, repetitive, narrowly defined versus broad scope with variety and complexity.
- Style of management – tight management versus loose. In particular, how specific the rules are about who has authority and freedom to act.
- Systems and processes.
- Recruitment and selection.
- Induction.
- Training and development.
- Communications.
- Appraisal.
- Employee relations.
- Counselling.
- Social activities.
- Redundancy.
- Terms and conditions of employment:
  - o Geoffrey Deith, then MD of Toshiba consumer products, described to prospective staff the new factory they were building in Plymouth: 'Everyone will be on monthly pay ... hourly paid will mean nothing in the future. There will be one dining room and the same type of coat for everyone. Why? To ensure that everyone in the company feels an important part

FIGURE 11.1 Activities for successful change management

of the team … we'll have the same holidays, the same sick pay entitlements … advisory board elected from all parts of the company' (4).

- Physical layout of the workspace to create effective communication patterns.
- Technology – interfaces to minimise errors and fraud.
- History – especially where things have gone wrong and resulted in new systems of control. Whilst historical events cannot be changed, their interpretation and the learning from them can.
- Risk appetite - social groupings at all levels from nations to families vary in terms of their willingness to take risks. The 'risky shift', as it is called, is a phenomenon where groups take more or less risk than any one of them would have taken, but due to the effect of the team, they go along with it.
- Symbols and totems – car park spaces, dining facilities, titles, uniforms and expenses policy:
  o A bank had an expense policy that ran to 30 pages and prescribed in great detail what you could claim for and the limit of any one claim. It encouraged an attitude of claiming up to the limit of what was allowed. People also saw it as symptomatic of a culture where no one was trusted to do the right thing. So, they changed it to 'every employee is entitled to claim reasonable expenses wholly incurred in the course of their duties and employees are reminded to spend the company money as if it were their own'. Initially expenses went up as people saw this as a licence to go wild. It was a reaction to previous constraints. In due course, more sensible behaviour emerged and expenses went down. Increasingly people felt they were trusted and acted responsibly.

Netflix has a similar expense policy but with certain checks (5).

- Stories and myths – the heroes and villains.
- Rituals – e.g., the Christmas lunch.
- Staff characteristics – prior experience, competences and prejudices.
- Reward systems – in particular, what is rewarded: performance versus long service/ loyalty?
- External perceptions – the media and competitors.

It was Tolstoy who remarked that 'revolutions seem impossible until they become inevitable'. There will come a time when the prospects of bringing about successful change are heightened. Whilst every situation is a unique product of a myriad of factors at a point in time and will require tailor-made solutions that are appropriate to that time, certain themes are critical for sustained and effective culture change. There are seven of these:

- Understand the context. Because culture is difficult to clearly define, it is likely that there will be many theories and offered solutions before a careful diagnosis is carried out of what is wrong and what is the cause of it. Off-the-shelf solutions are rarely fit for purpose, as they are unlikely to understand the full context and what has given rise to it.
- Gain agreement and clarity about the vision, values and goals, and ensure that every decision reinforces these. Metrics to determine how progress is being made should be in place.
- Define clear responsibilities that follow from the top and interlock across the organisation, ensuring that 'nothing falls between the cracks' and there are no overlaps. This in turn then leads to the next theme.

- Recognition of accountabilities for what and by whom. You may be responsible for department x, but are you also accountable for everything that goes on and the skills to deliver it?[1] 'Four factors will determine successful cultural change: clear communication, role-modelling, incentives and rewards, and the skills to act' (6).

- Define standards about expected behaviour, and the values to which the organisation aspires are spelt out. Ensure that there is timely and specific feedback about behaviour that is incongruent with what is expected.

- Increase transparency throughout the organisation so that decisions are open to all (and maybe open to challenge?). It is the hidden nature of decisions that often leads to corruption. It is said that sunlight is the best antiseptic and so too is transparency in terms of countering the germs of toxic behaviour.

- Clarify consequences when things go wrong. An unintended result of a greater willingness to forgive mistakes is that less attention is given to ensure that things are done right in the first place. However, there is a fine balance to ensure that no one is left in any doubt as to the seriousness of any breach, whilst at the same time not encouraging future breaches to be hidden from inspection. Too harsh a crackdown on bad behaviour runs the risk that fiddling expenses becomes falsifying invoices from (friendly) suppliers. Similarly, casual absence becomes hidden by fictitious sick notes.

THE C'S OF CULTURE CHANGE

A set of headings beginning with 'C' may act as a guide to activities for culture change.

CONTEXT AND CLIMATE

Culture change rarely comes about by itself – it is often a product of changes driven by significant (often disastrous) events, a new strategy, a business need, a fresh vision to change direction, etc. The first requirement then is to understand and explain the context, create a sense of urgency and why staying with the status quo is not an option. There may be goals that the organisation wants to achieve, and this can focus effort if it is seen as attractive and compelling to employees. There may also be situations to leave behind – for example, the 'burning platform', as it has been described. A combination of both can create the impetus for change.

As we saw in Chapter 9, a toxic culture will provide a toxic lens through which to view any initiative to bring about change, so we also have to create the climate for people to be willing to engage in the process. How you tackle the process is as important as what you do and say. More authoritarian styles need even greater deposits in the bank of goodwill in order to be deployed successfully. Even in tough economic times, people are no longer tolerant of having their views completely dismissed or ignored. The phrase in the leadership lexicon that is widely in current use is 'authenticity – but with more skill', particularly the use of more pulling behaviour congruent with the growth in Socratic coaching and the rise in mindfulness. Siegel (7) talks of the 'tripod of mindfulness' – stability from openness to others, objectivity in sifting information and observation of the world around us – then using that tripod to increase our awareness by looking inwardly more closely in order to sense the ebb and flow of energy within ourselves and our relationships with the world.

CLARITY

'I have a dream...' said Martin Luther King, a phrase that encapsulated the desires of millions of Americans. His vision set out a path to a desired future. So, a good start is to recognise where you are and then to identify where you want to get to.

- What will the organisation be like when the plan is implemented? What is our vision and the mission that underpins that? Vision and mission help to determine what we preserve and what we change.
- What do our different senses tell us – what will the organisation look like, sound like and feel like?
- What will be the impact on the people around us?
- What will they say in the newspapers and the professional press about the changes that have occurred?
- What might be said if it goes wrong?

A review of the Australian Public Service (APS) concluded that the following indicators of progress should be in place (8):

> This report calls for outcome-driven targets to measure the progress of the APS against its delivery of government priorities, satisfaction with services, ease of doing business, efficiency, citizen trust and employee engagement. Metrics that ensure the APS has a positive impact on the lives of all Australians and is accountable to the public. Action can begin immediately.

The organisation needs to achieve clarity about its mission, strategy, plan and process.

Mission

Mission defines what our organisation currently does and aspires to do. It is driven by the vision. It is the reason for our existence. It defines what we are here to accomplish. It is the overarching goal and the enduring purpose of the organisation. It is the benchmark against which we can compare the activities in which the organisation is currently engaged and future ones.

Strategy

Strategy is the route map for delivering our mission. It defines the choices of approach and the options for moving from where we are to where we want to be. There may be many different options for achieving the current mission, let alone a future vision. All this may be possible, but the mark of a successful strategy is that it achieves the current mission and along the way to the vision more efficiently and with less pain than the alternatives. Efficiency might include a better use of resources such as people, money and facilities,.

Plan

Real culture change will only come about when the drivers of culture - specifically systems of appointments, rewards, measures of performance, transparency of transactions and other activities along with accountability to independent bodies - are re-aligned to encourage good behaviour. At the end of the chapter is a template of a planning tool (Table 11.1).

Process

Below is a 11-step programme for cultural change of toxic environments:

1. The first step is to signal from the top of the organisation that change is coming. This might entail changing board members or encouraging existing ones to change their attitude and behaviour. If the former, recruit carefully to signal different values and a commitment to a new approach. If the latter, instigate an honest assessment of the issues, maybe a declaration of a *mea culpa* of what has gone before and a clear statement of board members' vision for the future and the values and behaviours to which they will be held to account. Traditionally the received wisdom is that you must start from the top, which is true to a certain extent. In large organisations the cultural transmission system from the top to the bottom is too long and diffuse for strong behavioural examples to be apparent at the bottom. If you only see the chief executive on a platform with many others, on a podcast or on the rare 'meet the people' walkabout, then their influence is limited and is often accompanied by cynicism: 'Those people up there don't understand the pressures we are under...' The key lever of change is middle management – they are more connected up and down the chain of command – knowing what is going on at the bottom and at the top. They are in a better position to influence both their staff and their management about solutions to the real issues people are facing (see the influence curve given in Figure 6.1 in Chapter 6). They need to be brought on board, empowered to act and rewarded for supportive behaviour, not punished for failing to achieve targets which are only achievable by bending the rules. Symbolic acts by senior management signals that real change is happening. This might include outlawing practices (pork-barrelling for politicians?), restitution for those wronged (financial compensation for bank customers?), changing privileges that are resented (everybody being on the same set of expense policies?) and a speedy response to critical reports (money laundering at Crown Casinos and sexual misbehaviour?).
2. Establish a clear statement about values and principles along with policies and rules about what is and is not acceptable. Much corruption starts with a lackadaisical approach to controls and rules. In time, a belief grows that these do not matter and this becomes almost a justification for ignoring the rules and forgetting that there was ever a different way. It is important to avoid an overbureaucratic approach. The aim should be to encourage everyone to internalise these rules and values by example and influence. Establishing due process to signal that legality and fairness are enshrined in the way in which things will be done builds confidence that new ways of working will endure.
3. Sort out the organisational design – structures to ensure a clear line of sight in the command structure in order to avoid any conflict of interest, and to focus on improving the design of processes that will mitigate any tendency to get around controls and rules. There is a simple test of organisational design called 'the water test'. Water flows down the easiest path and people do their jobs in the way that is easiest. If systems and structures obstruct people from doing their jobs in the easiest way, then when the pressure is on, they will find ways round the obstruction, like water round a rock. Structure and process in an organisation should be possible without compromising the espoused values of the organisation or values of employees.

4. Institute a wide-ranging, root-and-branch discussion of behaviours which support and those which undermine the espoused values throughout the organisations. The output of such discussions should form the basis of evaluation. In one organisation these workshops gave rise to a red card/white card system where everyone was encouraged to show a card if bad or good behaviours were shown. Whilst this approach initially met with scepticism, it soon entered the language in the company: 'That's a red card statement.' This raised people's consciousness about their behaviour and encouraged people to act more appropriately.

5. Create feedback mechanisms to build awareness of when behaviour is not congruent with the stated values and policies. Where rules are critical to safety or legal compliance, establish compliance staff who not only look out for any non-compliant transactions, but also where there is inappropriate behaviour, such as condoning bending of the rules. Identify key stakeholders and establish their role in maintaining compliance (see the example in given case study 3 in Chapter 5 of how one board tackled this). Demonstrate that it is OK to admit weaknesses and vulnerability, which encourages others to act differently. At Dun & Bradstreet, there is a 'failure wall' and at Credibility Corporation, there is the white board for admissions of falling short of targets (9). Establish a whistleblowing charter, maybe using some of the emerging platforms, such as Navex Global (10).

6. In all organisations there need for mechanisms to track performance across a spectrum of metrics, depending on what is critical to their success. This may involve hard measures of income and expenditure as well as measures that are more difficult to quantify, such as stakeholder satisfaction and engagement, adherence to the values and the climate of the organisation. In large public companies, compliance and audit need to be independent, and these functions should report to the audit committee of the board who comprise a majority of non-executive independent directors.

7. A key lever of change is the reward system, which needs to reflect what is achieved, but also how it is accomplished: 'No bonus if you double the business but don't live the values.' A significant shift in the culture of a construction company took place when the company's top salesman received no bonus because of his poor behaviour. Previously his behaviour had been condoned because of his sales record, which gave licence to others to indulge in these behaviours, especially bullying. Promotion processes should also reflect both behaviour and performance/potential in the criteria for selection. As we saw in Chapter 4, the higher proportion of sociopaths in senior management are more likely to ignore the collateral damage they create when pushing for higher performance.

8. To stick to rules that might go against your personal interest (i.e., to lose your bonus) takes considerable integrity and courage. Such selfless acts are helped by openness and transparency of transactions, and random checks on compliance. An independent complaints procedure is an early step to implement. To support openness, a whistleblowers' charter needs to be made explicit to give reassurance that such activity will not be punished. The fact that it is often resisted by organisations shows how effective it can be in exposing bad practice. Critics of whistleblowing point to the aggrieved person settling personal scores and exposing legitimate company secrets. Nevertheless, making it easy to expose behaviour is an important ingredient in a change process (though there must be safeguards against malicious acts).

9. Provide support in the form of behavioural coaching to get managers to 'walk the talk'. Where a manager or someone who has significant influence with their peers deliberately acts in a way that illustrates and confirms the aspired cultural norm, others will take their lead, which can help to reinforce the change. Most managers do not deliberately set out to be corrupt and so often deal with any unpleasant evidence by turning a blind eye to it - out of sight

is out of mind, which leaves the conscience clear. Subordinates, seeing the attitude of the manager, feel naturally emboldened to carry on with the fiddles and rule breaking. Developing the 'moral taste buds' and the capability to deal with poor behaviour helps to strengthen managers' willingness to confront these issues constructively.

10. Some activities that have helped organisations keep focused on customers include appointing 'Mr/Ms Customer' with the specific role of championing customer interests and again having access to transactions to check for their integrity. The 'mystery shopper' model is another useful tool in this respect.

11. Where part of the business is outsourced, a review should be instituted to determine whether there is sufficient retention of institutional memory to reliably evaluate performance. The service contract should again reflect behavioural measures as well as performance targets, which all too often are only costs and transaction times.

Such a programme takes time to fully embed, but the future benefits to the economy and society of all institutions (especially financial ones) that are trusted for their integrity are worth the effort.

Some points to consider are as follows.

CHAMPION THE CHANGE

Below is an account of a manager who had failed to change his organisation:

> *I knew we had to change fast to stay in the game, so I pushed and cajoled my staff to develop new products, streamline processes, let go colleagues and aggressively market our products to new markets. But we were beaten by the competition who changed faster and established a dominant position faster than us. As I tried to rouse my team to push on, they walked out. I had been unable to inspire them to stay with the journey and with that loss of talent I no longer had the drive to start again.*

Contrast this with another case where a champion for a change was vital for success:

> *An airline that ran into difficulty determined that it had to radically cut costs to survive. One of its competitors was in a similar situation and had let many hundreds of staff go with just a dismissal letter. Morale was low and the CEO was soon fired. The first airline's CEO resolved to face everyone who would lose their job and explain why. In the following weeks he went to every part of the organisation and talked directly to people about how the company had to cut costs if it were to survive, or no one would have a job. The result was that many lost their jobs, but those who were left saw a courageous visible leader in action and were prepared to redouble their efforts to get the airline back into profit.*

CEMENT THE CHANGES IN THE CULTURE

The Roman armies would burn the bridge behind them to cut off any possibility of retreat. Behaviour takes time to change (think how many of those new year's resolutions last beyond a few weeks!) and so any opportunity to slide back into the old ways should be discouraged. There is a need for clear standards set in an ethical framework, clear accountability for each person who has any responsibility in the system, and independent regulators who have the capability and capacity to investigate and rectify wrongdoing. Some countries have rules covering the period of time before politicians can use their contacts to lobby governments after leaving office. Similar rules should be encouraged when staff move from an institution like a bank to the market regulator. Personal relationships can get in the way of impartial judgement and may influence taking tough measures where required.

Transparency and feedback will help to expose those times when behaviour slips and to rapidly surface mistakes and failings so that they can be fixed. Rewards and celebrations are the positive incentives. One company introduced a 360-degree feedback process based on the espoused behaviours as part of its performance assessment and rewarded those who scored well. An insurance company in the UK had a party after a year of no policy or process breaches. None of these is a perfect solution, but the combination of sticks and carrots will in time shift behaviour.

CIVILITY

At the beginning of this book, we discussed how incivility provoked a problematic climate. A recent study (11) has shown how the effect of civility can enhance performance and creativity. They found that civility enhances 'thriving' at work, provided that it is within an organisation of supportive relationships.

CONSISTENCY

Changing personal behaviour is hard work and requires repetition (as anyone trying to lose weight or take more exercise will know!).

There are six levers that need to be working together to successfully change personal behaviour:

- Self-awareness of what to change.
- Willpower to do it.
- Belief that it is in my interests and is the right thing to do.
- Competence to make the change.
- Incentives to do it and penalties if I do not (sticks and carrots).
- Vision of what I might become once the change is accomplished.

One study indicated that you need to carry out the new behaviour many times over several months (12) before it becomes an ingrained habit. Consistency in applying the rules and processes along with persistence to stick with the programme are vital, as change takes time to really embed itself.

COLLEAGUES AND COALITIONS

A rule of thumb from organisational psychologists is that you need a third of affected staff to be on your side if change is to happen. You can assume that a third will be against and a third in the middle (the floating voter who needs to be won over). Finding colleagues who are with you and those who can form a coalition of supporters is an essential early activity.

Induction programmes are important steps in the onboarding process for new employees, yet they rarely go beyond explaining the company policies and the location of the toilets. It is an opportunity to establish norms early on through induction and training of such important behaviours as respect for others, fairness in all dealings and zero tolerance of abuse. Acculturation in organisations is accelerated because new people usually want to fit in. Even when people don't want to be there (for example, in prisons), there is still a strong desire to fit in and be part of the social network of relationships. Organisations placing more emphasis on the emotional connection by giving individual information and asking them for ideas from their first few days about what they liked and didn't like all results in higher retention and acceptance of the values and norms. The first 30 days is critical to retention.

CONSEQUENCES

Australian Prudential Regulation Authority (APRA) Chairman Wayne Byres in September 2018 said that senior executives of banks should 'feel a sting in their pay packets' when scandals occur on their watch. They squandered their reputations by focusing too much on profits (13). He argued for 'accountability maps' to identify who is responsible for what.

COMMUNICATIONS

In Chapter 9 we explored how communication can go wrong. One lesson is to ensure that those significant influencers inside and outside of the organisation are brought on board. They are the 'telephone exchanges', and the messages they pass can help or hinder the achievement of a correct interpretation of the messaging. Their circle of influence on others will decline the further away people are from them, so we have to build multiple channels. In transmitting culture through organisations by words and behaviours, we should never underestimate the power of unofficial channels, which are sometimes more trusted than official channels.

Here are some pointers for delivering an effective communication strategy, particularly in relation to values and the behaviours that underpin and undermine them:

- Everyone has a responsibility to role model behaviour in line with the espoused values (walk the talk).
- Give a voice to those who feel bullied and harassed and take their claims seriously. Be honest, transparent and sincere.
- The aim is to build trust and gain cooperation as in Figure 11.2 below.
- Encourage people at all levels to (respectfully) challenge bad behaviour when they see it.
- Be explicit in terms of what behaviour is encouraged and what is not.
- Clarify the consequences for bad behaviour.
- Be mindful that people who are suffering high levels of stress may misinterpret cues and may react badly.
- In areas of harassment and inappropriate sexual behaviour, promote a focus on developing gender equality, respect for all 'other' groups and educating young people on negotiating consent.
- Challenge language that minimises toxic behaviour or hijacks the issue for ulterior motives.

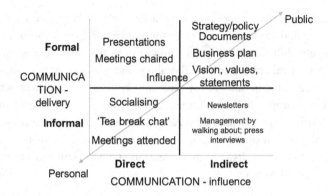

FIGURE 11.2 Planning communications

Used by permission of Farren Drury

Cooperation rises with trust. When trust is absent, defensiveness is shown by both the communicator and the recipient. As evidence mounts that this programme is for real and those managing it can be trusted, so cooperation rises and a more collaborative approach emerges.

When planning communications, there are many ways of accomplishing successful outcomes. Figure 11.2 shows two dimensions which yield four quadrants of activities. The more channels you can engage, the more likely it is that your message will get across[2].

COMMITMENT

Commitment to the goals and the process of achieving them is aided by involvement, but it is not the same as it. Rarely does change that you do *to* people stick, as opposed to doing *with* people. Giving people a role and a stake in the success of the change helps to build commitment. In times of change there will be rough spots which might well test even the most committed. This is when visible leadership (someone described it as 'walking *towards* the sound of gunfire') is crucial, especially when people get confused by continually changing situations and changing messages. Confusion also arises because the old ways of doing things clash with the new. When leaders are clear about the vision and goals, demonstrate understanding of people's worries and questions, and move to reassure them as honestly as possible without making false promises, commitment is more likely to endure.

CONCLUSIONS

One of the causes of culture conflict we have hardly touched upon here is the mismatch of cultural expectations. We make the mistake (or certainly native English speakers do) that because of a common language, beneath our differences there is a common cultural heritage and a shared set of meanings. Yet this is rarely true: after all, it is said that the Americans and the British are divided by a common language. With so many of the world travelling (the International Air Transport Association said that some 5 million people were in the air/transit at any one time before the COVID-19 pandemic), working with other cultures has become a common experience for millions. Cultural training is now on YouTube teaching people how to talk to those from a different culture. These illustrate how easily Western approaches of directness can easily offend politer or more discursive cultures. Conflicts over values can have a significant impact on organisational performance.

As we identified at the beginning of this book toxic cultures start with incivility. In our multicultural world, it is easy to cause offence, and once we view others with a measure of hostility, we interpret everything through that lens.

Perhaps we all need to walk a few more miles in each other's shoes. Organisations, like countries, show their values through what they care about and what they put their time and other resources into, especially for those who have no voice. The pandemic has shown how important our frontline workers are – roles that are often poorly paid and deemed to be at the bottom of the organisation. We should turn the pyramid upside down as we now realise how important these people are to our health and well-being.

Changing cultures at every level takes effort and time, yet the benefits of a helpful culture are well proven and likewise the costs of a toxic culture can be terminal. Each and every one of us has a responsibility to act with consideration to others and to play our part through our attitudes and behaviour in order to create a climate that is truly beneficial to all.

TABLE 11.1 Planning for behavioural change

This planning tool can be used as the basis for an individual survey or as a group discussion and then for the plan of action.

	Current position	Continue	Reinforce	Stop	Start
Visible signs	Different restaurants for different grades Reserved parking places Managers wear ties, others do not				
Attitudes	Positive about the company Negative about senior managers				
Beliefs	'The best way to succeed here is to get on with the job and don't rock the boat' 'The union will sort out any problems' 'Everyone works hard'				
Behaviours	Upward communication via the union rep Managers command and control Strong divisional lines of decision making				
Policies, processes, and systems	Leadership development only applies to very few Other areas to assess:				

- Key people
- Recruitment and selection
- Induction
- Training and development
- Communications
- Appraisal
- Reward
- Employee relations
- Counselling
- Social activities
- Redundancy
- Terms and conditions of employment

NOTES

1 Accountability is literally the ability and/or duty to report (or give account of) on events, tasks and experiences. While responsibility is an ongoing duty to complete the task at hand, accountability is what happens after a situation occurs. It is how a person responds to and takes ownership of the results of a task.

2 I am indebted to Farren Drury for sharing this model with me.

REFERENCES

1 Machiavelli, N. (1514) *The Prince*.

2 Fortune 100 best companies to work for (2021). Retrieved 27 May 2022 from https://www.greatplace-towork.com/best-workplaces/100-best/2021.

3 Williams, A. Dobson, P, and Walters, M. (1993) *Changing culture*. CIPD.

4 Williams, A. Dobson, P, and Walters, M. (1993) *Changing culture*. CIPD.

5 Hastings, R. and Meyer, E. (2020) *No rules rules*. W.H. Allen.

6 APS (2019) *Independent report into the public service*. Department of the Prime Minister.

7 Siegel, D. (2010, 4 February) Science of the mindful brain by Dan Siegel, MD. Retrieved 27 May 2022 from https://integral-options.blogspot.com/2010/02/science-of-mindful-brain-by-dan-siegel.html.

8 APS (2019) *Independent report into the public service*. Department of the Prime Minister.

9 Coyle, D. (2108) *The culture code*. Bantam Books.

10 See https://www.navex.com/en-gb.

11 Rukh, L., Hassan, Q., Babar, S. and Iftikhar, A. (2018) Impact of perceived organisational support and organisational reward on thriving at work: Mediating role of civility at workplace. *International Journal of Management Excellence, 12*(1), 1688-1699.

12 Clear, J. (2018) *Atomic habits*. Random House.

13 The comments about Crown come from Australian newspapers of 11th February reporting the 760-page report by former NSW Supreme court Judge Patricia Bergin to the Independent Liquor and Gaming Authority. A summary is given at Crown Resorts report set to be handed down by Bergin (casinoaus.net).

Name Index

Abrashoff, M. 152
Acton, Lord 45
Aitsi-Selmi, A. 2
Alderfer, C. 145
Amazon 23
AMP 61
Anderson, A. 3
Ang, Y.Y. 79
Apple 66, 130
Ardern, J. 59
Aristotle 157
Arpey, G. 136
Astra Zeneca 99
ATO 130

BAE systems 130
Baeten, X. 167
Bangladesh 4
Barings bank 100
Barker, S. 168
Barnardos 74
Barron, J. and Hannan, M. 101
Becket, T. 154
Berejiklian, G. 58
Bergin, P. 134
Bezos, J. 23
Bidon, J. 67
Black and Decker 61, 131
Blair, A. 93
Blau, P.M. 120
Board, B.J. and Fritzon, K. 64
Boyle, P.M. 130
Bray, T. 23
Broderick, E. 61
Brown, C. 167
Buffet, W. 60

Burlakoff, A. 168
Bush, H.W. 21
Byres, W. 183

Caius Petronius 92
Caldwell, C. 78
Carter, R. 151
Celcus, A. C. 50
Chamorro-Premuzic, T. 60
Chapman, G. 22
China Merchant Bank 161
Christies, R. and Geis, F. 63
Churchill, W. 94, 162
Cleckley, H. 64
Covey, S. 48
Coyle, D. 119, 150
Cummings, T.G. and Worley, C.G. 92

Darwin, C. 62
Davis, R. 17
Decker, A. 61
Diamond, J. 94, 129
Dilbert 18, 118
Ditton, J. 165
Drury, F. 15
Dun and Bradstreet 180

Edison, T. 98, 99
Einstein, A. 29
EMI 131
Engelland, C. 61
Enron 72, 129

Farrell, A.K. 45
Felps, W. 63
Ferguson, A. 160

Floyd, G. 132
Ford, H. 98
Friedman, M. 80

Gartner 53
Gekko, G. (The Wolf of Wall Street) 160
German Mittlestand 79
Ghan 162
Goffman, E. 66
Goldman Sachs 23
Google 66, 119
Grubbs, J. 77

H & M 130
Handlin, D. 1, 22
Harrison, R. 31
Hayne, Commissioner 167
Hazelton, D. 61
Hazlitt, W. 60
Hegel, G.W.F. 103
Helmsley, L. 60
Henry, K. 60
Hertz 148
Herzberg, F. 145
Hewlett Packard 96
Heydon, D. 122
Hickock, H. 59
Higgs 68
Hitler 58
Hoffer, E. 47, 97
Hofstede, G. 30, 47

Israel Dead Sea 129

James, H. 62
Jenkins, K. 122
John Lewis partnership 161
Johnson & Johnson 85
Johnsons 93
Joss, B. 162

Kant. E. 73
Kapoor 168
Kellogg 47
Kemp, V. 80
Khashoggi, J. 155
Kiefel, S. 123
King, M.L. 178
Kirana, R. 138

Klein, G. 96
Kuhn, T.S. 98

Lareau, A. 76
Leeson, N. 100
Lehman brothers 127
Lencioni, P. 38, 118
Levandowski, A. 66

Macmillan, H. 7
Makry, M. 135
Mao, T. 58
Marx, K. 16, 99
Maslow, A. 145
McClelland, D. 145
McDonnell Douglas 138
McGregor, D. 145
McLennan, J. 160
McNerney, W.J. 136
Meyer, E. 30
Microsoft 53
Morrison (General) 58
Moses 91
Moshagen, M. 63
Mueller, C.M. 96
Murthy, N.R. 80

NAB 167
Navalny, A. 155
Negroni, C. 137
Netflix 176
Nigeria 80
Nike 130
Nolte, D.L. 75

O'Farrell, B. 134
Ohno, T. 93

Packer, J. 134
Pahari, Bo 61, 74, 167
Papas, B. 63
Parkinson, N. 103
Pearson, C. and Porath, C. 9
Pentlands 119
Piff, P.K. 76
Pink, D. 147
Popovich, G. 61
Porter, L. and Lawler, E. 146
Putnam, R. 16

Ramaswamy, V. 80
Ratner, G. 101
Rausch, J. 78
Red Robbo 113
Rock, D. 115
Roethlisberger, F.J. and Dickson,
     W.L. 112
Roosevelt, F.D. 149
Rousseau, J.J. 21

Sarbanes-Oxley 3
Sartre, J.P. 21
Schein, E. 18
Senge, P. 29
Siegel, Dan 177
Smith, A. 16, 129
Smithers, A. 161
Snowden, E. 82
Soichiro, H. 51
Sony 1, 22
Spock, B. 77
Stalin 58
Suzman, J. 16

Tajer, Captain 137
Taylor, F.W. 112

Templeton, J. 24
Tolstoy, L. 176
Toyota 93
Trompenaars, F. 15, 30
Trump, D. 59, 68, 102

Uighurs 130
Urwick, L. 145

Verdun 17
Victoria 101
Vroom, V. 146

Weber, M. 16
Weick, K. 18
Weinstein, H. 1, 68
Wellington (Duke of) 157
Wells Fargo 162
Westpac 162
Wetlaufer, S. 96
Wilde, O. 72
Williams, K. 98
Williams, S. 152
Wolf, N. 122

Xianjiang 13

Subject Index

Abigail and the river 73
Abilene paradox 118
absenteeism 32
accountability 186n1
Administrative Procedures Act 129
Affordable Care Act 136
aged care 127
American airlines 136
AMP61 *see* NML and AMP
amygdala hijack 149, 151; *see also* neuroscientists
Anglican church 87; *see also* values and religion
APRA 183
Arabic saying 127
ASIC 79
asymmetric power relations 127
Australia: parliament 1: Federal government 34; Public
　Service 178; Royal commission into banking and
　financial institutions 79, 160
Australian Recording Industry association 23

banks and poor service 15; Barings 101
behavioural committed speaking 103
beliefs 21, 118
Benfold, USS 152
best companies to work for 174
black hole 8
Black Lives Matter 129
Black Swan 98
Boeing *see* case studies and other examples
boundary management 94, 103
bribery 126, 130
British Airways waterside 99
British parliament 1
bully 50; gender differences 52; as strong management
　51; suppliers 126

cancel culture 133
case studies and other examples: author recruiting
　for a position 66; bullying a secretary 51: Caius
　Petronius 92; car hire company 20; case study
　1 (chapter 5): Changing the ethical landscape
　83; case study 1 (chapter 8): Crown resorts 134;
　case study 3 (chapter 5): Measuring behavioural
　change 86; case study 3 (chapter 8): The Boeing
　737 max story 136; case study 2(chapter 5): The
　case for ethics in business (Tylenol) 85; case
　study 2 (chapter 8): The US health industry
　135; control of capital expenditure 100; Crown
　resorts 134; empowering staff to act 105; Google
　and Levandowski (*see* Google, Levandowski);
　government and the biscuit contract 162;
　government and the IT system 17, 168;
　government merger of two departments 47; Indian
　fable 147; Insys 168; Interviewing research study
　67; Italian sandwich bar in London 120; journalist
　in London 157: Mary and the dilemma of aged
　care 128; naval ship 50; NML and AMP 24; noisy
　factory 100: planes with bullet holes in WW2
　94; purchasing department of an airline 132;
　redundancy and voluntary turnover 115: repair
　shop 93; retailer and customer service 126; ring in
　the gutter 32; role of blame *vs* a learning culture
　148: a senior person who lost their job 151: airline
　CEO champion of change 181; airline purchasing
　department 30, 132; airline ramp handling staff
　148; Amnesty international 149; Australian
　Defence Force 34; Australian Federal Government
　and the 'bonk ban' 33; steam train in the Midwest
　104: Tavistock institute and milk delivery 106;
　tech company 77; US health industry 135; whistle
　blower and the ATO 130

Catholic church and devil's advocate 99
caveat emptor 129
CBA 167
change: activities for success 175; challenge of 97;
    change to 174; the Cs of 177; difficulties 114,
    174; the levers of 175; personal behaviour 182;
    requirements for 123
Chicago music school 152
Chinese Communist Party 130; saying 16
Christians and values 87
climate, working 120; *see also* government case study of
    merger of two departments
cohesion, lack of 5
committees 103
communication 153–154; deficient 5; distortion
    157–158; effective strategy 183; transmission system
    100, 156; why it goes wrong 154, 156; *see also*
    organisation
compliance 164
conflict 98; of interest 101
corruption 79; and relatives 80; *see also* bribery
COVID-19 45, 101; and power 52; societal
    implications 54, 126–28
Crown *see* case studies and other examples
c's of culture change 177; cement the change in
    the culture 181; champion the change 181;
    civility 182; clarity 178; colleagues and coalitions
    182; commitment 184; communications 183;
    consequences 183; consistency 182; context and
    climate 177; *see also* change; communication;
    culture
culture definitions of 15; audit questionnaire 36;
    change 174; counterculture 24; diagnosis of
    differences 31; economic activity 15; formal
    19; good and bad consequences 5; informal 20;
    ingredients 17; male dominated 122; mapping 46;
    measurement 29; myths 174
CV 102

Daily Mail test; pub test 80
dark triad 25
dead sea 129
decision making 91
delegation 91
derivatives 100
deviant behaviour 6, 21; *see also* toxic culture
diagnosis of toxic culture 34
discretionary effort 120

discrimination laws 132
drivers of toxic cultures 2, 18

entitlement 75, 173
equifinality 92
ESG 61; social licence 61
ethics: advantages 81; enforcing ethical standards 81;
    positions 73; roots of 75; subverted 82
eustress 150

FASEA 82
fear 5, 62, 133, 149–150; dealing with 151; loss
    from 150
Federal Aviation Authority (FAA) 136, 137
feedback and criticism 152–153
fentanyl 168
Foreign Corrupt Practices Act 130
France Telecom 26

gaslighting 116
gini coefficient 166
goals 152
great resignation 53
greed 149; is good 3, 134, 160, 173
grievances 33
Guardian newspaper 22

hadron collider 22
harassment 3, 122
health consequences 3
hiding transactions from legal and tax authorities 126
homeless charity 18
home working 52–53; effects of 53
HR human resources 23; enforcing standards 82, 98,
    102; practices 25; *see also* unconscious bias
humour 117; clowning 117; death of Stalin 18; Dilbert
    18; *see also* satire
hygiene conditions 153

IATA 184
imposter syndrome 60
impression management 49, 68
incivility 2, 10, 21–22
indigenous people in Australia 133
influence curve 95–96
innovation 95, 96; and creativity 113; inhibitors of
    96–97
Islamic norms 123

John Hopkins Hospital 135
jokes *see* humour
Judaeo-Christian 23

kaizen 98
key performance indicators (KPIs) 166

labour turnover 32
law: boundaries of legality 58; legal implications
    25–26; regulatory frameworks 126
leadership: destructive styles 58, 59; effective 59;
    inadequacies 62; moment of truth 62; reluctance
    to confront 151; toxic characteristics 60; *see also*
    dark triad; Machiavellian; narcissism; psychopath;
    sociopath
lean manufacturing 93
Lion Air 137
listening 62; test of 155
little emperor syndrome 77

Machiavellianism 63; and *Mach iV* test 63
management philosophy 15, 58; scientific management
    and the human relations school 112; strong 112;
    style 5, 78
manipulation 49
MBWA 52; *see also* management philosophy
MCAS 137
Me Too 1, 68, 129, 173
mind map 92
Minutemen missiles, 'Missileers' 150
misbehaviour 113
Mittlestand 79
moral compass 72
motivation theories 4, 145–147
MPs 1, 3
muck up day 76

narcissism 68, 102; dealing with them 69; gender
    differences 76
Navex global 180
neurological explanations 22
neuroscientists 22
NHS 77
norms 21, 110; and boundaries 103; change
    114; conflict growth 102; design 91, 94, 101;
    disruption of social networks 114; and drinking
    111; dysfunctional 93; informal 113; testing 94–95

organization sociology 23
ostracism 3, 22
outplacement 102

parable of the talents 149
passive aggressive behaviours 3, 115, 116
patriarchal society 76
pawahara 51
performance assessment 165; and potential 165; related
    pay 165; and values 75
personality factor D 63
peter principle 66
Phoenix memo 98
Plum creek timber 94
police use of force 132; *see also* Floyd, G.
power: balance of 126; contingencies 48; distance 30;
    imbalance 33, 45, 122, 126, 127, 174; mapping 46;
    ways of exerting 49
psychological contract 53, 111; positive 75; and
    trust 111
psychopath 64, 108; checklist 65; pawns and patrons
    67, 108; and Peter principle 66; types 64; why
    tolerated 65

racism 132
red teams 95
relationships 18; history of 127; shift to a more
    transitory 112
remote working 52
reward: at different times of life 163; extrinsic and
    intrinsic 160; share schemes 161; toxic 163–164;
    see also performance related
rotten apple theory 63
Royal Commission into banking and the financial
    sector 1 160
rules: crisis 105; fiddling 106; role of 4, 104

sabotage 3, 107
Sarbanes Oxley 3
satire 117
scenario planning 95
sexual behaviour 120, 121; mating
    manoeuvres 121
shaming 3
Sherlock 155; *see also* listening test
SHRM survey of toxic cultures 9
Singapore and gambling 135
six sigma 98
social exchange theory 47; cohesion 53; *see also*
    psychological contract
sociopath 64
stakeholders 96, 101
status 113; symbols 4
stress 62
Swedish approach to COVID-19 59

tax 130; evasion 79; hiding transactions 126
team cohesion 120; assessment 39; dysfunctional 118; flex 104; good behaviour 119; and problem solving 114; sabotage 3
time recording 115
toxic diagnosis 34, 35; change of 123; signs of 2–3, 31
toxic positivity 5
toxic workplaces: team culture 118
Toyota; lean manufacturing 93
trade unions 25, 99, 104, 114, 126
tragedy of the commons 126, 129
transparency 129; Transparency International 129
trust 16, 101

unconscious bias 102
upbringing 75

US Health Care *see* case studies and other examples
utilitarian 73

values: compromising 126; cultural differences 123; individual differences 73; moral compass 72; rating my acceptance 85; and religion 87
Volkswagen, 'dieselgate' 45, 131

whistle blowers 23, 123; charter 180
WH Smith 152
wilful blindness 58, 173
wokeism 133
working from home (WFH): effects 126–128
wrong, blatant 33

Printed in the United States
by Baker & Taylor Publisher Services

Printed in the United States
by Baker & Taylor Publisher Services